THE LIMITS OF BODILY INTEGRITY

The Limits of Bodily Integrity

Abortion, Adultery, and Rape Legislation in Comparative Perspective

RUTH A. MILLER
University of Massachusetts, Boston, USA

ASHGATE

Published by
Ashgate Publishing Limited
Gower House
Croft Road
Aldershot
Hampshire GU11 3HR
England

Ashgate Publishing Company
Suite 420
101 Cherry Street
Burlington, VT 05401-4405
USA

Ashgate website: http://www.ashgate.com

British Library Cataloguing in Publication Data
Miller, Ruth A.
The limits of bodily integrity : abortion, adultery, and rape legislation in comparative perspective. - (Law, justice and power series)
1. Sex and law 2. Body, Human - Law and legislation 3. Women - Legal status, laws, etc. 4. Women - Crimes against 5. Sex crimes
I. Title
342'.0878

Library of Congress Cataloging-in-Publication Data
Miller, Ruth Austin, 1975-
The limits of bodily integrity : abortion, adultery, and rape legislation in comparative perspective / by Ruth A. Miller.
p. cm. -- (Law, justice, and power)
Includes bibliographical references and index.
ISBN 978-0-7546-7061-2
1. Sex and law. 2. Women--Legal status, laws, etc. 3. Civil rights. 4. Human reproduction--Government policy. 5. Sex and law--Europe. 6. Women--Legal status, laws, etc.--Europe. 7. Civil rights--Europe. 8. Human reproduction--Government policy--Europe. I. Title.

K487.S65M55 2007
342.08'78--dc22

2006100197

ISBN-13: 978 0 7546 7061 2

Reprinted 2008

Printed and bound in Great Britain by MPG Books Ltd, Bodmin, Cornwall.

Contents

Acknowledgements

This book owes its existence to a symposium on "gender relevant legislative change in Muslim and non-Muslim countries" that was sponsored by the Islamic Legal Studies Program at Harvard Law School in the fall of 2005. I am grateful to Louise Halper for having organized the symposium and for having encouraged me to present my research there. I am likewise grateful to the other participants in the symposium whose insightful comments and questions helped me to reformulate my ideas into the foundation for a book-length project. Susan Slyomovics, especially, has been uncompromisingly generous in her support of my work.

This book is also a product of the atmosphere of intellectual freedom and scholarly exchange that I have enjoyed at the University of Massachusetts, Boston. Woodruff Smith has been particularly sympathetic to my research agenda, and the conversations that I have had with him have been invaluable. I have benefited similarly from exchanges on and off campus with Alex Des Forges, Pratima Prasad, Ana Aparicio, Shirley Tang, Amy DenOuden, Elora Chowdhury, Gretchen Umholtz, Jalal Alamgir, Steve Silliman, Rob Lublin, Heike Schotten, and Arjun Jayadev.

To the extent that this book represents an attempt to engage not just with scholars of Islamic Legal Studies, but with scholars of Legal Studies in general, I am indebted to academics in this latter field for their willingness to converse with me and to respond with patience to my questions. My discussions with John Parry have opened up countless areas of analysis that I had not considered previously. Austin Sarat and Pnina Lahav have also been tolerant, generous, and understanding as they have introduced me to this fascinating new field.

Finally, I would like to thank Miles and Betsy Miller for their sympathy and their unwavering support of my work in all of its—sometimes unexpected—manifestations.

Chapter 1

Introduction

Introduction

The subject of this book is the intersection between citizenship and reproduction in modern and post modern European states. This intersection—between law and politics on the one hand and sexuality or biology on the other—has been analyzed and debated for well over 200 years.[1] The gendered nature of classical liberal political belonging has likewise been well established, if the beneficiary of a less extended historical tradition.[2] My primary purpose in this book is therefore to engage in what has become an ongoing discussion, to look a bit more closely at the creation first, of citizens, and second, of citizens with distinctly sexual or reproductive identities.

At the same time, I intend to take this discussion in a new direction. I should explain first of all, for example, what I mean by "intersection." When I talk about the intersection between citizenship and reproduction over the following pages, I will not be talking about a metaphorical relationship between abstract notions of gender and abstract notions of political belonging. Nor will I be concerned with the modern development of biopolitical structures focused on the procreation and health of a given population *per se*—although each of these scholarly frameworks will play a significant role as I develop my argument. Instead, my focus in this book will be on the concrete, physical, solid, and material collision of law and sexuality—the formulation of the womb as a political space, and as a space more often than not sliced out of a given citizen for the sake of political expediency. Over the next chapters, I will indeed seek to demonstrate first and foremost the physicality of the politicized womb—the way in which it has been defined upon a distinctly material planc.

Given this emphatically not metaphorical understanding of "intersection," my working definitions of both "citizenship" and "rights" will also necessarily be concrete. It is true that my starting point with regard to each is the liberal tradition, with its idealization of individual rights and the rational state-citizen relationship. It is equally true that the geographical and chronological reach of this study will extend to more recent twentieth century authoritarian and twenty-first century "spectacular"[3] variations on the same theme. Once again, however, I will understand rights and

1 As noted by Pedersen 1996, 673-698. See also Duben and Behar 2002, 181-2. And, more broadly, Pateman 1988, *passim*. Among others.

2 See Pateman 1988, *passim*. Brown.1992, 7-34. One could argue that the tradition of feminist critiques of liberalism is as old as liberalism itself, however, if we consider the work of Mary Wollstonecraft and others.

3 As it has been termed by Agamben 1998, 10.

citizenship above all as instruments of cutting, splicing, and stitching—as tools in the construction of the physical, flesh-bound citizen, rather than in the construction of the abstract, law-bound citizen. Indeed, a second fundamental argument that will recur throughout this book is that it is precisely the relentless granting of rights that we have seen since the eighteenth century that has turned the womb into a political space.

A third theme that will appear with frequency is related to this process of rights-granting and concerns the nature of the modern and the post-modern. When I talk about modern and post-modern states over the following chapters, I will be referring both to states operating within certain basic chronological boundaries—the late eighteenth century to the present—and also to states situated within the more complex and shifting ideological framework that developed over this same period. The twenty-first century "spectacular post-democratic society," as a society in which "politics knows no value (and, consequently, no non-value) other than life,"[4] is arguably a post-modern society. The mid-nineteenth century post-Enlightenment society, with its emphasis on rationality, legal formalism, organization, and meaning, is arguably a modern one. The authoritarian and fascist states of the mid-twentieth century served, again arguably, as a bridge between the two—appropriating the vocabulary of formal law and rational legalism in the name of a politics of spectacular bare life.

This gradual process will form the principal backdrop for my discussion of reproduction and citizenship. Indeed, two aspects of it will be vital. The first is the collapse of the modern, supposedly distinct categories of law, politics, and war into a single, overreaching category.[5] The second—one that has received less attention—is the related collapse of abortion, adultery, and rape into a single, overreaching category. As political violence and political belonging were stripped of any meaning but "life" and reformulated into a monolithic unit, I will argue, abortion, adultery, and rape were also reformulated into a single category. This was not, however, the conflation of, say, adultery and rape that we see in medieval and early modern legislation—not the "traditional" interpretation of sexual crime that came under attack in the modern period because it privileged what was apparently a religiously defined community over a politically defined consenting individual. It is instead, I will suggest, a new, modern, and post modern collapse of sexuality into reproduction, derived precisely from the liberal idealization of the consenting individual and a direct legacy of the liberal rights granting state.

Finally, I should explain what I mean by Europe. The states that interest me particularly in this book are France, Italy, Turkey, and the Ottoman Empire. Upon first glance, these may seem like odd choices. Indeed, if we define Europe as the contemporary European Union, Turkey would obviously not be included in the

---

4 Ibid.

5 This process has received a great deal of commentary over the past century. I will be relying primarily on Agamben 2005, *State of Exception* and Schmitt 1996 [1932], *Concept of the Political*, Schmitt 1985 [1922], *Political Theology: Four Chapters on the Concept of Sovereignty*, and Schmitt 2004 [1932], *Legality and Legitimacy*. For an analysis that brings Marxist theory to bear on the phenomenon, see Hardt and Negri 2004, *passim*.

picture, and Italy would be only peripherally relevant.[6] Similarly, although the Ottoman Empire was never officially colonized, it was without question engaged in a *quasi*-colonial relationship with a self-consciously external Europe,[7] and thus no more "in" Europe than Turkey is today.

At the same time, the nature of my argument, my focus on reproduction and citizenship, and my focus in turn on political and biological, permeable and impermeable borders, boundaries, interiors and exteriors make a discussion of Europe using these case studies perhaps more meaningful than one using more obviously "European" European states. Indeed, the nature of colonial and post-colonial political belonging is and has been such that both Italy and France have had to deal with an ongoing process of defining and redefining their position within Europe as well as what they themselves are as European nation states.[8] Similarly, Turkey's torturous process of becoming European—a legacy of the Ottoman Empire's tenuous, included/excluded membership in the nineteenth century Concert of Europe—is in a very basic way an argument between the Turkish government and various European Union officials about what Europe is. A final theme that will run throughout this book is therefore that these intersections between politics and reproduction, these collisions between law and sexuality, produce not only the flesh bound political subject, but also a Europe in a constant process of redefinition.

My primary points will thus be, first, that the post-eighteenth century intersection of citizenship with reproduction has produced a concrete, physical political space situated within the womb. This space is neither metaphorical, nor merely the signifier of gendered citizenship, but is materially productive of a distinctly flesh bound rather than law bound political subject. Moreover, it has been the granting of modern rights above all that has led inexorably to this biologically defined citizen. Second, as this political space has been defined, and as modern politics have gradually given way to post-modern politics, legislation on issues related to the womb—in particular legislation on abortion, adultery, and rape—has collapsed these

6 On Italy as a state at the margins of "civilization" and thus Europe see, for instance, Sassatelli 1998, 108, who argues that Italy is a country on the periphery of the "modern West," and "a Mediterranean and Catholic country where the lack of a bourgeois revolution, the persistence and transformation of family allegiances and patron-client loyalties have informed both the political and the economic transition to modernity." For an earlier, and more blatantly exotic analysis see, among others, the following *fin de siècle* discussion of corruption in Italy: "Secret of Crispi Favor: Africa is the Answer to the Vexing Italo-English Enigma—Aggression, Adventure, and Ruin: Most Cruel, Inquisitorial, and harrowing of All Imposts" 1898, 2, where it is asserted that "the [Italian] government majority are as much mercenaries as the negro battalions of Baratieri."

7 See, for instance, Inderpal Grewal's discussion of the perception of the Ottoman Empire as "feminine": "Though refuting the argument that enfranchisement of women was emasculating to the nation, Fawcet believed that Turkey was a feminine nation, showing that she too saw the colonized and Eastern countries as effeminate, and also upholding the claim that the project of colonization was a virile one." Grewal 1996, 69.

8 The invention of the so-called "refugee problem" in both states (predicated as it is upon implicit assumptions of French and Italian racial purity) is an obvious example of this process of definition.

same issues into a single, uniform category. Just as law, politics, and war became one and the same throughout the twentieth century, so too did any and all crime relating to sexuality and reproduction. Finally, each of these processes has played and continues to play a key role in defining Europe. The sexual and reproductive implications of drawing and redrawing borders or boundaries are, again, not simply symbolic or allegorical—they are concrete, and they produce tangible consequences for the bodies of European citizens as well as for the bodies of those subjects defined against, or apart from, Europe.

Liberalism, Authoritarianism, and Biopolitics

Most discussions of citizenship, and particularly rights-based citizenship, are situated within a narrowly defined liberal political tradition. The citizen as a rights bearing individual is seen as the product of a particular eighteenth century moment, and whether or not this idealized citizen has ever actually existed outside of the realm of political theory, he[9] is depicted as active, free from coercion, and operating within structures that exist to preserve his liberty. At the same time, since this same eighteenth century moment, a second citizen, the legacy of a more authoritarian take on the sovereign relationship, and usually held up as somehow the opposite—or even the shadow—of his liberal counterpart has become equally prominent. This citizen is engaged in an equally intimate, similarly modern relationship with state authority, but his rights are passive, and his individuality—if granted—is subordinated to some variation on collective identity.

The interplay—and apparent dichotomy—between the liberal citizen and the authoritarian citizen has been the subject of a number of analyses and discussions. One of the most cogent of these is Talal Asad's in his book *Formations of the Secular*. In an examination of identity cards and citizenship in Europe, Asad argues that

> in Britain, identity cards are thought of as a threat to the liberty of individual subjects (that is, *citizens*), and in the European Union states they are seen as a guarantee that a collective object (that is, the *population*) will be provided efficiently with equal welfare. The former focuses on liberty as an active right, the latter on welfare as a passive one.[10]

Although Asad associates the "citizen" primarily with the liberal political relationship in this passage, the basic tension that he describes is between the two camps that I mentioned above—the issue at stake is differing notions of rights, active versus passive, individual versus collective, liberal versus statist or authoritarian. The issue at stake, in other words, is the opposition between our two eighteenth century sovereign subjects, each caught up in an apparent and eternal opposition to the other.

I mention this apparent dichotomy both because it has served as the foundation for political debate in all four of my case studies—the Ottoman Empire, Turkey,

---

9 See below, Chapter 5, for a discussion of gendered citizenship in classical liberalism and how this notion has been re-interpreted in the modern and post modern periods.

10 Asad 2003, 140.

France, and Italy—and also because one of the primary corollaries to the argument that I sketched above will be that the opposition between the post-eighteenth century liberal and the post-eighteenth century authoritarian is a fantasy. Indeed, I will be suggesting over the following pages that when we place reproduction at the center of modern and post modern political relationships, these two groups become, eventually, one.

At the same time, I am not the first person to note the convergence of these two forms of sovereignty in the twentieth and twenty-first centuries. Michel Foucault and Giorgio Agamben have both convincingly criticized the purely juridical approach to the modern state-citizen relationship, the logic of which leads inexorably to an assumed dichotomy between the liberal and the authoritarian. Arguing first that the eighteenth and nineteenth century classical juridical subject gave way in the twentieth century to a biopolitical subject, both Foucault and Agamben suggest that this twentieth century sovereign focus on biological (rather than legal) life has in turn rendered the classical juridical categories of sovereignty (left, right, liberal, authoritarian) irrelevant. In his series of lectures, *Society Must Be Defended*, Foucault described what he called a gradual "penetration" of the classical juridical sovereign right to take life or let live by a new sovereign right "to make live or let die."[11] He discussed, in other words, the movement from politics to what he defined as biopolitics, from a focus on the rights of the individual to a focus on the health of the population. The transition from the right to life to the right to death obliterated the line between active and passive citizenship, between rights and duties writ large. All that was left was the health of the population, which rested in turn upon the biological integrity of the citizen.

Giorgio Agamben, using Foucault's work as a starting point, takes this transition to its logical conclusion. With regard to rights, for instance, he argues that "declarations of rights represent the originary figure of the inscription of natural life in the juridico-political order of the nation-state."[12] It is precisely the granting of rights that in this analysis moves biology to the center of politics. Likewise, this centering of the biological renders, Agamben notes, left and right, liberal and authoritarian meaningless:

> only because biological life and its needs had become the *politically* decisive fact is it possible to understand the otherwise incomprehensible rapidity with which twentieth century parliamentary democracies were able to turn into totalitarian states and with which this century's totalitarian states were able to be converted, almost without interruption, into parliamentary democracies. In both cases, these transformations were produced in a context in which for quite some time politics had already turned into biopolitics, and in which the only real question to be asked and to be decided was which form of organization would be best suited to the task of the care, control, and use of bare life.[13]

If, in other words, we assume a biopolitical rather than a juridical model of rights and citizenship, the divisions between liberalism and authoritarianism become irrelevant.

11 Foucault 2003, 241.

12 Agamben 1998, 127.

13 Ibid, 121-2.

Moreover, the biopolitical model shifts the very context in which debates surrounding citizenship and rights occur—the issue at stake becomes not who has rights and who does not, but rather the extent to which the granting of rights has successfully inscribed "natural life" or biological "bare life" into the juridico-political order.

We are left, therefore, with the absence of a dichotomy—nothing to fight about. Although neither Foucault nor Agamben write anything explicit in this direction, however, I would suggest that the gaping hole in political discourse that they describe is the most overt and the most obvious in the realm of reproduction.[14] It is in the womb that the biopolitical subject is formed, in the womb that liberalism and authoritarianism collapse into each other, and in the womb that distinctly modern and post-modern sovereignty is articulated. Although I am without question interested in this book in the—at this point very well theorized—relationship between *gender* and citizenship, therefore, I am far more interested in the relationship between *sexuality* and *reproduction* and citizenship. Similarly, although I am concerned with the liberal and authoritarian construction of political space—the public, the private, and the fantasy of the distinction between the two—I am far more concerned with the construction of biological space, with, again, the womb as a setting for political subject formation.

Consent and Bodily Integrity

I am thus particularly concerned with the ways in which markers of political identity have joined together with markers of reproductive or biological identity to produce biopolitical, rather than liberal or authoritarian space. I am interested, in other words, in the ways in which a citizen's political status as a consenting individual collides with a citizen's biological status as a being possessed of bodily integrity. Indeed, I would argue that consent and bodily integrity have come together as *the* twin pillars of appropriate sexual, reproductive, and political structures[15] only as law has become a function of biopolitics. I would argue, moreover, that since this moment, the consent/bodily integrity formula has been critical to the obsolescence of the juridically defined citizen.

The invocation of this formula has been the most obvious in recent national and international interpretations of rape. Rape, in fact, has been articulated as a "crime against humanity" precisely as the "conception of the material integrity of the body as a right" has developed, and as the crime has come to be understood first and foremost "as a violation of autonomy."[16] As we shall see in the following chapters,

14 Foucault's *History of Sexuality* is, of course, a history of biopolitics, and in this sense he is without question writing explicitly about these issues. At the same time, however, my focus on gender and on reproduction specifically, as well as my emphasis on rights-granting as key to the creation of biopolitical space, takes my argument in a significantly different direction from his. Foucault 1990, *passim*.

15 I will discuss various "inappropriate" structures in Chapters 4 and 5.

16 Or as "as a failure to recognize the victim's civil rights of self determination," (i.e. a crime against the ability to consent). Campbell 2003, 508-9. For a further analysis of Campbell's argument, see below, Chapter 3.

however, consent and bodily integrity have been equally key to the criminalization and decriminalization of abortion and adultery, as well as to more broadly defined discussions of gender and citizenship. As Drucilla Cornell has argued with respect to the conditions necessary "to transform ourselves into individuated beings who can participate in public and political life as equal citizens," only "1) bodily integrity, 2) access to symbolic forms sufficient to achieve linguistic skills permitting the differentiation of oneself from others, and 3) the protection of the imaginary domain itself"[17] are sufficient for full, equal political participation. Bodily integrity and consenting individualism, in other words, are for Cornell central to overcoming the gender hierarchy implicit in post-Enlightenment conceptions of citizenship.

But they are also, as I mentioned above, central to supplanting political space with biopolitical space, to exploding the classical-juridical categories of citizenship and to rendering them largely meaningless. I will elaborate on this argument more fully in the following chapters, but for now I would like to sketch three analyses of the consent/bodily integrity formula that point to a significant transformation in the relationship between sexual and reproductive identity on the one hand and political identity on the other. The first of these analyses suggests that sexual and reproductive legislation has been instrumental to the formulation of lawless space. The second suggests that that the citizens who inhabit this space are subject, in the name of security or even national security, to a constant, intense, and intimate regulation of every aspect of their biological lives—that sexual and reproductive legislation is promulgated precisely for the purposes of this regulation. The third suggests more broadly that the consent/bodily integrity formula itself has produced a situation in which citizens can be known only biologically and sexually, and that juridical status alone is irrelevant to contemporary politics.

Modern consent, then, is a very specific, narrowly defined legal concept developed at the end of the eighteenth century in part to differentiate full citizens from partial citizens or non-citizens. It is not a vague or open idea: citizens—mature, sane, politically active individuals—are capable of consent. Partial citizens, passive citizens, or non-citizens—those below the age of maturity, those declared insane, or the politically inactive—are not. In the realm of sexual crime, the most obvious manifestation of this notion is in legislation on statutory rape[18] where, whether or not a child[19] consents to sex according to conventional standards, the activity is still criminal because the child has not become a full citizen and thus capable of consent according to political and legal standards.

Children, however, are not the only partial citizens or non-citizens regulated by national or international political structures, and it is here that the consent/bodily integrity formula becomes problematic. Another increasingly recognizable non-citizen or partial citizen is the (internal or external) refugee—mature, sane, regulated,

17 Cornell 1995, 4. For a further analysis of Cornell's analysis, see below, Chapter 2.

18 Statutory rape as a criminal category has been the subject of increasing criticism in a number of fields over the past 30 years. In the Italian context, for example, see the discussion of the issue in Everhart 1998, 688. In the United States context, see MacKinnon 1989, 175-6.

19 Or (notoriously) anyone declared an imbecile or incompetent.

but not in any way a full political actor. Indeed, what recent national and international interpretations of consent and bodily integrity have produced from the perspective of refugees—even, or especially, to the extent that they have been endowed with ersatz rights—is a situation in which any and all sexual or reproductive behavior on their part has become criminal. Sex has become rape and reproduction has become criminal abortion and/or criminal procreation. I will elaborate on this point in detail in Chapter 4, but for now I want to emphasize that this is not just a verbal game that I am playing. The coming together of the political and the biological, consent and bodily integrity, has produced precisely these results in the states that I am examining and precisely these results in the transnational and international context.

A second aspect of the consent/bodily integrity formula that I would like to consider in brief now and explore in more detail later on is the process by which consent has become the instrument used to excise any meaningful right to bodily integrity—and has thus become a means, again, of criminalizing all sex. The simultaneous invocation of bodily integrity and consent in contemporary legislation has, I will argue, defined non-criminal sex as an activity in which a citizen consents specifically to a violation of his or her bodily integrity. By consenting to this violation, however, this same citizen effectively transfers sovereign power—transfers the sovereign's unique ability to waive a citizen's rights—to his or her sexual or reproductive partner.[20] The only choice on the part of individuals engaging in sexual activity has therefore become a criminal one: 1) an individual can violate another individual's right to bodily integrity without his or her consent and thereby commit the traditional liberal crime that is rape, or 2) an individual can violate another individual's right to bodily integrity with his or her consent, usurp the sovereign prerogative, and thus commit a biopolitical act of treason.

Once again, this is not a simple word game. As Agamben points out in his discussion of the political philosophy of the Marquis de Sade:

> not only philosophy but also and above all politics is sifted through the boudoir. Indeed, in Dolmancé's project, the boudoir fully takes the place of the *cité*, in a dimension in which the public and the private, political existence and bare life change places. The growing

20 This relationship between the citizen and his or her rights does not even make sense in a classical-juridical context. If we consider, for instance, the right to life of the individual in the classical-juridical model, it is the sovereign, and the sovereign alone, who is capable of overriding it. Moreover, should the sovereign choose to violate an individual's right to life, consent has nothing to do with the process. The subject is deprived of the legal protection of full citizenship before his or her life is taken. It is true that many legal systems describe situations in which a citizen's right to life is forfeit—"honor killing" being an obvious example of this process in the nineteenth century French, Italian, and Ottoman criminal codes. It is likewise true that the contemporary debate surrounding euthanasia—although arguably more a biopolitical than a political debate—largely has to do with whether or not a citizen can consent to a violation of his or her right to life. But even so, there has been no moment in either of these debates at which the classical juridical sovereign has given up the monopoly on the right to life, or in which the biopolitical sovereign has given up the monopoly on the right to death. There is no question of consent on the part of the citizen—beyond, some might argue, the consent that tied this citizen into an original social contract—because it is the sovereign's right alone to "choose."

> importance of sadomasochism in modernity has its root in this exchange. Sadomasochism is precisely the technique of sexuality by which the bare life of a sexual partner is brought to life. Not only does Sade consciously invoke the analogy with sovereign power ("there is no man," he writes, "who does not want to be a despot when he has an erection"), but we also find here the symmetry between *homo sacer* and sovereign, in the complicity that ties the masochist to the sadist, the victim to the executioner.[21]

When we bring together political consent and biological bodily integrity, in other words, we produce a state full of precisely the sovereign subjects described by Sade and Agamben—a state in which public and private, political existence and bare life collapse into one another, in which a citizen's only choice is between committing violent assault and committing treason. We create a biopolitical arena, centered around the womb, and in the constant production of likewise biopolitical subjects.

The final aspect of the consent/bodily integrity formula that I would like consider in short here and in more detail later on is the extent to which it assumes a body of citizens known only by their sexual and reproductive identities. As Asad suggests in his discussion of identity cards in Europe, the basic tension between the British and the continental interpretation is a tension between liberal understandings of citizenship and authoritarian understandings of citizenship. In the first, identity cards represent a violation of the rights of the citizen in that he or she is forcibly incorporated into a national collective. In the second, the rights of the citizen can be violated only by insufficient access to the state welfare guaranteed by the identity card. When consent and bodily integrity are brought together, however, the identity card dilemma shifts and takes on a very different meaning.

Indeed, the question at stake becomes not what sort of juridical identity a citizen might carry, but instead what sort of bodily borders and reproductive identity a citizen will bear. As Deniz Kandiyoti has noted in her analysis of the Turkish transsexual community, for example, "there is now an established medical-legal procedure that culminates in the award of a pink identity card (to replace the blue identity card held by men) which confers on its holder the full legal status of a woman."[22] The Turkish government, in other words, is not remotely interested in the legal activity or in the juridical identity of its citizens; it is interested in their reproductive activity and their reproductive identity: are the citizens of Turkey men or are they women? Have they consented legally to their existence as one or the other? And have they fulfilled medically the bodily and biological requirements for membership in one or the other category? This coming together of the medical and the legal, along with the insistence upon a physical and sexual male/female divide is not a product of politics. It is a product of biopolitics—and of a universe in which consent and bodily integrity operate together to bolster the citizen's broader biopolitical rights.

---

21 Agamben 1998, 134-5.

22 Kandiyoti and Robert 1998, 22.

Gender

The argument that I have sketched until now has relied primarily upon theories of rights, citizenship, biology, and reproduction that explore gender only tangentially. Obviously, however, this book is also indebted to a half century tradition of scholarship that addresses gender and citizenship directly, and I would like to take some time now to explain how my analysis engages with this work. The gendered nature of political belonging in liberal and neo-liberal states became a subject of scrutiny particularly during the 1980s and 1990s. Scholars such as Carole Pateman, Nancy Fraser, and Wendy Brown, for example, were all instrumental in exposing and analyzing "the [Euro-American] state's masculinism," especially in its juridical form.[23] Yeşim Arat and Deniz Kandiyoti have likewise produced groundbreaking work on similar issues within the Turkish context, examining the ways in which rights and citizenship have been gendered within a specifically Turkish political framework. What I would like to do over the next few paragraphs is therefore to summarize what I see as the major themes in this work, and then to explain how my reliance upon a biopolitical, rather than political understanding of rights complements and challenges it.

In general, the scholarship of the 1980s and 1990s looked first of all at the relationship between gendered citizenship and the public/private distinction, and second, at the relationship between gendered citizenship and the granting or denial of rights. Thus, Carole Pateman sees modern patriarchy as a function of the original "social contract," modern "civil freedom" as a "masculine attribute" described incorrectly as "universal," and women incorporated into the civil order in such a way that they "attain the formal standing of civil individuals, but as embodied feminine beings … [are] never 'individuals' in the same sense as men."[24] She likewise argues that

> women, womanhood and women's bodies represent the private; they represent all that is excluded from the public sphere. In the patriarchal construction of the difference between masculinity and femininity, women lack the capacities necessary for political life … [I]n the story of the creation of civil society through an original agreement, women are brought into the new social order as inhabitants of a private sphere that is part of civil society and yet is separated from the public world of freedom and equality, rights, contract, interests, and citizenship.[25]

Brown and Fraser focus more directly on the apparent granting, but actual denial, of "rights" to the woman citizen. As Brown notes, for instance, "even when women acquire civil rights, they acquire something that is at best partially relevant to their daily lives and the main domain of their unfreedom."[26] She further links the incomplete

---

23 As Brown notes, "the *juridical-legislative* or *liberal* dimension of the state encompasses the state's formal, constitutional aspects. It is the dimension Marx, in his early writings, criticized as bourgeois, it is central to Catharine MacKinnon's and Carole Pateman's theorization of the state's masculinism, and it is the focus of the rapidly developing field of feminist jurisprudence." Brown 1992, 13.

24 Pateman 1988, 1-2, 224.

25 Pateman 1989, 4.

26 Brown 1992, 17.

acquisition of rights on the part of women to the public/private divide, arguing that, "for the most part rights do not apply in this [the private] sphere; rather this realm is firmly governed by norms of duty, love, and custom, and until recently, has been largely shielded from the realm of law."[27] Fraser, in a nearly identical move, likewise argues with reference to social welfare systems that the "subject of the 'masculine' subsystem has a right to benefits and is protected from some legally sanctioned forms of administrative caprice, whereas the subject of the 'feminine' subsystem largely lacks rights."[28] Each of these scholars, in other words, critiques the public/private distinction, posits the construction of this distinction as the foundation for a partial or incomplete acquisition of rights or civic identity on the part of women, and thus explains the gendered nature of modern citizenship.

There has been similar innovative work on gender and citizenship in Turkey. Throughout the 1980s and 1990s, scholars such as Yeşim Arat and Deniz Kandiyoti, for example, critiqued the gendered nature of Turkish citizenship. In a manner comparable to Pateman's, Brown's, and Fraser's, they contextualized their studies within a largely classical-juridical model, highlighting the tensions and internal contradictions in the notion of the public/private divide,[29] as well as designating some state activity as "progressive," and some as "backward" with regard to women's rights.[30] The result was a situation in which, again, the issue at stake was to what extent the liberal state had lived up to its rhetoric of equality. Moreover, as Arat concluded in 1996, both "citizen" and "feminist" were words that had meaning only in a secular, middle class context—neither "Islamists" nor "carpet weavers" belonged in this juridically defined world because political belonging was solely and uniquely an issue of the liberal individual and his or her rights:

> Unlike carpet weavers or Islamists, feminists act politically to expand their citizenship rights in pursuit of personal liberation in a secular context. Women's experience of citizenship reveals, in Turkey, that the seemingly neutral concept of citizenship is indeed gendered. Whereas citizenship is irrelevant for women where rights are communally defined, others use it as a means to promote a religious worldview in which the secular concept of citizenship is irrelevant.[31]

Again, these discussions have been hugely important in recent feminist critiques of the liberal and neo-liberal state. Their focus on the political rather than the biopolitical, however, has led them in many ways in a direction nearly opposed to the one that I shall be taking in this book.

---

27 Ibid, 18.

28 Fraser 1989, 154.

29 For example, "Perhaps what throws more light on the gendered nature of citizenship in Turkey was Tansu Çiller's public announcement that Özer Çiller, her husband, is the head of their family at home, despite Özer Çiller's objections and his insistence that decision making is democratic in their home … [S]he must publicly affirm that in the private realm she plays the role of a woman while in the public realm she plays the role of a man." Arat 1996, 29.

30 For example, "thus, although the secular reformers of the Turkish Republic may have had a set of nationalist goals as their ultimate objective, they have nonetheless had a progressive impact on women's rights." Kandiyoti 1987, 334.

31 Arat 1996, 31.

Whereas Brown, for instance, argues that "the liberal state does not recognize the family as a political entity or reproduction as a social relation,"[32] I shall attempt to demonstrate the opposite: the liberal (and authoritarian) state explicitly recognizes the family as a political entity, and relies heavily upon the notion that reproduction is a social (and political) relation. Perhaps more important, however, is her conclusion that, first, "women have been culturally constructed and positioned as the creatures to whom this pursuit of power and glory for its own sake stood in contrast: women preserve life while men risk it," and second, that this cultural construction set a foundation for the masculine nature of political belonging.[33] Again, my argument, situated in biopolitics rather than in politics, will stand in direct opposition to this statement. Biopolitical sovereign power is explicitly a power founded upon the right to "*make live*" rather than on the right to "*take life*." It is a power linked inextricably to the "feminine attribute"—preserving life—that Brown holds responsible for the marginalization of the female citizen. Indeed, I shall argue throughout this book that when we shift from a political framework to a biopolitical framework, the unquestioned given of nearly all late twentieth century scholarship on gender and political belonging becomes untenable. In a biopolitical framework, where reproductive identity rather than legal identity is key, where a citizen's sole right *and* duty is to produce and be part of a healthy national population, it is rather the female citizen, possessed of a womb, who become the norm. If anything, in fact, it is male citizens who must conform, who are artificially supplied with a uterus.

Thus, whereas Pateman describes a contradiction between the modern political focus on population and the gendered nature of citizenship, arguing that "the performance of women's duty is vital for the health of the state, yet the duty lies outside citizenship—indeed motherhood is seen as the antithesis of the duties of men and citizens,"[34] I once more will suggest the opposite. I will attempt to show that reproduction as a political duty is one of the most basic attributes of citizenship—motherhood indeed made identical to citizenship. Finally, when we understand citizenship within a biopolitical framework, Arat's communally oriented "carpet weavers" and politically religious "Islamists" are no longer remotely "irrelevant." Communalism is only apolitical or extra-political when we assume a (liberal) juridical model of sovereignty reliant upon and, more important, *distinguished by* the rights bearing individual. Likewise, the politicization of religion is only "dysfunctional" when we assume 1) a meaningful public/private divide and 2) an argument about whether religion should operate in the public sphere or whether it should operate in the private. When, contrarily, bare life, reproduction, and the health of the population become the markers of political belonging, when the issue at stake is not who may or may not be granted rights, inclusion and exclusion of this sort become meaningless.

In other words, whereas each of these scholars criticizes the liberal or neo-liberal state for, essentially, its exclusionary nature—rights *seem* to be granted equally but in fact are not, political identity *seems* to be gender neutral but in fact it is not—I

32 Brown 1992, 19.

33 Ibid, 28.

34 Pateman 1989, 11.

will be arguing that the sexual and reproductive nature of modern citizenship lies in the modern state's relentless *inclusion*. I see not a partial granting of rights, but a full granting of rights—not an incomplete acquisition of civic identity, but a complete acquisition of civic identity. And it is this rights granting and citizenship formation in and of themselves that move political discourse away from the classical "public" or "private" and toward the modern and post-modern reproductive and biological—moves it away from the urban square where demonstrations take place and toward the womb, where biopolitical subjects are formed. The result is thus a situation, again, in which citizens possessed of a womb become the norm, and civic identity apart from this womb becomes meaningless.

Colonialism

This is not to say, of course, that all scholarship on gender and citizenship has operated within this classical-juridical model. Discussions of gendered political belonging in the colonial context, for example, have necessarily grappled with the question of biology, blood, and reproduction, given the central and overt role that race has played in the formulation of imperial sovereignty both "at home" and "abroad." Likewise, more recent scholarship on sexuality, reproduction, and citizenship in Turkey has situated the Turkish experience more overtly within colonial and neo-colonial frameworks.

As Ann Stoler has argued, for example, it was precisely in the colonial "laboratories of modernity," that "those most treasured icons of modern western culture—liberalism, nationalism, state welfare, citizenship, culture, and 'Europeanness' itself [were] clarified."[35] It was in the colonies, in other words, that the issues analyzed by scholars such as Pateman, Brown, and Fraser were tested and articulated. At the same time, however, the biopolitical aspects of modern citizenship were equally overt in this context, their antecedents likewise formulated in the colonial "periphery" before ever appearing at the metropolitan "center." As Stoler argues elsewhere, "the management of non-conjugal sex was implicated in a discourse on 'the defense of society' much earlier than [Foucault] suggests, not as a coherent and comprehensive regime of biopower, but with many of its incipient elements"—indeed, "in this age of empire, the question of who would be a 'subject' and who a 'citizen' converged on the sexual politics of race."[36] Laura Briggs, in her analysis of "race, sex, science, and U.S. imperialism in Puerto Rico" posits a similar process, in which, for example, "the [Contagious Diseases] Acts and their analogues served to organize 'disorderly' women, often limiting their mobility to segregated districts, enrolling them as imperial citizens through the essentially bureaucratic process of registration, and sometimes restricting their clients by race."[37]

For both of these scholars, in other words, juridical models of citizenship were crucial, but blood, biology, and race were equally so. Moreover, both Stoler and Briggs suggest that the imperial relationship was a relationship central to citizenship

35 Stoler 2002, 146-7.

36 Stoler 1995, 40-1, 133.

37 Briggs 2002, 27.

formation both in the colony *and* at the metropole—an argument that will be fundamental to my discussion of reproduction and political belonging in France, Italy, Turkey and the Ottoman Empire. Although the first two states are most often seen as colonizers and the second two as colonized, I will ground my analysis in the fact that all four have spent the past 300 years grappling with this imperial reality, and that a discussion of sexual and reproductive legislation in any of them must take this reality into consideration. My discussion will therefore engage perhaps more unambiguously with work such as Stoler's and Briggs's than it will with work such as Pateman's, Brown's, and Fraser's.

My discussion will also necessarily engage with recent scholarship on gender and political belonging in Turkey, much of which has also moved away from the classical-juridical model. Ayşe Parla's work on virginity examinations, for example, explicitly highlights the simultaneously biological and political nature of citizenship in the modern Turkish nation state. By arguing first that, "virginity examinations must be viewed as a particularly modern form of institutionalized violence used to secure the sign of the modern and/but chaste woman, fashioned by the modernization project embarked on by the Turkish nationalist elite under the leadership of Kemal Atatürk,"[38] Parla discards both the juridical language of full or partial citizenship and the earlier reliance upon a progressive/backward dichotomy that looked solely at rights obtained or rights denied. She indeed suggests a process of citizenship formation similar to that described by Stoler and Briggs, in which what is at stake is not (or not just) the legal and the political, but the biological and the "racial"—in which political belonging is an issue of reproduction far more than of rights. When she continues that "the state's routinized intrusion into women's bodies comprise a fundamental facet of its sovereign claim over social relations in the home or the nation,"[39] she is likewise emphasizing the extent to which the liberal and neo-liberal creation of public and private space has been augmented (or even replaced) by the creation of a biopolitical space situated in the modern citizen's body—or, as I argue, in the modern citizen's womb. The sovereign power that she describes is directly related to the sovereignty assumed by the consent/bodily integrity formula that I outlined above—a sovereignty resting upon the notion that sexual and reproductive activity are not *related* to political activity, but in fact *identical* to it. When I argue, therefore, that it is precisely the relentless rights-granting that occurred in the Ottoman Empire, Turkey, France, and Italy over the nineteenth, twentieth, and twenty-first centuries that led to the womb defined and delimited as the new, and sole, biopolitical arena, I am conversing directly with work such as Parla's.

An Outline

This book is divided into two long chapters and two short chapters. Each of these chapters addresses in a different way the key role that sexual and reproductive legislation on the one hand and sexual and reproductive rights on the other have

38 Parla 2000, 66.

39 Ibid, 66.

played in the articulation of biopolitical space—and in the inscribing of this space upon the bodies of women citizens. The first of the long chapters, on reproductive rights and legislation, is couched in a discussion of "race suicide"—the nineteenth century fear that a declining birthrate or a debauched population would lead to the disappearance of a nationally and biologically defined political collective. The threat of race suicide horrified French, Italian, Ottoman, and Turkish politicians throughout the late nineteenth and early twentieth centuries, prompting an increasing regulation of reproductive activity over these decades and the blanket criminalization of abortion. The result was, first, the opening up of the womb as a public and political arena, and second the forging of an inextricable link between reproductive identity and political identity.

Most histories of abortion legislation see this moment as a brief if influential one, ending with the Second World War, the gradual decriminalization of abortion, and the likewise gradual articulation of consent and bodily integrity as fundamental rights. I question these analyses in this chapter, however, suggesting that in fact the late twentieth and early twenty-first century emphasis on rights—especially the right to consent and the right to bodily integrity—has in fact defined women and their wombs more relentlessly as spaces, and as spaces subject to regulation, than the earlier legislation had. Engaging in particular with analyses of consent and bodily integrity that posit each as a barrier against trespass rather than as a protection against violent attack, I argue that the invocation of, and the increasing reliance upon, these rights has turned reproductive legislation and reproductive rights into issues far more about collective or national security than they had ever been even during the era of "race suicide."

The second long chapter, on sexual legislation and sexual rights, follows a similar trajectory. Framed within a discussion of Foucault's 1977 proposal that rape be understood as a crime absent any sexual meaning, the feminist critique of this proposal, and the influence of this feminist critique on recent national, transnational, and international legislation, it suggests that post-eighteenth century rape and adultery law has, like abortion law, defined women above all as biopolitical space. After a brief discussion of the medieval conflation of rape and adultery, I turn in this chapter to a more detailed examination of the nineteenth, twentieth, and twenty-first century overlap between the two—an overlap, I argue, that owes its existence to the invention of the modern, rights-bearing citizen and, again, to this citizen's status as biopolitical space. Moreover, I argue throughout the chapter that it has been, once more, precisely the elaboration of consent and bodily integrity as rights central to modern citizenship that has turned women's bodies into space. If anything, their bodies have become subject to more extensive searches and to further regulation as bodily integrity especially has become the central right to protect—their (mute) biological testimony central to contemporary notions of legitimate governance and democratic process.

The final two chapters of the book examine various implications of these juridical processes. One of the most obvious purposes of the repeated redefinition of sexual and reproductive crime and, more basically, sexual and reproductive identity, for example, has been to define civilization—and especially European or "Western" civilization. In the first of these final short chapters, therefore, I go into detail analyzing the role played by reproductive legislation and sexual legislation in defining Europe, along with the role played by abortion, adultery, and rape law in drawing civilizational lines between it and the outside. In particular, I suggest that it is the perception of a "successful" biopolitical citizenry possessed of "secure" sexual and reproductive rights in Europe or the West that has served to separate this region (or ideological construct) from the rest of the world.[40] The most immediate result of this perception has been the attempt to draw those outside of this self-described Europe—in particular refugees or stateless people—into the political sphere influenced by these norms. Indeed, I argue, the invention of "refugee sex"—a highly regulated variation on the sexual and reproductive behavior of citizens of European nation states—has been the direct result of this process.

The second of these final short chapters discusses in more detail the type of citizen who inhabits this sexually and reproductively defined Europe. Drawing especially on Agamben's and Carl Schmitt's analyses of the state of exception, I argue that the collapse of law into politics into war that each of these theorists describes has been accompanied by a simultaneous collapse of abortion into adultery into rape. Indeed, the trajectory of sexual and reproductive legislation over the past three centuries has produced, I conclude, a situation in which sexual/reproductive crime has come to be seen above all as an assault on the exceptional sovereignty defined by the collapse of law, politics, and war. To that extent, I likewise conclude that the neutral citizen—the citizen assumed by the biopolitical state of exception—has necessarily become the citizen possessed of a womb.

40 I should emphasize that my purpose in this chapter is to discuss the *perception* of difference between Europe and not-Europe or the West and the not-West, not any actual difference that may or may not exist.

Chapter 2

Reproduction and Race Suicide

Introduction

Most histories of modern European abortion legislation begin with the late nineteenth century fear of depopulation and the intensifying state focus on reproductive behavior that resulted from it. The question of "race suicide" had become a pressing concern among intellectuals, scholars, and policy makers all over Europe and North America by the turn of the twentieth century, and biological purity, how to preserve it, and how to fortify it appeared regularly on the agendas of apprehensive national parliaments. The criminalization of abortion was in many nation states the first step in a series of laws aimed at protecting the integrity of the nation and, in some later codes, this same beleaguered, suicidal "race."[1] In France, for example, "by the fin de siècle,"

> anxiety over depopulation had become what one historian has called a "master pathology," and in 1920, shortly after World War I, the Assemblée Nationale passed what another historian has called "the most oppressive laws in Europe against contraception and abortion" … [G]iving or getting an abortion had been illegal in France since 1810; the law of 1920 continued the practice of seeing private decisions about family size as matters of public policy by instituting penalties for anyone who recommended abortion, sold instruments which could induce abortion, sold or distributed contraceptives, or discussed birth control.[2]

Although abortion had been defined as a criminal act in the 1810 Napoleonic Code, in other words, it was only at the end of the century that it was linked to "depopulation anxiety," and legislation concerning it held responsible for the (implicitly inappropriate) overlap between "private" reproductive decisions and "public" policy ones. What these analyses suggest is thus a gradual process over the late nineteenth and early twentieth centuries by which the French state began to regulate that most private of activities—reproduction—and to turn the womb into a public as well as a political depository for the "health of the population" and, by the 1940s, the "integrity of the race."[3]

---

1 See, for instance, "Crimes Against the Integrity and Health of the Race" in *Penal Code of the Kingdom of Italy* 1931, Part X.

2 Pedersen 1996, 675-676.

3 Andres Horacio Reggiani, for example, argues that French abortion legislation "raises the question of the prominent role of the French State—the INED [Institute National d'Études Demographiques] is a public institution under the joint supervision of the ministries of Research and Social Affairs—in identifying pronatalist goals with demographic policy." Reggiani 1996, 726.

It is not my purpose to cast doubt on these conclusions. Without question, early twentieth century French (and Italian, and Ottoman, and German, and United States) abortion policy was linked to fears of race suicide and to the dire political and military consequences of depopulation.[4] I would also argue, however, that this fin de siècle moment was a long time in the making—itself the product of eighteenth century notions of citizenship in which the rights-bearing individual (even more so than the evolutionarily besieged "race") was the inviolate entity in need of protection and fortification. Indeed, the linkage between inappropriate reproductive (as opposed to, or in addition to, sexual) behavior with inappropriate, and eventually self-destructive, political behavior was formulated much earlier than many have argued. Long before interwar French parliamentarians on both the left and the right were calling for the death of purveyors of contraception, and even before Napoleon had criminalized abortion in France in 1810, for example, F.C.H. Pouqueville, a French consul in the Ottoman Empire, was already writing the following about unhealthy reproductive habits, depopulation, and their political (and civilizational) consequences in Ottoman lands:

> Although [Muslim Moreote women] are often Greeks themselves, unlike the latter they rarely have a large number of children. This may be explained, on the one hand, by the institution of polygamy and, on the other, by the frightful art of abortion, which is familiar to them. Nowhere have the effects of abortion been so harmful [as among the Turks] nor so solemnly consecrated. Avowed publicly in the family of the Sultan, who condemns his sisters and nieces to sterility, these horrible means of depopulation pass on to different strata of society. When suspected of infidelity, the wives of a Turk do not hesitate to commit the crime. They even resort to it, without remorse, with the sole object of conserving their attractiveness and protecting the beauty that gives them an empire over their rivals, with whom they never cease to be at war.[5]

Immediately following France's liberal revolution, in other words, abortion joined polygamy as *the* sexual/reproductive behavior most indicative of the disordered, self-destructive Eastern state.[6] As Pouqueville makes clear, the Ottoman political/

---

4 As Nathan Stormer has argued in the United States context, "whereas the wrangle over women's versus fetal rights takes center stage in debates today, in the early struggle the procreativity and health of the white, bourgeois body politic was at the forefront. Physicians declared abortion a threat to civilization and promulgated rules for safe, adequate procreation … [N]ot only did a woman carry the fate of her kin in her womb, now she also carried the fate of an entire class, ethnicity, race, and nation, as improper or insufficient reproduction among white middle and upper classes was marked as a 'national threat.'"Stormer 2000, 115-116

5 Pouqueville 1805, 265. As quoted in Stoianovich 1962, 630-1.

6 The relationship between inappropriate familial and sexual relationships—embodied especially in the harem and in polygamy—and inappropriate political relationships so central to Enlightenment era political philosophy has received a great deal of attention. Inderpal Grewal provides one of the most cogent analyses of this phenomenon when she writes "if despotism embodies this opacity, then the harem, as a displacement of European monarchy, becomes a space that most clearly depicts this mode of control. Such a view is apparent in its earliest forms in Montesquieu's *Persian Letters*. There the harem is in disarray, with fomenting rebellions, wives with no love for the husband/master, intrigues, and crises.

familial relationship was precisely the sort of political/familial relationship against which revolutionary liberalism stood in opposition—a relationship in which a tyrannical sovereign who respected neither the rights of the individual (whom he "publicly" condemned to sterility) nor the health of what would eventually become the race (which he allowed to depopulate) could continue to hold sway. By 1865, the question of Muslim or Turkish depopulation had indeed become such a widespread trope that European statisticians, less interested in the rights of the citizen than in the "truth" of the population crisis,[7] were attempting to combat it with studies of the "On the Supposed Extinction of the Turks and the Increase of the Christians in Turkey" sort.[8]

These efforts proved for the most part ineffective. Throughout even the 1960s it was still argued that "the practice of polygamy and abortion and the spread of venereal disease reduced the reproductive powers of the Turks," which in turn led to political, military, and economic "decline."[9] Indeed, as recently as 1999, we learn from one scholar that "the Ottoman Empire declined not solely as a result of the vice, indolence, and lack of interest of the Sultan or the endless intrigues in the harems … [W]hile European countries and Russia grew in economic and military strength, the Ottoman leaders allowed their empire to fall further behind. What is more, largely because of the widespread practice of abortion, the Turkish population declined."[10] The "actuality" of the late eighteenth century Ottoman Turkish race suicide thus

---

Such despotism in the domestic space embodies the orientalist view of the harem. To this, in Montesquieu's inaugural text of the European Enlightenment, is compared the dream of a transparent society, one where self-government is done out of love." Grewal 1996, 49. The question of *reproductive* rather than familial or sexual disarray in eighteenth century orientalist texts of this sort has, contrarily, received relatively little attention.

7 And what it meant for their own, now biologically defined national collectives.

8 "It is alleged by many authorities that Turkish women and their husbands generally countenance abortion and infanticide for various reasons—the women to save the trouble of pregnancy, and the men to get rid of children they cannot keep, and in the belief of the decline of the race. That abortion is resorted to for various motives in Turkey, by women married and unmarried, as in our own and other countries, may be admitted as it is admitted for other countries; and the medical evidence to be found never goes further than this. To suppose a general practice of abortion among the higher and upper classes, is opposed to open facts. In Turkey, the position of mother is higher than that of wife, and the first female personage of the empire is the mother of the Sultan, the Valideh Sultan. Among men and women there is an earnest desire for children, and whenever I have inquired, I have found husbands or wives have had children." Clark 1865, 265.

9 Stoianovich 1960, 250. See also, "the upward attack against persons in authority and the downward assault upon the peasants by merchants, artisans, soldiers, brigands, officials, and vagabonds were paralleled by action of another nature on the part of the Muslim townswomen. We allude, in particular, to the adoption by Muslim women of birth control measures about which we know unfortunately next to nothing … [W]e should like consequently to reformulate our hypothesis: After the Ottoman conquest the Balkan family grew larger and stronger. The Muslim Ottoman family (the Albanian Muslim family perhaps excepted) on the contrary, became both psychologically and biologically weaker after the close of the sixteenth century." Stoianovich 1962, 630-1.

10 Edgerton 1999, 37-8.

became the foundation and backdrop for later discussions of the "threat" of race suicide on the part of European and North American populations. The Ottoman sovereign respected neither liberal rights nor the authoritarian race; this lack of respect was manifested most obviously in the apparent, unnatural joy he took in widespread abortion displaced onto widespread polygamy, and the result was a weak state in a constant process of decline.

This is not, of course, to say that the Ottoman government itself was unconcerned with depopulation and its relationship to abortion by the late nineteenth century. In 1889, for example, the daily newspaper *Sabah* ran an articled entitled "'Memalik-i Osmaniyye'de tezayüd ve tenâkı-ı nüfus' (Population increase and decrease in Ottoman lands)." As Alan Duben and Cem Behar note,

> the anonymous author of the article upholds the mistaken though widespread view that the population of the Ottoman Empire had considerably declined since "olden times," and stresses that this decline had been particularly dramatic for the Muslim population as compared to other religious communities. Alongside very high infant mortality, venereal diseases, and "disproportionate and thoughtless marriages," the author does not hesitate to mention abortion as one of the main reasons for what he perceives as the especially rapid decline of the Ottoman Muslim population.[11]

In the same year, the Sultan Abdülhamid II convened a committee to look into "the unhealthy practices of abortion which have been increasing recently in our dominions and have been causing a decrease in the Muslim population."[12] The question of abortion, its relationship to depopulation, and the ways in which it signified both inappropriate political violence and inappropriate political relations was thus both the product of an eighteenth century liberal context, and a foundation for nineteenth century concerns about the quantity of the race, its quality, and how the state was going to protect it. By the 1920s and 1930s, Turkey, much like France and other European nation states, had become the possessor of a modern, authoritarian policy toward abortion—the "gentler" criminalization from the Ottoman period having fallen by the wayside.

The only obvious difference between the Turkish and the French cases in fact seems to be the way in which they were analyzed in hindsight. Scholars of the French situation, while seeing the interwar attitude toward depopulation as "pathological," have nonetheless left unquestioned the underlying assumption that the French population was in fact in a steady state of decline. Scholars of the Ottoman case—with exceptions of the sort noted above—argue, contrarily, that the Ottoman impression

11 Duben and Behar 2002, 181-2. They likewise state that "another long article appears the same year in *Sabah*. It is simply entitled 'İskat-ı cenin' (Abortion), and contains the following: 'Abortion is perhaps not the most important reason for population decline, but it is surely the most terrible. Abortion is not an error or an offense. It is a terrible crime … [A] child is a creation of God from the very moment it is conceived. Article 193 of our Criminal Law concerns abortive practices. If a pregnant woman with or without her consent, uses or is made to use drugs or any other means in order to abort, the perpetrator of this crime is punishable by six months to two years imprisonment. If the criminal is a doctor, surgeon or apothecary, he would be sentenced to hard labor.'"Duben and Behar 2002, 181-2.

12 Ibid, 183.

was "mistaken." I will discuss the implications of these differing approaches in more detail in the final chapter of the book. For now, I simply want to emphasize that the modern criminalization of abortion in the Ottoman Empire and Turkey was linked just as securely to fears of depopulation as it was linked to similar fears in states like France. Indeed, if anything, the Ottoman situation was perceived as more dire, given the apparent relationship between *actual* "decline" and *actual* abortion practices so central to post eighteenth century colonial rhetoric.

This is the first half of the story of modern European abortion legislation. The second half usually begins with the conclusion of the Second World War—the European trauma that, according to various national (and colonial) narratives, illustrated beyond any doubt the folly of political structures based in authoritarianism and the necessity for tolerant replacements that would protect the rights of the individual.[13] By the 1960s, feminist movements had also adopted this post-Second World War language of rights and liberties in their efforts to de-criminalize abortion. Thus, in the late 1960s in Turkey,[14] and in the late 1970s in France and Italy, the "right to health" became the foundation for a partial decriminalization of abortion for therapeutic reasons,[15] and in the early 1980s all three states based a more extensive relaxation of the law on the "right to bodily integrity." As one scholar of the French process argues,

> when the Socialist Party (PS) won the 1981 elections, a change was presaged for women's policy. The PS had undergone a transformation of sorts, when its own Secretariat des Droits des Femmes sponsored a congress for party delegates on women's rights in 1978; a rewritten platform on abortion was just one result. By 1979, PS had proposed a new abortion rights agenda that started with the proclamation that "la liberté de disposer de son corps est un droit inalienable"—"the freedom to control one's body is an inalienable right."[16]

Opponents of this process similarly abandoned their earlier authoritarian vocabulary and also took up the rhetoric of rights, privileging, however, the "right to life" of the fetus over the "right to bodily integrity" of the mother. The health of the nation or race in this way disappeared almost completely from the discourse, remaining if

---

13 Among others, see, for example, Mark Mazower's *Dark Continent: Europe's Twentieth Century*. It is a perplexing book, the title of which seems to acknowledge the relationship between rights-based European liberalism (sometimes conflated in the text with "democracy," in the usual "fascism v. democracy" dichotomy) and colonial violence, but the contents of which constitute a straightforward progress narrative of European rights and freedoms since the Second World War. As the book concludes, "globally, Europe has lost its primacy, and perhaps that is what most Europeans find hard to accept. Yet compared with other historical epochs and other parts of the world today, inhabitants of the continent enjoy a remarkable combination of individual liberty, social solidarity, and peace. As the century ends, the international outlook is more peaceful than at any time previously." Mazower 1998, 403.

14 Tezcan 1980, 5.

15 Very limited abortion for therapeutic reasons had been made legal in France in 1955.

16 Robinson 2001, 95.

anything an unpleasant reminder of mid-century politics nearly as inappropriate as the eighteenth century Ottoman Sultan's tyrannical, polygamous despotism.

Once again, my purpose is not to question the basic outline of this story. The rhetoric surrounding abortion did change following the Second World War, and the partial or complete decriminalization of abortion in the 1970s and 1980s rested squarely upon a vocabulary of individual rights rather than upon a vocabulary of racial or national integrity. At the same time, however, I would also like to suggest that the late twentieth century decriminalization of abortion was in no way a departure from, and was indeed in many ways a continuation of, the mid-nineteenth century process of rendering the womb a political—and then a biopolitical—space. Both the criminalization of abortion, with its attendant placement of the health of the nation or the race in the womb, *and* the de-criminalization of abortion, with its placement of the rights of the individual in the same location, assumed that "reproductive space" was a separate, political, public arena, in which the modern sovereign-subject relationship would be articulated. In the same way, in other words, that both rights-based liberal states and race-based authoritarian states were founded upon late eighteenth and early nineteenth century sovereign declarations of rights[17]—be they the various revolutionary or Napoleonic French Constitutions or the various edicts produced during the Ottoman Tanzimat—both the late twentieth and early twenty-first century rights rhetoric that surrounds the "abortion debate" *and* the late nineteenth and early twentieth century race rhetoric that surrounded the same debate owe their existence to eighteenth century writers like Pouqueville.

Once abortion joined polygamy as the dysfunctional Eastern practice that served as both metaphor and concrete manifestation of inappropriate, uncivilized governance—in other words, once the womb joined the family as the place in which political relations would be hammered out—the womb, like the family, remained politicized. Indeed, as its political meaning gave way to a more overtly biopolitical meaning, the *type* of rhetoric produced there—liberal or authoritarian, progressive or conservative, left or right—became irrelevant. All that mattered was the continuing process of citizenship formation and population management key to the biopolitical state.

Historical Context

At the same time, abortion did not suddenly and for the first time become a legislative issue in the late eighteenth and early nineteenth centuries. In France, what would become Italy, and the Ottoman Empire, it had been the subject of debate among jurists for centuries. Ottoman legislators, for example, were the inheritors of a well established Islamic legal tradition, and largely followed the Hanafi school's approach to the issue, allowing abortion in the first 120 days of pregnancy.[18] At the same time,

---

17 Agamben 1998, 126-131.

18 "The majority of scholars from the Hanafi and Zaydi schools allow abortion before 120 days; they argue that the fetus is not ensouled until the 120 days pass. The Hanbali school allows abortion before 40 days. The Shafi'i school is divided: some scholars allow abortion until 80 days (as sperm and blood clot); some allow it before 120 days. Others, including the

at least three of the four major Sunni schools of law were well represented within Ottoman borders, and so the fundamental debate among these schools—the moment at which the fetus became "ensouled"—would have been well represented as well. As Donna Bowen notes,

> there are two basic opinions: (1) abortion at any point following conception is murdering a created entity and is thereby forbidden; and (2) the fetus is created at a point following conception—some say 40 days, some 90 days, some 120 days. Before creation, abortion is permitted; following this point, it is forbidden .... [I]n a hadith the Prophet adds the explanation that 40 days is assigned to each stage: the fetus is held as a drop of sperm for 40 days, as a blood clot for another 40 days, and then as an embryo for a final 40 days, at which point the fetus is "created"—the point, by extrapolation, at which some jurists consider the soul enters the fetus. Other hadiths give 40 days as the time of creation.[19]

Marion Katz has also pointed out that in medieval and early modern analyses, deliberate abortion undertaken by a woman receives less attention than accidental or culpable miscarriage. In such cases, she argues, the debate, still linked to the question of the moment of ensoulment, is whether compensation for the loss of the fetus "due to such culpable actions as blows to the stomach" should be treated as the equivalent of wounding, with payment going to the woman,[20] or as the equivalent of murder, with payment going to the "heirs" of the fetus.[21] Two further questions that appear with frequency in discussions of abortion are thus, first, to what extent negligence, deliberation, or responsibility should be considered relevant to the criminal nature of the act and, second, whether abortion as a "violent act" has more to do with wounds inflicted on the woman or the taking of the life of the fetus. Leslie Peirce, in her analysis of law and gender in one sixteenth century Ottoman court, suggests that Ottoman authorities of this period, at least, could answer these questions with some certainty: abortion was something done to rather than by the woman (as Katz argues), although the payment (*diyet*) was compensation for the life of the fetus rather than compensation for a wound to the woman.[22] By the nineteenth and twentieth centuries, as we shall see, all three of these issues—

Muslim theologian and Shafi'i jurist al-Ghazali, prohibit it at any time." Bowen 1997, 164. The majority Ottoman school was the Hanafi school, although there were significant Shafi 'i and Maliki minorities in the Empire.

19 Bowen 1997, 164. See also, "Almost the only possible generalization about the opinions of the four schools of Sunni *fiqh* is that they all hold abortion to be forbidden after ensoulment (literally 'the inbreathing of the spirit') which is held ... to occur after 120 days of gestation. The only exception to this rule is in the case of peril to the life of the mother, which is held to take precedence over the potential life of the fetus." Katz 2003, 30.

20 Ibid, 25.

21 Avner Giladi has also noted that "in many sources, coitus interruptus ('azl) and abortion (ijhad) are mentioned in the same breath as infanticide ... [A]bortion, like infanticide, was regarded from the juridical point of view, as a severe crime against a living creature, especially if it took place in the later stages of pregnancy. Otherwise it was tolerated by some jurists." Giladi 1990, 190.

22 The source that Peirce cites for this is not a court record, but Colin Imber's discussion of the jurist Ebu's-Su'ud. Peirce 2003, 147.

the moment of ensoulment, the question of responsibility, and the nature of the injury—were re-appropriated and reinterpreted in the service of modern political and biopolitical goals.

The medieval and early modern history of abortion legislation in France and Italy was the product of similar scholarly debate. Unlike jurists in the Sunni Islamic world, however, who were relatively free to interpret law independently, constrained for the most part only by the dictates of their schools or the political realities of the states in which they were operating, jurists in the Catholic world were tied closely to the Vatican's dictates on canon law. Although there may have been differing ideas about whether and when abortion should be allowed, therefore, these ideas were for the most part subsumed under binding declarations made by various Popes. As Marina Calloni notes,

> in the Middle Ages, abortion started to be condemned as culpable homicide and punished according to canon law. The fetus was in fact considered as a *person*, meaning a body supplied with a soul … [T]he Church adopted over the centuries two different approaches to this question: the idea of *immediate animation* and that of *late animation*. While under the former idea, supported by the Popes Sisto V and Gregory the XIV in the sixteenth century, the fetus is considered as having from the beginning a life or a soul, under the latter, supported by Pope Innocent III, in the twelfth and thirteenth centuries, the fetus is considered as having a life or a soul only when the quickening of the fetus can be felt. This second interpretation derives from Aristotle's philosophy, which states that a male fetus acquires a soul 40 days after his conception while a female fetus obtains hers 80 days after.[23]

Like their medieval and early modern Muslim counterparts, in other words, medieval and early modern Catholic legislators were similarly concerned first and foremost with the moment of ensoulment—the point at which the fetus became a "person." Unlike the debate in the Islamic world, however, the debate in the Catholic world took place over time rather than over schools of thought—in the twelfth and thirteenth centuries, the approach to abortion was closer to what we see among Hanafi scholars, whereas in the sixteenth century, it was closer to the Shafi'i interpretation. Moreover, unlike scholars of Islamic law, who debated issues of responsibility and injury in addition to the moment of ensoulment, scholars of Catholic canon law were interested almost exclusively in whether or not the fetus was a person. Indeed, in 1532, around the same time that Ottoman authorities were defining abortion as, simultaneously, something external that happens to a woman, if nonetheless something that requires compensation to the heirs of the fetus, Charles V, the Holy Roman Emperor, was stating in a criminal code that extended to all of the land under his control, the far more succinct argument that "abortion was homicide and was therefore to be prosecuted."[24]

Whereas the modern and contemporary invention of reproductive consent and bodily integrity could develop out of multiple and related medieval and early modern traditions of responsibility and injury in the Ottoman Empire, therefore, in France

23 Calloni 2001, 181.
24 Ibid, 182.

and Italy, it was linked more overtly to the basic problem of "life." In the twelfth and thirteenth centuries, life began at 40 days, in the sixteenth century, it began at conception, by the late nineteenth century it was linked to the perpetuation of the race or nation, and by the late twentieth century it was linked to the protection of the rights of the individual citizen. As Calloni notes, it was in 1839 that "Pope Pius IX chose definitively, on the basis of the new dogma of the 'immaculate conception' of Mary, the version of the immediate animation of the fetus."[25] At precisely the moment, in other words, that pronatalism was taking off in Europe and race suicide was becoming a new national threat, the immaculate nature of ideal reproduction[26] became the basis for a religious reinforcement of the criminal nature of abortion.

This is not, however, to say that Ottoman/Turkish approaches to abortion did not resemble French and Italian approaches by the mid to late nineteenth century. All three states, for example, have had similar histories with regard to developing an official terminology for speaking of abortion. In France and Italy, for example, "abortion" (*avortement, aborto*), from the Latin "to miscarry" (*aborior/aboriri*), was replaced in twentieth century legislation by "voluntary interruption of pregnancy (IVG)" (*l'Interruption voluntaire de grossesse*,[27] *Interruzione Volontaria della Gravidanza*)[28] both because the term "abortion" had become associated with feminist "radicalism"[29] and because it was considered insufficiently technical. In the Ottoman Empire and Turkey, the original Arabic term used in legal discourse, a variation on "labor" (*ijhad*), was replaced by the Ottoman Turkish term, "abortion," or literally "the rejection of the fetus" (*ıskat-ı cenin*) by the early nineteenth century. In the early twentieth century, this Ottoman Turkish term was replaced by the modern Turkish for "abortion/miscarriage," literally "causing a child to fall" (*çocuk düşürme*), suggesting a much more deliberate act than previous words for "miscarriage"[30] The French, Italian, and Turkish governments have all, in other words, deliberately altered the legal terminology (and to some extent the popular terminology) by which abortion has been understood over the past century.[31]

---

25 Ibid, 181.

26 For more on "the idyllic image of the fetus … organized by the model of pure self-willed conception" in modern abortion rhetoric, see Stormer 2000, 128.

27 Robinson 2001, 110.

28 Calloni 2001, 182.

29 Robinson 2001, 110.

30 *Türk Ceza Kanunu* 1994, 128–130. "*Düşürmek*," "to make fall," is the causative of "*düşmek*," "to fall." Recently the word "kürtaj," from curettage, has been used with frequency in popular and official discussions.

31 It is worth noting the deliberate confusion that has been created in the French and Italian context between abortion (IVG) and artificial insemination or in vitro fertilization (IVF). In Italy, for example, "Once abortion was raised in the context of the IVF [in vitro fertilization] controversy [in 1981], [abortion opponents] posed the moral question of the life of embryos inside and outside the womb … [E]ventually [Marida] Bolognesi [Chair of the Commission to prepare the IVF bill] resigned because the majority of the Chamber of Deputies approved an article of the bill which neglected the *fecundazione eterologa*, which meant that only gametes belonging to married couples could be used for IVF." Calloni 2001, 196.

I would indeed like to emphasize the broader shift in attitude that these changes in French, Italian, and Turkish terminology represent. As Lealle Ruhl argues with regard to "birth control" in general,

> the term implies that spacing, regulation, and otherwise "interfering" with supposedly natural processes (the biological processes of reproduction) are not only possible but indeed desirable and even necessary. Seen in this light, women's reproductive capacities are unruly and damaging to women's liberty—a view epitomized by the writing of de Beauvoir, who denies the very possibility of agency in the physiological processes of pregnancy.[32]

This argument could be applied with equal credibility to the changing language of abortion. Whereas "abortion" might be considered "natural," if also a "failure,"[33] part of the "biological processes" of pregnancy, IVG and *çocuk düşürme*, the latter with its causative tone and the former with its explicit invocation of both the liberal "voluntary" and the artificial "interruption," make clear that the behavior is anything but natural. The implication is that what had once belonged to the realm of nature and biology had moved (or been moved) into the realm of politics and law. As Ruhl argues, biology is held up in distinct opposition to law—a woman's reproductive capacity is specifically damaging to her legal identity as a citizen. Freedom, in other words, becomes the opposite of biology.

At the same time, however, I want to suggest that this voluntary interruption, even as it implied a separation of the reproductive or biological from the political, simultaneously inscribed both reproduction and biology effectively into legal and political structures. By turning pregnancy into something that *could* be regulated, for example, the unruly v. controlled (reproductive v. political) dichotomy broke down. Rather than being a place best left alone, in which the politically irrelevant or dangerous occurred, the womb became instead an explicitly relevant place, open to and in need of intervention, a place where the well controlled pregnancy could and should be subject to politics instead of nature—a place subject to control by the sovereign rights-bearing citizen, the citizen capable of responsible, voluntary behavior. The phrases IVG and *çocuk düşürme* thus represent one aspect of the womb as biopolitical space. Again, however, this reinterpretation of the womb could not have occurred without a centuries long process of earlier legislation—a process in which variations on "life," the relationship among law, politics, and life, and the proper arena in which this relationship ought to play out had already been theorized time and time again.

---

32 Ruhl 2002, 650.

33 *Aborior/abriri* also means "to fail." I should note as well that the "natural," or at least non-deliberate, nature of the term "abortion" depends on a reading of *ab-orior/oriri* that defines the preposition *ab* as "away from" rather than as "at the hands of." *Orior/oriri* means "to be born."

The Biopolitical Womb

I have been using the term "biopolitical space" throughout this chapter without providing a working definition of it, and I would like to pause now to discuss in more detail the ways in which I see it relating to my argument. When I talk about biopolitics, I am referring first of all to the theory of sovereignty (and eventually governmentality) that Foucault developed in his 1975–1976 lectures, "Society Must be Defended," and in the first volume of his *History of Sexuality*. As I mentioned in the introduction to this book, the aspect of Foucault's theory of biopolitics that interests me particularly is the movement he describes from a classical-juridical sovereign right "to let live and make die" to a biopolitical right "to make live and let die." As this movement takes place, Foucault argues, the disciplined body and the managed population gradually come to replace the rights-bearing citizen and the sovereign, territorial state: "after a first seizure of power over the body in an individualizing [disciplining] mode, we have a second seizure of power that is not individualizing but, if you like, massifying, that is directed not at man-as-body but at man-as-species ... [W]e have at the end of [the eighteenth] century, the emergence of something that is no longer an anatamo-politics of the human body, but what I would call a 'biopolitics' of the human race."[34]

Obviously, there are a number of implications to this approach to modern sovereignty. After first introducing his theory of biopolitics in outline, for example, Foucault immediately notes that in the eighteenth century "we also see the beginnings of a natalist policy, plans to intervene in all phenomena relating to the birth rate."[35] He continues, however, that it is not just fertility, but also morbidity that becomes of interest, and indeed death ceases to be something sudden and definitive (for an individual), but instead an issue for the population, "something permanent, something that slips into life, perpetually gnawing at it, diminishes it and weakens it."[36] Finally, a third major issue that he sees as a function of biopolitics is the issue of the "environment" and its effect on populations—"the problem, for instance, of swamps throughout the first half of the nineteenth century. And also the problem of the environment to the extent that it is not a natural environment, that it has been created by the population and therefore has effects on that population."[37]

In *The History of Sexuality*, Foucault further develops his theory, arguing that,

> for the first time in history, no doubt, biological existence was reflected in political existence; the fact of living was no longer an inaccessible substrate that only emerged from time to time, amid the randomness of death and its fatality; part of it passed into knowledge's field of control and power's sphere of intervention. Power would no longer be dealing simply with legal subjects over whom the ultimate dominion was death, but with living beings, and the mastery it would be able to exercise over them would have to be applied at the level of life itself; it was the taking charge of life, no more than the threat of death, that gave power its access even to the body ... [F]or millennia, man remained

34 Foucault 2003, 242-243.
35 Ibid, 243.
36 Ibid, 244.
37 Ibid, 245.

> what he was for Aristotle: a living animal with the additional capacity for a political existence; modern man is an animal whose politics places his existence as a living being in question.[38]

The defining characteristics of biopolitics that interest me here are thus 1) the transformation of sovereign right and the shift in focus from the citizen to the population, 2) the emergence of fertility as well as morbidity (but not death) as subjects of political interest, 3) the linkage of "the environment" to politics, and 4) the modern subject as "an animal whose politics places his existence as a living being in question."

A number of interpretations of biopolitics have addressed these four aspects of Foucault's theory over the past 30 years. Ann Stoler, for instance, has used the theory of biopolitics as a context for analyzing the relationship between modern (colonial) racism and bourgeois sexuality. In her *Race and the Education of Desire*, she argues that,

> one of the more riveting themes of the lectures, on the production of "internal enemies" within the body politic, alters our reading of *The History of Sexuality* in yet another way. Foucault's finer tracing in the lectures of a "racism that a society will practice against itself" provides a strong rationale for two of his claims: that the biopolitical management of life was a critical bourgeois project and that the management of sexuality was crucial to it.[39]

Here, in other words, the transformation or alteration of sovereign right and the sovereign subject produces a situation in which the enemy becomes internal, and in which the management of fertility as well as morbidity rests squarely on a self-referential racism. As Mitchell Dean likewise notes with regard to biopolitics and racism, "the life of the population, its vigor, its health, its capacity to survive, become necessarily linked to the elimination of internal and external threats … [B]ut this last example does not necessarily establish a positive justification for the right to kill, only the right to disallow life."[40]

Both Stoler and Dean thus implicitly or explicitly link biopolitics to law. In this way, they bring me back to Giorgio Agamben, on whose interpretation of biopolitics I will be relying heavily throughout this book. It is Agamben, again, who suggests the elimination of classical categories of sovereignty in the biopolitical state,[41] as well as the central role played by rights in inscribing bare life or biology into political structures.[42] I will discuss these issues in more detail below. For now, I would like to focus on his description of biopolitical *space*, which he sees manifesting itself most

38 Foucault 1990, 142-143.

39 Stoler 1995, 92.

40 Dean 1999, 140.

41 Noting for instance that "only within a biopolitical horizon will it be possible to decide whether the categories whose opposition founded modern politics (right/left, private/public, absolutism/democracy, etc.)—and which have been steadily dissolving, to the point of dissolving, to the point of entering today into a real zone of indistinction—will have to be abandoned …". Agamben 1998, 4.

42 Ibid, 126-131.

clearly in the twentieth century concentration camp. He argues with reference to the Nazi *lagers*, for example, that:

> Whoever entered the camp moved in a zone of indistinction between outside and inside, exception and rule, licit and illicit, in which the very concepts of subjective right and juridical protection no longer made any sense … [I]nsofar as its inhabitants were stripped of every political status and wholly reduced to bare life, the camp was also the most absolute biopolitical space ever to have been realized, in which power confronts nothing but pure life, without any mediation. This is why the camp is the very paradigm of political space at the point at which politics becomes biopolitics and *homo sacer* is virtually confused with the citizen … [T]he bare life into which the camp's inhabitants were transformed is not, however, an extrapolitical, natural fact that law must limit itself to confirming or recognizing. It is, rather, a threshold in which law constantly passes over into fact and fact into law, and in which the two planes become indistinguishable.[43]

In addition to biopolitical space as space in which the right to make live and let die holds sway, in which fertility and morbidity are of central concern, in which the environment becomes a political trope, in which the Aristotelian human animal's politics call his biological existence into question, in which the racialized enemy becomes internal, in which racism becomes self directed, and in which the right to disallow life supersedes the right to kill, it is thus also a space in which outside and inside, exception and rule, licit and illicit are conflated, in which every citizen becomes *homo sacer*—capable of being killed but not sacrificed—and in which, most fundamentally, law and fact collapse into one another.

Again, Agamben associates this biopolitical space most directly with the concentration camp, questioning Foucault's choice not to use the camp as his paradigmatic example.[44] Throughout the remainder of this book, however, I will similarly question Agamben's choice of the camp as the fundamental biopolitical arena. More so than the concentration camp, I will suggest, it is the womb that has become the paradigm of this particular form of sovereignty. It may seem strange to shift the realm of biopolitics from an area that, if indefinite, is nonetheless real in a way that the womb is seemingly not. But I will nonetheless argue that the very collapse of fact and law that is fundamental to biopolitics produces a situation in which the womb is just as much a real space as the *lager*—just as much a real space as the sports arena turned into a detainment center for refugees.

I do, however, want to make absolutely clear that when I say that the womb is the paradigmatic example of biopolitical space—that it is essentially more concentration camp than the concentration camps—I am *not* making an argument about the fetus as an inhabitant of that space, or about the fetus as a being with rights or as a person subject to legal protection. As we shall see over the following pages, the fetus as an issue of juristic (and biological) debate was completely irrelevant by the mid-nineteenth century, except to the extent that it served as a signifier of the larger population, nation or race. Indeed, the fetus reappeared as an "individual" only in the late twentieth century—a moment that I will address below. Rather, I will argue

43 Ibid, 170-1.

44 Ibid, 4.

that, given the various defining characteristics of biopolitical space sketched above, the womb exemplifies this space the most obviously. The woman citizen thus in turn becomes both biopolitical subject *and* biopolitical setting, with all that each of these roles imply.

Defining Nineteenth Century Reproductive Space

I would like to turn now to nineteenth century abortion legislation in France and the Ottoman Empire. Abortion was codified as a criminal act in France with the 1810 Napoleonic penal law and in the Ottoman Empire with an 1859 law based loosely on the Napoleonic model. Both of these codes, I will argue, were fundamental to transforming the womb into a setting for biopolitical subject formation, although at this early stage the issue at stake was primarily the role that rights would play in linking reproductive behavior to citizenship. At the same time, I should note that France and the Ottoman Empire were not unique in this respect and that I am certainly not alone in emphasizing this characteristic of modern abortion legislation. Stormer, for example, in his discussion of "Prenatal Space" in the U.S. context argues similarly that "through discourse on abortion in the United States, women's bodies have become scenes of national biopolitics."[45] Since Stormer is focusing primarily on the period after the Second World War, however, the construction of the fetus as rights-bearing individual is central to his discussion. One major theme that reappears in his essay, for example, is the notion that "occluding women from reproduction results in a void inhabited by an autonomous fetus. Thus, for biomedical rhetoric that privileges a fetal individual, the disappearing woman is the condition of fetal visibility and publicity."[46]

Once again, although I am arguing from a similar starting point, in many ways my discussion of nineteenth century abortion legislation in France and the Ottoman Empire is quite different from Stormer's analysis of the United States. Indeed, I will suggest that this legislation first and foremost privileges the woman as space or setting *over* the fetus as individual. Indeed, I will argue that the fetus for the most part disappears altogether. The womb as a political environment is what is at issue in the new legislation—the womb as a place in which the sovereign right to disallow life supersedes the sovereign right to kill, in which "the race" is defined explicitly, and in which law and fact, rule and exception collapse into one another. With that in mind, let me turn now to the 1859 Ottoman code and the 1810 French code upon which it was modeled.

The 1859 Ottoman Criminal Code addresses abortion in two articles—192 and 193—of a larger chapter entitled "Abortion, sale of falsified drinks, and sale of toxic

---

45 Stormer 2000, 135. He continues, "explicitly acknowledged or implicitly assumed, one theme of this research is that biomedical discourse transforms the womb into a *social space* in that it is a *site* of discourse about life, rights, and the essence of 'woman.' Understanding how this embodiment has occurred requires that we ask how discursive practices have brought together the womb and the public as a coincident location, as prenatal space." Stormer 2000, 109.

46 Ibid, 112.

substances without demanding the guarantee of the buyer."[47] These articles state that anyone who violently brings about a pregnant woman's abortion will pay *diyet*—translated into French as "the blood price"—as prescribed by Islamic law. He will also be condemned to forced labor if his intent was to cause the abortion. Second, anyone who brings about an abortion with drugs or medicine will be imprisoned from six months to two years, even if he did so with the pregnant woman's consent. If the condemned is a doctor, surgeon, or pharmacist, the punishment will be hard labor. The rest of the chapter—articles 194 to 196—discuss aiding a suicide, practicing medicine or pharmaceuticals without a license, and producing toxic or poisonous substances.[48]

The French text from which these passages were adapted is similar in detail, but differs in some key broader aspects. First of all, abortion in the Napoleonic Code appears in a much longer chapter, entitled "Threats"[49] and follows 10 articles discussing intimidation through violence, voluntary wounding, and various types of blows. The immediately preceding article, 316, addresses the "crime of castration"[50] and its punishment. Finally, the one article that focuses on abortion, 317, states that anyone who brings about a pregnant woman's abortion by any means—violent or non-violent, whether or not the woman consented—will be imprisoned. A woman who procures her own abortion will be punished in the same way. Finally, doctors, surgeons and other health officials, as well as pharmacists, will be punished with hard labor if they aid in bringing about an abortion. The same article then continues with a discussion of aiding suicide. The final article in the chapter, 318, discusses poisonous substances, although there is no mention of operating in the medical profession without a license.[51]

I would like to focus first of all upon aspects of the two passages that are similar to one another. The most basic point to note, for example, is that, again, neither concerns itself primarily with the rights or life of the fetus. By placing the article on abortion into the chapter on criminal threat rather than into the chapter on homicide, by surrounding it with articles on castration, voluntary wounding, and suicide, French jurists clearly conceived of abortion as a different sort of violent crime. It was voluntary or self-destructive at best and sexualized at worst. Unlike homicide, the line between victim and perpetrator was unclear, and the crime was the implicit result of an illness or an imbalance rather than the greed, passion, or desperation that would prompt a normal murder. The point of the legislation was indeed not to protect the individual from attacks on life, but instead to protect the collective from inappropriate, inexplicable biological or sexual violence. From the very beginning, in other words, modern French abortion legislation ignored the notion of the fetus-as-individual and concerned itself instead with the ways in which 1) the womb might

47 "*Avortement, débit de boissons falsifiés, vente de substances toxiques sans exiger de garantie de l'acheteur.*"

48 "Code pénal ottoman" 1905-6, Chap. 2, Art. 192-193. [All translations from Ottoman, Turkish, and French are mine unless otherwise noted.]

49 "*Menaces.*"

50 "*Crime de castration.*"

51 "Code pénal Napoléon" 1849, Chap. 2, Art. 316-317.

act as a cover for the inappropriate behavior of abnormal individuals, and 2) the womb must therefore be opened and regulated.

The Ottoman take on the disappearing fetus is not as clear cut as the French take, but it is still a departure from medieval and early modern Hanafi interpretations. In the Ottoman code, as in the French code, the primary issue of concern is inappropriate behavior on the part of women and doctors, not the moment at which the fetus becomes ensouled and thus a person who has lost his or her life. At the same time, however, it is evident that earlier Ottoman and Hanafi legislation did play a role in the adaptation of the Napoleonic text. To the extent, for example, that abortion is simultaneously an act of violence, *diyet* must be paid. The question of who will receive the payment—the woman or the "heirs" of the fetus—is, however, left open, thereby also leaving open the question of whether the behavior is criminal because of the wound to the woman or whether it is criminal because of the death of the fetus. The fact that when abortion occurs non-violently, *diyet* is not prescribed seems to imply that the issue at stake is wounding (as it was in the sixteenth century). But the further fact that any punishment at all is then stipulated for non-violent (but also non-homicidal) abortions likewise indicates that there is more going on here than there had been in the earlier legislation.

Indeed, by leaving the question of the recipient of *diyet* open and by both criminalizing non-violent abortion *and* placing it outside of the framework of homicide law, Ottoman jurists, like their French counterparts, are defining the crime as something different—arguably as an attack on a space rather than as an attack on a person. The *diyet* to be paid in the 1859 law, for example—nebulous as it is—can be seen as compensation for simultaneous physical assaults on the fetus as a person and the womb as a space. The imprisonment of those who engage in non-violent abortion, however, is a response solely to a political and biological attack on the womb as a space. The crime results in neither death nor wounding, in other words, but *diyet*, even in its absence, is playing a role here in the elaboration of Ottoman rather than French abortion legislation. If anything, it is in fact the appropriation and reinterpretation of *diyet* that makes possible an Ottoman, as opposed to French, construction of liberal citizenship.

First of all, the appearance of *diyet* links modern Ottoman legislation to a notion of Ottoman/Islamic "tradition" in the same way that the modern Napoleonic legislation had been linked to French/Catholic "tradition" in the early nineteenth century. In the medieval period, for example, one method of calculating the *diyet* to be paid for an illegal abortion was to value a miscarried fetus and a male or female slave equally—suggesting, as Katz argues, "a rough symbolic equivalence between the potential life that has been lost and the life of the enslaved human being who is to be delivered in restitution."[52] Before the modern period, such an equivalence would have made good economic and political sense, political subjects defined communally in relation to various economic, social, and political structures.

When we view this approach to abortion through the lens of eighteenth and nineteenth century liberal rhetoric and the discourse of the rights-bearing citizen, however, the coming together of the enslaved human being (with his or her potential

52 Katz 2003, 27.

but not actual political life) and the unborn fetus (with its potential but not actual biological life) takes on a new salience. The basic liberal transformation, after all, was one in which political space was defined above all as an arena in which "slavery" was not an option[53]—in which, as the trope went, a slave became free upon setting foot within the boundaries of x or y "free," modern nation state.[54] When the jurists responsible for the 1859 Ottoman code reinterpreted *diyet* within the context of early nineteenth century liberalism, therefore, they were making a distinct, if implicit, statement about the simultaneity of political and biological life in their own modern state. They were thus also delimiting the womb—just as their French counterparts had—as the place in which these two aspects of nineteenth century sovereignty would be articulated, and in which the modern relationship between biological identity and political or legal identity could and would be expressed.

Indeed, the Ottoman legislators responsible for the 1859 law were not the only jurists within the empire to be concerned with the juridical and political implications of abortion and reproduction—with the relationship between modern legal identity and modern biological identity. As Katz notes,

> the prominent Hanafi jurist Ibn 'Abidin (d. 1842 CE) presents an interesting discussion of this issue [of *takhalluq*[55]] while commenting on the statement that a woman's 'idda (waiting period after being widowed or divorced) expires with the miscarriage of a fetus that displays some aspect of the human form, such as a hand, foot, finger, nail, or hair; and that "its form does not become apparent until after 120 days" have passed … [T]he connection between the fetus's displaying some aspect of a recognizably human form and its right to protection under the *Sharia* is a somewhat complex one. On the one hand, it may be understood as expressing an underlying attitude towards the nature of human life: a living thing is human if it displays human form. This would seem to be the idea behind Ibn 'Abidin's terse statement that before this point "it is not a human being." However, the importance of the criterion of formation (*takhalluq*) is also connected to the rules of evidence: no legal ruling can be applied to a being whose very existence is in doubt … [I]bn 'Abidin, for instance, admits that the contention that the formation of the fetus begins only at the end of three months is problematic; he cites a source stating that "it has been observed that its form appears before this period of time [has expired]."[56]

---

53 Rhetorically, if not in practice. I am not in any way denying the complexity of, for example, Locke's defense of slavery as a practice within the broader context of liberalism as a theory.

54 This trope appears in France, for example, in a vast array of contexts, from the political theory of Emmanuel-Joseph Sièyes to the novels of Alexandre Dumas. As Sarah Hanley has noted, "The maxim 'there are no slaves in France' supported the legal cases of enslaved African women and men who were brought from the colonies into France, filed suits of freedom in French courts, and won." Hanley 1997, 45. Within the framework of gender studies, Pateman has argued that "most liberal theories would with to argue that there is one relationship, at least, to which consent ought not to be given. A person ought never to consent to be a slave, because this totally negates the individual's freedom and equality and hence, in a self contradiction, denies that the individual is capable of consent." Pateman 1980, 162-163. I will engage with this last statement in more detail in the next chapter.

55 "The emergence of discernibly human features" which is said "to coincide with the moment of ensoulment."

56 Katz 2003, 32-33.

There are, in other words, three political relationships formulated in the womb in this mid-nineteenth century discussion of biological—and *thus* political—identity: the marital relationship (a marriage can occur when a divorced woman miscarries a fetus with a "human form"), the sovereign-citizen relationship (an individual has a right to legal protection if he or she displays a "human form"), and the more basic sovereign-subject relationship (*no* legal relationship can occur if an individual's [physical] existence is in doubt). Moreover, although each of these relationships is articulated through an analysis of the development of the fetus, I want to emphasize that in this modern as opposed to medieval discussion, the primary questions raised are not about a specific fetus and its specific legal role. The issue of what the miscarried fetus is worth—what the *diyet* ought to be, for example—is either sidelined completely or tied to abstract questions of rights, sovereignty, and legal identity. The primary question is instead about the status of the fetus as a human being *to the extent that this status can help in delimiting the womb as a political space*. The fetus exists in this variation on modern abortion legislation, in other words, only as the signifier of a new role for the womb.

The third point that Katz makes, for instance, is for all intents and purposes a point about *habeas corpus*. Legal rulings can happen only if the object of those rulings is a "real" and existent political subject. Rather, however, than focusing on the political subject whose existence is in doubt because he or she is, say, in a different land or bearing a different name, the *habeas corpus* formula here is focused on the political subject residing (or hiding, or taking on a different name) in reproductive space—and thus reproductive space as a (democratic or proto-democratic) repository for political relations. As Agamben argues with regard to the notion of *habeas corpus* in the European tradition:

> nothing allows one to measure the difference between ancient and medieval freedom and the freedom at the basis of modern democracy better than this formula. It is not the free man and his statutes and prerogatives, nor even simply *homo*, but rather *corpus* that is the new subject of politics. And democracy is born precisely as the assertion and presentation of this "body": *habeas corpus ad subjiciendum*, "you will have a body to show." The fact that, of all the various jurisdictional regulations concerned with the protection of individual freedom, it was *habeas corpus* that assumed the form of law and thus became inseparable from the history of Western democracy is surely due to mere circumstance. It is just as certain, however, that nascent European democracy thereby placed at the center of its battle against absolutism not *bios*, the qualified life of the citizen, but *zoē*—the bare, anonymous life.[57]

By linking *habeas corpus* in turn to reproduction, the womb becomes explicitly a pre-eminent space in which both the post-revolutionary French and the Tanzimat era Ottoman "battle against absolutism" would be fought. It became the arena, in other words, in which biopolitical sovereignty and a citizenship predicated simultaneously on law and bare life would be created.

---

57 Agamben 1998, 124. I have elaborated on Agamben's (much contested) interpretation of *habeas corpus* in another article, "On Freedom and Feeding Tubes: Reviving Terri Schiavo and Trying Saddam Hussein," forthcoming in *Law and Literature*.

Ibn 'Abidin's nineteenth century interpretation of abortion legislation—with its focus not necessarily on the fetus, but on abstract political relationships as they are articulated through the status of the fetus, with its concern about modern, scientific analyses of the fetal "human form," is therefore operating within an intellectual context that overlaps clearly with that of contemporary Ottoman and French jurists. All three discussed, analyzed, and (in the case of the latter two) legislated on abortion in such a way that the fetus gave way to the womb as the new target of jurisdiction. In the French code, abortion is made not-homicide, moved into a separate chapter, and turned implicitly into a crime against the collective and *consequently* the "self." In the Ottoman code, the same transition occurs via the appropriation and reinterpretation of *diyet*. In all three, the womb is gradually clarified as a separate, legal arena in which the modern, biopolitical citizen will be formed.

There are other aspects of the codes, however, that also facilitate this transformation. In both France and the Ottoman Empire, for example, it is primarily within the context of abortion legislation that the medical establishment is tied to legal structures—a relationship key to the creation of institutions out to protect a biopolitically defined collective. In both texts, doctors or pharmacists who perform abortions are punished more heavily than others who do so. In the Ottoman code an extra article is added to the chapter, penalizing any medical practitioner without a license. The decision to include legislation on unregulated doctors within the section on abortion and reproduction was, moreover, not an arbitrary one. It was indeed a necessary precursor to the delimitation of the womb as a space in which modern sovereignty would be articulated. With the entry of doctors and medical practitioners into legal texts focusing on reproduction, for instance, it necessarily becomes imperative both to create a cohort of medico-legal experts—modern physicians—capable of overseeing this space and to criminalize anyone—"traditional" practitioners—with the knowledge or ability to obscure, hide, or misrepresent it.

Once again, however, the Ottoman and French governments were not unique in instituting this process. Throughout the nineteenth century, as various national legislatures criminalized abortion, they simultaneously criminalized and/or regulated doctors, pharmacists, or midwives insufficiently aware of their central role in citizenship formation. In nineteenth century Italy, for instance, "in response to successful lobbying by physicians, increasingly extensive legislation not only subjected midwives to more careful control by state-appointed medical authorities, but also limited their use of surgical instruments and manual versions."[58] In the United States, "the criminalization of abortion was one of the first legislative successes won by the AMA [the American Medical Association], marking a connection of law and medicine through the management of the womb. In medico-legal discourse, the womb was the representational ground of interconnection."[59] In semi-autonomous Ottoman Egypt, Clot Bey, a French Physician employed by the governor Mehmet Ali to nationalize the Egyptian medical establishment, set up schools of medicine and midwifery, producing a situation in which "sexuality and reproduction were defined

58 Triolo 1994, 260-261.

59 Stormer 2000, 123.

as the proper concern of a number of modern professions: medicine, education, and criminal justice."[60]

Both the medico-legal overlap and the opening up of the womb, both the construction of a basic biopolitical sovereign-subject relationship and its articulation through a legalistic reproductive rhetoric had become, in other words, an international trend. Indeed, we can see in Ottoman, French, and other abortion legislation a quite distinct conflation of morbidity and fertility as well as a collapse of legal rule into political exception. As Leslie J. Reagan argues with regard to the criminalization of abortion in the United States, by 1857 the AMA had begun lobbying against abortion, by 1867 Illinois had criminalized the activity, and by the end of the nineteenth century, every state had done so. She further argues that as abortion was gradually criminalized, the state of Illinois began to use "dying declarations" from women in order to prosecute abortionists—bringing about a subtle transformation of the legal system as a whole. She notes with regard to "dying declarations" in Chicago, for example, that:

> the dying declaration was an unusual legal instrument that allowed the words of the dead to enter the courtroom. Legally a dying declaration is an exception to the hearsay rule … [C]ommon law allowed the admission of dying declarations as evidence in homicide cases, and states permitted this exception in abortion cases as well … [t]he state's attorney also provided a standardized format for the dying woman's answer. She should answer "I am Miss ______. Believing that I am about to die, and having no hope of recovery, I make the following statement, while of sound mind and in full possession of my faculties." To be considered valid in court, the statement had to establish that the woman believed she was near death … [A]lthough most women who had abortions were married,[61] the state's prosecutors focused on abortions by unwed women, and this formulaic dying declaration assumed that the dying woman would be unmarried.[62]

Mervat F. Hatem describes a similar situation in Egypt in the 1830s, in which the obstetric knowledge of *dayas* ("traditional" midwives) was questioned, but in which they were seen as skilled in "uncovering the secrets of infertility" and providing "quick abortions." She continues that Clot Bey set up the school of "professional" midwives to "put an end to this practice."[63] Eventually,

> the graduates of the school of midwives were to play a big role in the surveillance and criminalization of abortion. Upon graduation, the professional midwives served as agents of the state's relentless pursuit of *dayas* who performed abortions. As members of the district medical staff that spread into different regions from 1840 onwards, they were charged with "sanitary policing." As part of this task, the new midwives were required to register births and verify and record the cases of death among women … [T]hey were to

60 Hatem 2000, 68, 70.

61 See also, "whereas in the first half of the [nineteenth] century the practice [abortion] was viewed primarily as an exceptional act—the last resort of the unwed mother—in the latter half it was increasingly acknowledged as a married woman's back-up method of birth control." McLaren 1978, *passim*.

62 Reagan 1991, 1254.

63 Hatem 2000, 70.

> receive one piaster for each verification of death ... [U]nder these new policing rules, the professional midwives would recognize abortions that went wrong and would list them as the cause of death. In such cases, the state would charge and prosecute the *dayas* for murder.[64]

Finally, in early twentieth century France,

> government reports after the war [World War I] referred to three hundred thousand to five hundred thousand abortions a year ... [D]octors who were opposed to *all* forms of fertility control found it politic to attribute the entire shortfall in French fertility solely to abortion. Secondly, doctors hostile to midwives and popular practitioners used these figures as evidence of the need to sharply curtail unsupervised medical practice. Finally, doctors angered by an emerging feminism responded by blaming France's "race-suicide" not on a decision made by husband and wife but on the selfish act of the independent woman.[65]

In each of these cases, the most obvious point to note is the close relationship between (both biological and legal) birth and death. In a basic way, we see a transformation over these years in the role of the obstetric doctor or midwife. Associated before with birth or, at most, birth gone wrong, they were increasingly called upon to witness death. Again, however, the "death" that was to concern them in their professional capacity—to the extent that in Egypt they were paid on a per-death basis—had nothing to do with the fetus. Instead, registered midwives and doctors were expected to verify illegitimate tampering with the womb—unregulated entry into a political space, in other words—as the cause first, of a woman's demise, and second, of a collective race suicide. The "quick abortion" became in this way identical to "infertility" writ large, and therefore a national attack as much as an individual one. The focus on a lack of sanitation as the cause of abortion-related death likewise cast abortionists as enemies of hygienic environments fit for collective (rather than necessarily individual) "health."[66] The death of an individual woman thus became of far less importance than the cause or setting of her death. Breaking into the womb, desecrating it, and committing murder there, indeed, became uniquely horrifying in the same way that breaking into, desecrating, and committing murder in any other public space—a school or a courtroom, for example—is horrifying. The issue at stake was a collective one—and now one in which the womb would become a setting

---

64 Ibid, 73-4

65 McLaren 1978, 479.

66 See also an Ottoman commentator from the 1880s who, "after severe condemnation on moral and hygienic grounds ... writes 'we constantly hear of cases of abortion causing the death of many women. Such illegal abortions are performed with the help of numerous instruments, all as unimaginable as they are unhygienic.'"In Duben and Behar 2002, 183. Again, the precise cause of the individual woman's death (the "unimaginable" instrument) is marginalized here in favor of a larger commentary on sanitation (its "unhygienic" nature). Such commentary is not unique to writers in favor of criminalizing abortion, however. One could similarly argue that late twentieth century lobbying in favor of legalizing abortion, with its reliance on the coat hanger theme, is making use of an identical sanitation discourse. See below for an elaboration this argument.

for the regulation of individual birth *and* death, as well as for collective fertility *and* morbidity.

As the prominent role played by doctors and midwives in the policing and regulation of abortion collapsed morbidity and fertility into a single issue, however, it also collapsed legal exception and legal rule into the same category. The most overt manifestation of this process is in the reliance on dying declarations by the Chicago police in the mid-nineteenth century. As Reagan argues, the use of the dying declaration was explicitly an exception—a suspension of the hearsay rule—but it was a "permitted exception" that quickly became the norm in trials against abortionists. In admitting dying declarations as evidence, she continues, it was assumed that the victim of homicide would not lie about his or her attacker when he or she knew that death was at hand. What was not "true" in other cases, that is, became "true" with the use of dying declarations.

I would also argue, however, that the exceptional quality of abortion-related dying declarations went much deeper than this. Reagan notes, for instance, that the dying declaration was "an unusual legal instrument that allowed the words of the dead to enter the courtroom."[67] But these words carried legal weight only if they had been spoken while the witness/victim/perpetrator was hovering on the threshold between life and death. The use of the dying declaration in abortion cases was an exception, in other words—and a normalized, commonplace exception—that by definition ignored basic biological "facts." It was an exception that presumed a witness/victim/perpetrator's legal identity *only* to the extent that her biological identity was indeterminate—*only* to the extent that her body was fluctuating between life and death, to the extent that she was in the indefinite state, "dying." This legal/biological identity was not analogous to the identity of an individual who, for instance, makes a will that carries legal weight after his or her demise, or who enters into a contract that remains in effect after death; it is not simply the continuation of civic or legal relations after the cessation of biological relations. It is instead a continuation of legal relations explicitly predicated and reliant upon the *suspension* of biological relations—upon their being rendered, in other words, exceptional. It was thus a situation in which, quite distinctly, an individual's politics placed his or her existence as a living being (neither alive nor dead) into question. The fact that the dying declaration in abortion cases also overrode any pre-existing marital status merely reinforces its exceptional quality. The individual making the declaration may or may not have been married. Once her body entered the indeterminate state—somewhere between death and life, in the process of both reproduction and decay—her legal status was lifted and made irrelevant, she became "single," and no provisions were made for any other legal identity.

Another way to think about this process is to return to Ibn 'Abidin. In a basic way, what we see with the use of dying declarations is the exception becoming the rule for at least two of the legal relationships that he placed into the womb. Marital relationships, for instance, were still articulated through reproductive space, but in this case the legal status, "married," was eliminated as soon as the womb was illegally entered. Thus, in precisely the same way that entry into the space

67 Reagan 1991, 1254.

represented by the concentration camp stripped an individual of his or her status as "citizen,"[68] entry into the womb stripped a woman of at least this particular legal or political identity. Hovering between life and death, "normal" civic identity of this sort was impossible. Instead the exception, "single," became the rule. Likewise, to the extent that the dying woman was a perpetrator as well as a victim and witness to the abortion, the right to *habeas corpus* was, if not eliminated, then rendered inchoate. The body existed and it did not exist—as did the dying-woman, legally relevant, her words politically valid only because she was dying, in the process of ceasing to exist. The dying declarations thus turned the womb into a preeminent biopolitical space—into *the* framework for the sovereign exception. They became ideal arenas for the process described by Agamben, wherein "law refers to life and includes it in itself by suspending it," in which,

> the relation of exception is a relation of ban. He who has been banned is not, in fact, simply set outside the law and made indifferent to it but rather *abandoned* by it, that is, exposed and threatened on the threshold in which life and law, outside and inside, become indistinguishable.[69]

Abortion legislation and the role of the now regulated doctor in this way turned the woman-citizen into both an inhabitant of biopolitical space and also into the setting in which this space would be carved out. Her womb became an arena both regulated and forbidden, a space excluded by its inclusion, as Agamben puts it—where death and life, rule and exception remained in a permanently suspended state.

The most overt example of this process in nineteenth century Ottoman and French abortion legislation is not, however, the way in which the fetus was re-positioned, nor the way in which doctors became a primary focus of the legal codes. Instead, it is the proximity of legislation on suicide to legislation on abortion. In the Ottoman code, the article on suicide follows the two articles on abortion and operates under the same chapter heading. In the French code a single article covers abortion *and* suicide. The biopolitical implications of this placement could not be more obvious: whereas the text on suicide reinforces the modern state's sovereign right to "let die," the text on abortion reinforces its sovereign right to "make live." Suicide and abortion are thus as much attacks on biopolitical sovereign right as homicide had been on juridical sovereign right. I would like to pause here, however, to emphasize the implications of rhetorically and juridically linking suicide and abortion in this way. First of all, doing so brings together once again death and birth, morbidity and fertility. The threat and deterrent represented by death alone in the classical juridical

68 "Whoever entered the camp moved in a zone of indistinction between outside and inside, exception and rule, licit and illicit, in which the very concepts of subjective right and juridical protection no longer made any sense. What is more, if the person entering the camp was a Jew, he had already been deprived of his rights as a citizen by the Nuremburg laws and was subsequently completely denationalized at the time of the Final Solution. Insofar as its inhabitants were stripped of every political status and wholly reduced to bare life, the camp was also the most absolute biopolitical space ever to have been realized." Agamben 1998, 170-1.

69 Agamben 1998, 28.

system is superseded by the regulatory power represented by death and life together in the biopolitical system.

Second, and more important, the conflation of suicide and abortion clarifies even more effectively the womb as a separate, politically defined space. Again, the usual take on the modern criminalization of abortion is that it occurred as a response to fears of population decline and race suicide. But this take is for the most part one sided—similar to analyzing the criminal nature of homicide solely as function of an individual's right to live and not taking into consideration the simultaneous, and equally illegitimate, appropriation of the classical sovereign's right to kill. Abortion, in other words, is problematic, yes, because it is an attack on a healthy population. But it is also, if not more so, problematic because it appropriates the sovereign right to make live—just as suicide appropriates the sovereign right to let die. Whereas suicide, however, occurs for the most part in classical juridical space—the private domicile or the public square, for instance—abortion occurs in biological space, in a womb where public and private are meaningless concepts. Unlike the domicile or the square, the womb is secret, closed off, and inaccessible. It is a place where a constant, wanton disregard for sovereign right can occur, situated—despite its centrality to modern political and legal relations—completely outside of sovereign relations. The modern criminalization of abortion is therefore not just about protecting the new rights of the population or race; it is equally, if not more so, about including within sovereign territory an excluded space—about turning biological space into biopolitical space,[70] about creating an arena, if not defined by law, at least bounded by it.

Indeed, the final aspect of the Ottoman and French legislation on which I want to focus—the inclusion of articles on poison and toxic substances in the chapter on abortion and suicide—reinforces the importance of space, rather than necessarily rights, in modern approaches to reproduction. The emphasis on toxic substances is more apparent in the Ottoman code—where it is part of the chapter heading—than it is in the French code, but it nonetheless plays a central role in both. In both texts, for example, the question of toxicity is almost more important than the question of poison—poisonous threats to the individual are thereby subsumed under toxic threats to the environment. This environment subject to an increase in toxicity, however, is not simply the public space of classical juridical law, but, again and almost more so, the biological space of reproductive law. By creating a slippage between toxic substances, which presumably affect an external environment, and abortifacients, which by definition affect an internal environment, the external and internal collapse once more, and the womb is rendered yet again a pre-eminent biopolitical space.

One might in fact argue that this mid-nineteenth century French and Ottoman legislation is a direct antecedent of the late twentieth century anti-abortion rhetoric described, for example, by Laury Oaks in her study of "Smoke-Filled Wombs and Fragile Fetuses." Like Stormer, Oaks is concerned primarily with post-war U.S. approaches to abortion, and the fetus is therefore more central to her discussion of the legislation than it would be in a study of the nineteenth century. But her analysis

70 Rather than, as with the concentration camp, turning political space into biopolitical space.

of late twentieth century anti-smoking messages—and the criminal prosecution in the United States of pregnant women who engage in drug-related practices "unhealthy" to their fetuses[71]—is nonetheless relevant to this earlier period. Indeed, what we see in these messages is a situation in which the violent act of the classical juridical system is almost completely marginalized—in which, despite the rhetoric, the individual rights of the fetus are of little importance. Instead, the fetus is fragile and under attack in these narratives in the same way that the population is. It is not a blow or wound that threatens it, but instead an increasingly toxic environment.[72] The fetus is thus no more an individual in these scenarios than any other subject of the biopolitical state might be—it is one small component of a collective population. Even when rights-rhetoric returns to center stage in the late twentieth century, in other words, it is linked inextricably to nineteenth century fears of race suicide. Even in the twentieth century, it is still the environment/population relationship rather than the violent act/individual relationship that is of concern. And even in the twentieth century, the womb remains what it had become 150 years before—a biopolitical space, an "environment," subject to regulation, cleaning, and purifying.

The fact, for instance, that in the 1880s, the Ottoman Sultan was concerned explicitly with the "unhealthy practices of abortion which have been increasing recently … and have been causing a decrease in the Muslim population,"[73] rather than, say, the *criminal* practice of abortion and its assault on the rights of the individual emphasizes the extent to which the womb-as-environment had become the dominant trope in discussions of the issue. Indeed, along with the re-situation of the fetus as a signifier of the population or race rather than as a being in and of itself, the centering of the medical establishment, and the overlap of legislation on suicide and legislation on abortion, the appropriation of "environment" related vocabulary to discuss reproductive issues simply defined further the nature of the politicized womb. In both France and the Ottoman Empire, legislation on abortion appears to have played a critical role in gradually sidelining the individual and his or her juridical rights and centering the collective and its biopolitical health.

Consent and Interwar Reproduction

The marginalization of the rights-bearing individual in modern abortion legislation did not mean, however, that rights became irrelevant. Indeed, just as Agamben suggests an indissoluble link "between the rights of man and the new biopolitical determination of sovereignty,"[74] between declaring rights and inscribing biology into

---

71 Oaks 2000, 63-65.

72 A revealing example of this process might be found in the media flurry surrounding the actor Tom Cruise's purchase of a sonogram machine for his pregnant girlfriend Katie Holmes. What had begun as an attempt to render Holmes's womb a celebrated (public, healthy, normal) environment eventually generated a heated debate over whether Cruise's zeal in delimiting this space was in fact inadvertently poisoning or sullying it. See, for example, Kritz 2005.

73 Duben and Behar 2002, 183.

74 Agamben 1998, 130.

political structures, I will suggest that the two rights fundamental to modern sexual and reproductive legislation—consent and bodily integrity—have likewise been essential to the determination of the womb as biopolitical space. Over the next two sections, I would therefore like to discuss in more detail the role, first, of consent and second, of bodily integrity in twentieth century abortion legislation. Both consent and bodily integrity appear with frequency in analyses of rape especially—and I will certainly return to them when I address rape legislation in the following chapter. But I also want to suggest that they are equally, if not more so, central to the criminalization and de-criminalization of abortion. Each has indeed been key to the politicization of reproductive space—each responsible for the placement of both honor and liberty into the womb and for the delimiting of the womb as an arena in need of regulation.

Discussions of consent or consent theory, for example, usually highlight three issues. First, consent is seen as the product of liberal (or sometimes "liberal democratic") political theory—a manifestation of post-Enlightenment notions of individual liberty that stand in opposition to what is often described as a "traditional" conservativism. Thus, Martha Chamallas, for instance, sees a twentieth century movement from a traditional/moralistic approach to "the law of sex," with its emphasis on the marital status of the participants,[75] to a liberal approach, with its emphasis on privacy, consent, and (the prevention of) harm.[76] From understanding sexual behavior as a matter of communal interest, in other words, we gradually come to understand it as something private. It becomes "free," a "right" even, and is held up as the quintessential activity in need of protection from political intervention—unless, of course, it is shown to cause harm to a third party. Consent is central to this liberal transformation—its apparent absence is, for example, at the heart of the implicit criticism of the early twentieth century French "practice of seeing private decisions about family size as matters of public policy" that started this chapter.

At the same time, a second major aspect of many analyses of consent involves a critique of this liberal approach—an accentuation of either the internal contradictions within consent theory itself or of the impossibility of invoking consent given the "reality" of social, economic, and political power imbalances. As Carole Pateman has argued, "despite the apparent importance of women's consent, it is legally and socially declared irrelevant within marriage, and a woman's explicit 'no' is all too

75 "The traditional view is the familiar moralistic notion that the only sexual conduct that is acceptable is sex that occurs within marriage … [W]hen the traditional view is expressed in the law, the critical fact tends to be the status of the participants, rather than the purpose or nature of the sexual encounter. Legal regulation in the traditional mode regards non marital sexual activity, whether consensual or not, as properly subject to legal sanction." Chamallas 1988, 781.

76 "Under this [liberal] view, sexual conduct is quintessentially private conduct with which the law should not interfere. This conception of private sexual activity tolerates nonmarital sex in some circumstances. In place of marital status, the concept of consent emerges as the central demarcation line to separate lawful from unlawful sexual conduct. The liberal definition of consensual conduct in turn defines the sphere of protected private conduct. The liberal view finds no warrant for legal intervention with consensual sex unless external harm to third parties can be proven." Chamallas 1988, 782.

frequently disregarded or reinterpreted as 'consent.'"[77] Chamallas likewise notes that "since liberalism's primary concern is with limiting government coercion, feminists charge that it is incapable of producing equality for women,"[78] and that, "in the abstract, consent may be gender neutral. But as long as women do not in fact have the opportunity to initiate sexual relationships on equal terms with men, the concept of consent continues to suggest that women are appropriately the passive parties in sexual relationships."[79] Outside of the realm of gender studies, we see similar challenges to the liberal theory of consent. When consent comes into play in discussions of "just punishment," for instance, at least one scholar has argued the following:

> consent is a trump card in liberal theory, with the power to convert an otherwise unfair distribution of burden into a justified one. And one who commits a crime consents to punishment because he has acted voluntarily with knowledge of his act's legal consequences, that is, the punishment prescribed for that act … [P]ut differently, the consensual theory of punishment justifies any punishment, even if the punishment is severely disproportionate (in terms of the action's deserts) to the severity of the crime. There is no proportionality limit to consensual punishment.[80]

Once again, we therefore have a critique on two levels—first, consent theory not only ignores, but even reinforces an unfair power differential, and second, it is self-contradictory in that the lack of proportionality severely undermines "rational" approaches to individual freedom.[81]

A final aspect of these discussions thus usually involves a reassessment of the role of consent, and possible alternative approaches to the liberal ideal of the consensual relationship. The analysis of consent and punishment above, for example, ends with a call to re-institute retribution as at least one aspect of criminal law, while Chamallas advocates an "egalitarian" view of sexual relations, in which the key defining characteristic of "legal sex" would be mutual pleasure or intimacy.[82] The alternative or addition to consent that will interest me the most is, again, the "right

---

77 Pateman 1980, 162.

78 Chamallas 1988, 783.

79 Ibid, 814.

80 Alexander 1986, 178-179.

81 To bring this back into the context of reproduction and rationality, see Lealle Ruhl's statement: "my analysis explores several themes surrounding the willed pregnancy. First, I examine the idea of the willed pregnancy as a by-product of a liberal paradigm of subjectivity that stresses rationality and self-discipline as guiding principles." Ruhl 2002, 642.

82 "The principal difference between the egalitarian view and the liberal view of acceptable sexual encounters centers on their differing understandings of the relationship between individual choice as manifested in sexual behavior and the broad goal of sexual freedom *per se*. Under the liberal view, the characterization of an encounter as sexual tends to relegate it to the private sphere and insulate it from legal regulation, absent strong evidence of physical coercion or harm to third parties. The maximization of individual choice in the liberal view reasserts maximum freedom in society as a whole. The egalitarian perspective, in contrast, is more reluctant to equate individual choice with sexual freedom and is consciously directed toward expanding the choices actually available to women." Chamallas 1988, 841.

to bodily integrity"—but this is an issue that I will address in more detail in the next section. For now, the point that I want to emphasize is that each of these discussions of consent relies implicitly or explicitly upon a distinct progress narrative—on a story that moves us from the traditional to the liberal to some alternative to liberal. Over the next few pages I will be challenging the validity of this narrative and suggesting various alternatives to it.

Indeed, I will see consent, first of all, as a product not of a single liberal moment but of nearly all modern interpretations of the sovereign relationship. In the realm of reproductive legislation, for example, consent becomes for the first time central and fundamental in a self-consciously *fascist* context—occupying relatively little space in nineteenth century liberal codes such as the Napoleonic and Ottoman laws. Rather than a progression or movement from a traditional focus on marital status to a liberal focus on individual freedom or privacy to a post-liberal focus on bodily integrity, therefore, the situation that I will be describing involves an overlap of all three. And I will further argue that it is in the arena of this overlap that the biopolitical subject is formed—that it is, in other words, the blurring of these political boundaries that allows for reproductive space to become pre-eminent modern political space.

With that in mind, I would like to turn to one final interpretation of consent and sovereignty—Elaine Scarry's "Consent and the Body: Injury, Departure, and Desire." Although Scarry's interest in this article is specifically consent in the realm of medical ethics, her discussion of the sovereign relationship writ large—and the way in which she contextualizes her analysis within a vignette on nuclear war—makes it without question relevant here. Indeed, her basic position is, first of all, that consent has always been grounded in the body and that the modern sovereign relationship rests squarely on the notion that "the substratum of all other political and civil rights is the relation of the person to his or her own embodied personhood."[83] Consent and bodily integrity, in other words, overlap in this interpretation from the beginning.[84] Moreover, starting from this foundation, Scarry suggests three further corollaries: first, that the physical and legal borders of the body and the physical and legal borders of the nation state are—both theoretically and in practice—one and the

83 Scarry 1990, 868-9.

84 See also, "the body is, then, the thing protected. But the body is also the lever across which sovereignty is gained, authorization achieved. This carries us to the third feature of this portrait, the emphasis on citizenship." Scarry 1990, 871. For more on periodization, see Alan Hyde's analysis of "bodies of law," in which he argues that "it appears that the body did not exist as a subject of legal analysis until the early nineteenth century. In the early years of that century, a distinctively modern body takes shape in legal and popular culture, a body that represents an individuated, human spirit that is the person inside it, a person that controls the body but is not identical to it … [T]he nineteenth century body is legible to others, is the object of the empathy or sympathy of a viewer, feels pain, but also bears legible signs that may call for its expulsion from society. In the twentieth century, this body continues to be constructed in legal discourse, but coexists with other bodies that are represented in abstraction for their relations with others: 'dehumanized' constructions of the body that are distanced, anonymous, rejected or unavailable to us. These modern legal discursive bodies include property bodies awarded legal damages, container bodies with tax deduction, bodies as 'interests' weighed against search warrants." Hyde 1997, 9.

same;[85] second, that given the necessarily weak, often physically passive position of the supposedly actively consenting citizen, theories of consent destabilize any practical, conventional categories of "active" and "passive;'[86] And finally, that,

> active and passive are so mystified in consent that the phenomenon of consent actually calls into question the reality or usefulness of the categories of passive and active. Each time "consent" emerges, it is an alarm bell saying something is wrong with these categories; they do not refer to anything that actually exists. Or, alternatively, it may be that consent itself acts to explode, or at least disturb, these categories; and this disturbance of categories might be seen as one of its negative or instead one of its most attractive features.[87]

Scarry's analysis, in other words, situates consent, consent theory, and approaches to consent at the very basis of the collapsed categories that define biopolitical space: the biological and the political, the bodily and the national, the active and the passive, and—counter-intuitively—the consenting and the non-consenting. Consent thus presupposes a modern citizen whose political activity is directly inversely proportional to his or her physical or biological activity. I will further argue that the prominent role that consent plays in interwar fascist or *quasi*-fascist legislation on abortion likewise breaks down the boundaries between the traditional, the liberal, and the authoritarian, the public and the private, and honor and liberty. Consent therefore operates in this legislation to produce a single, monolithic biopolitical sovereign/subject.

In 1926, the recently formulated Turkish Republican government adopted the self consciously liberal 1889 Italian criminal code as a means of emphasizing its new European identity. This code remained in effect in Turkey for less than a decade and in Italy for approximately 40 years, but I would like to pause now to highlight three aspects of it that carried over into the legal reforms of the 1930s. First of all, the code

---

85 For example, "though in each instance one is only disposing of a relatively tiny piece of matter—one's own body—in fact by having absolute authority over what can touch, or pass across, the boundaries of one's own person, and conversely, to be able to exercise authority over the world space in which one places or displaces oneself, one has just gained absolute authority vis à vis the world." Scarry 1990, 880.

86 For example, "situations of sickness, injury, or operation often entail heightened forms of the passive and the active. The patient is in a situation of extreme passivity; the physician or surgeon extreme activeness … [Y]et is it precisely here—in the injured, sleepy, anesthetized, dying body—that we have the sudden granting of rights, sovereignty, dignity." Or "William Macy's account of consent 'encourage [ing] full respect for the dignity of the patient who has not, through illness, forfeited his [or her] sovereignty as a human being.' Has not forfeited it through illness, and we can add, or through anesthesia, or unconsciousness, or even death. The whole issue of consent, by holding within it the notions of sovereignty and authorization, bears within it extremely *active* powers. Yet it often arises precisely at the point where by any conventional description, there seems an extreme of passivity." Or finally, "in general, the whole notion of consent stands the distinction between passive and active on its head, since consent theory claims that it is by the will of the apparently passive that the active is brought into being." Scarry 1990, 873, 881.

87 Ibid, 883.

went into more detail on abortion than the Napoleonic law had, and indeed placed the articles on reproduction into a separate chapter entitled "On Abortion." Second, the articles created an explicit hierarchy of culpability for women who consented to, did not consent to, or actively sought abortions, as well as for anyone who might have aided them. Finally, the chapter dictated harsher penalties for "a person exercising a profession or an art regulated in the interest of public health" who brought about an abortion, but a two thirds reduced penalty for anyone who "brought about [the abortion] in order to save his own honor, or that of his wife, his mother, his daughter, or his sister."[88] In addition to the key role played by the medical establishment that we saw in the Napoleonic code, in other words, two new issues came to the fore in this legislation: consent and honor.

The 1889 law was repealed in Italy in 1930/31 in favor of a new, explicitly fascist criminal code written by Mussolini's Justice Minister Alfredo Rocco. Between 1933 and 1938, the Turkish government likewise replaced large sections of its 1926 law with relevant sections from the Rocco code. By 1938, therefore, both the Turkish and the Italian populations were subject to a new chapter on criminal reproductive behavior entitled "Crimes Against the Integrity[89] and Health of the Race." The majority of this chapter concerns abortion. Two additional articles, however, also criminalize sterilization (consenting or non-consenting), "procured impotence to procreate," and rhetoric against procreation on the part of citizens "of either sex." Doctors are likewise specifically targeted. Finally, an article in the Italian law that does not appear in the Turkish adaptation also criminalizes deliberate or negligent infection with syphilis or blennorhagia.[90]

The substance of these articles is, given earlier legislation, what one might expect. First of all, there is the now explicit placement of the rights of the race into reproductive space—with the added stipulation now that the *only* crimes that a citizen can apparently commit against a biological collective are procreational. It was not just that patriotic reproductive behavior was serving as a pillar of national integrity in other words; it was that reproduction was *the* pillar of national integrity. At the same time, however, the articles also dwell on and indeed dissect the notion of consent. After first differentiating among active, passive, consenting, and non-consenting women, there is, for example, a further elaboration of these categories, in that a consenting woman under the age of fourteen, lacking understanding or volition, or under threat of violence is legally understood to be "not-consenting." Finally, in a "return" to what many would regard as tradition, the articles likewise emphasize honor and the need to protect it—indeed, the protection of honor is broadened to include both "one's personal honour [and] that of a near relative."

French legislators between the first and second World Wars were operating in a similar—in some ways identical—legal and political framework. As early as 1920, French parliamentarians passed almost unanimously a new law that criminalized

88 Code pénal turc 1927, Art. 468-472.

89 In the Turkish version of the code it is "perpetuation" rather than "integrity."

90 *Penal Code of the Kingdom of Italy* 1931, Art. 545-555. The Turkish chapter is also slightly different in that bodily harm caused to a woman during an abortion receives a three to eight year penalty rather than a ten to fifteen year penalty.

both "contraceptive propaganda" and "inducement to abortion."[91] By the late 1930s, a commission was formed to examine "the possibility of expanding the definition of acts against the national security so that it might include 'criminal abortion'... within the emergency decrees concerning the internal and external security of the country."[92] Finally in 1942, "law 300" was passed, which allowed for abortionists to be tried by "the Tribunal d'état, a special jurisdiction created by Vichy and empowered to give exceptionally harsh punishments without regard to the provisions of the Penal Code," and which likewise turned abortion into "a crime against the embryo, the society, the state, and the 'race.'"[93] Just as in Italy and Turkey, in other words, in France too, abortion legislation was linked explicitly to the health of the nation and the race—bodily boundaries and national boundaries overtly and irrevocably intertwined. Moreover, just as in Italy and Turkey, the precise "moment of fascism," 1942, was for the most part meaningless. The precedent set by earlier abortion legislation in the decades leading up to the predominance of the Vichy government created a situation in which fascist ideology *per se* was not in any obvious way a departure.

I would like, therefore, to return now to the points raised by Scarry in her discussion of consent. In particular, I will be interested in collapsing political categories, in the creation of biopolitical space, and in how each plays out in this interwar reproductive legislation. Again, the primary categories that interest me here are 1) the body and the nation, 2) the consenting and the non-consenting, 3) the active (citizen) and the passive (citizen), and 4) honor and liberty. My basic

---

91 "On 31 July 1920, the Chamber passed by five hundred voters to fifty-three a new law making both contraceptive propaganda and inducement to abortion illegal. A second law passed on 27 March 1923 made abortion a misdemeanor subject to the criminal courts, and no longer a felony; the lawmakers thus tried to avoid the acquittals often given by juries." Reggiani 1996, 731.

92 "During the years 1938-39 the pronatalist campaign reached its climax. The Alliance nationale contre la dépopulation turned to more direct, sensationalist propaganda that sought to single out birth-control practices as a threat to the integrity of the nation. Meanwhile, the recently created Haut comité de la population studied the possibility of expanding the definition of acts against the national security so that it might include 'criminal abortion' ... within the emergency decrees concerning the internal and external security of the country." Reggiani 1996, 735-6.

93 "The ideology imposed in the summer of 1940 by the National Revolution maintained and expanded some of the policies begun under the Third Republic. The harsh measures advocated by the pronatalists to curb the decline of the birthrate met with success when law 300 of 15 February 1942 returned to the policies of the Napoleonic Code, again defining abortion as a crime ... [T]he law called for two measures against prescribed abortionists: first, the Ministry of Interior or the prefect could order their administrative arrest; second the authorities could turn any suspect over to the Tribunal d'état, a special jurisdiction created by Vichy and empowered to give exceptionally harsh punishments without regard to the provisions of the Penal Code. The new political circumstances turned Doublet's earlier advocacy for criminalizing abortion into policy, making it a 'social crime.' Law 300 turned abortionists into 'murderers of the fatherland;' abortion became a crime against the embryo, the society, the state, and the 'race' ... [A]ccording to a historian of the family, it was Doublet who proposed the term "Family" for Vichy's motto 'Work, Family, Fatherland.'"Reggiani 1996, 748-750.

position will be that the destabilization of the first two turns the body—and more specifically the womb—into a political space, and that the destabilization of the last three renders this space explicitly biopolitical, in need of regulation. Furthermore, I will suggest that the central role played by reproductive legislation in this process of destabilization is by no means arbitrary—or at least not any more arbitrary than its nineteenth century role in linking together modern medical and modern legal structures.

Once again, the intertwining of bodily boundaries and national boundaries—or reproductive space and political space—is relatively overt in the Italian, Turkish, and French legislation. Criminal reproductive behavior—abortion, sterilization, contraception, and the spreading of venereal disease—is a crime against the race and the nation above all, as well as a threat to both internal and external security. I want to emphasize, however, that this take on the womb, the nation, and their overlap—although indebted to earlier, nineteenth century fears of population decline and race suicide—is very much a twentieth century phenomenon. It is not *just* that the failure to reproduce and to reproduce in a healthy manner is responsible for a population decline, in other words—a decline that will in turn lead to military and political weakness. It is also—and indeed more so—that the attack on biopolitical sovereignty implied in the nineteenth century legislation has become overt in its twentieth century counterpart.

Abortion, in other words, is not just an attack on collective health, it is also, and again more so, an assault on the sovereign right to make live. The right to make live is now likewise explicitly at the basis of modern citizenship (i.e., without birth, there are no "natural" rights in the liberal *or* fascist sense).[94] And abortion is therefore very precisely a threat to both the political interior and the political exterior. Abortion is murder, that is, not because it ends the life of the fetus, but because it renders impossible the future existence of the citizen. It is likewise treason not because the population might decline, but because it undermines the basis of each and every state-citizen relationship. In every conceivable way, therefore—legally, politically, and perhaps most important, physically—the womb *is* the nation, and the borders of the womb are political boundaries.

When the nineteenth century French pronatalist Bouverat "compared with morbid detail the fetus killed by the egg piercing probe to the torments suffered by criminals in ancient China,"[95] therefore, his point was not that any one individual fetus might suffer pain and torment and that abortion should therefore be prevented. It was that France should not allow illegitimate sovereign relationships of the sort

94 For example, "At the same time, however, the very natural life that, inaugurating the biopolitics of modernity, is placed at the foundation of the order vanishes into the figure of the citizen, in whom rights are 'preserved' (according to the second article [of the Declaration of 1789]: 'The goal of every political association is the preservation of the natural and indefensible rights of man'). And the Declaration can attribute sovereignty to the 'nation' (according to the third article: 'The principle of all sovereignty resides essentially in the nation') precisely because it has already inscribed this element of birth in the very heart of the political community. The nation—the term derives etymologically from *nascere* (to be born)—thus closes the open circle of man's birth." Agamben 1998, 127-8.

95 Reggiani 1996, 737.

"common" to China—a nation repeatedly held up as a lawless space, where torture was the norm, and individuals had neither rights nor recourse[96]—to proliferate within its own borders. *And in particular within its own reproductive borders*. Likewise, when Edouard Ignace, a member of the French republican left declared in July 1920 that, "on the day after a war where almost 1,500,000 Frenchmen sacrificed their life so that France would have the right to live in independence and honor, it is intolerable that other Frenchmen have the right to draw substantial incomes from the multiplication of abortions and anti-conceptional propaganda,"[97] the issue at stake was not simply that the First World War had depleted the French population and that abortion was adding to the problem. Ignace's statement was more than that. It was a comment about life—both biological and political—and how to preserve it within collapsed national and reproductive boundaries. "France" maintained its honor and liberty in two interdependent arenas—the battlefield where individuals made an apparent "choice" (or "sacrifice") to die, and the womb where the population, as we shall see, likewise made an apparent choice to live. The two spaces had become interchangeable, and the seamless transition from one to the other in this rhetoric barely worthy of comment.

I would likewise suggest, however, that the boundaries of these overlapping arenas were defined first and foremost by consent. As Stormer argues with regard to reproductive space in general, by the end of the eighteenth century, the womb had become a pure, neutral area in which "purified order f[ed] purgative symbolism. It punctuate[d] valid consent in democratic theory and circumscribe[d] the space where consent form[ed], the public sphere."[98] It makes sense, therefore, that when this space took on more hyperbolic political importance in the early twentieth century, the notion of consent should be foregrounded in the legislation dealing with it. At the same time, however, the role that consent played in delimiting reproductive space was not as straightforward as it might originally appear.

Indeed, even the most basic aspect of consent that appears in the legislation—the defining of the active citizen as an individual capable of consent—becomes problematic when considered more carefully. In the nineteenth century, the question of whether a woman consented to an abortion could be resolved with a "yes" or a "no." By the 1930s, however, issues of maturity, responsibility, sanity, and coercion had all entered the picture. Starting in the 1930s, in other words, there was a concerted (fascist) effort to link "choice" or "consent" on the one hand to (what many would regard as a liberal conception of) citizenship on the other. In the same way that maturity, responsibility, sanity, and coercion each played a role in determining who could or could not enjoy post-Enlightenment political rights—who could or could not attain full v. incomplete or active v. passive citizenship—that is, they were also

---

96 For examples of the late nineteenth and early twentieth century trope of "Chinese torture" linked to inappropriate Chinese governance, see, among others, "Chinese Punishment Methods" 1894, 5, "Torture in Chinese Trial: Peking Officials Use Forbidden Methods" 1908, 4, Dunlop 1889, 516-524, "How China is Governed" 1892, 2, Foord 1900, 401, Leroy-Beaulieu 1899, 43-74, and others.

97 As cited in Pedersen 1996, 690.

98 Stormer 2000, 128.

playing a role in determining those capable of reproductive consent. And for those operating within a classical juridical framework, this was as it should be: children, the insane, and those under external coercion could definitely claim welfare, but could never, and should never, claim liberty, or the right to consent.

For those operating within overlapping reproductive and political boundaries, however, the issue became more complicated. One result of this new interwar approach to reproduction, consent, and citizenship, for instance, was the 1939 arrest of "the Neo-Malthusian and radical feminist Madeleine Pelletier" in France, who was "described by the presses as 'physically incapacitated,' and who was committed "by means of a 'placement d'office' to an asylum for the insane, where she was to die eight months later."[99] Madeleine Pelletier, in other words, was arguably on the receiving end of a new, and relentless, biopolitical interpretation of consent. It is true that one can see this incident as exceptional, a travesty of justice, and meaningless within the larger, normal context of liberal (or fascist) political theory. But if we look at the specific details of the incident—an individual advocating population control, and in particular abortion, is declared insane and thus necessarily incapable of consent—its centrality to the new legislation is clear. Indeed, it returns us in an oblique way to the contradiction at the heart of classical liberal theory described by Pateman above: "there is one relationship, at least, to which consent ought not to be given. A person ought never to consent to be a slave, because this totally negates the individual's freedom and equality and hence, in a self contradiction, denies that the individual is capable of consent."[100] A free individual who consents to his or her own enslavement, in other words, becomes incapable of consent. But there are two ways in which this incapacity might occur. The first is that the individual, by choosing slavery, declares him or herself enslaved and/or insane, and therefore incapable of making a choice. The second rests on the notion that by declaring every citizen free, a sovereign is simultaneously declaring his or her right to grant freedom. The free individual who persistently seeks to enslave him or herself thus undermines not just his or her own rights but, more importantly, sovereign right.[101] There is, in other words, no actual choice with regard to being a slave or being free. A free individual who undermines these rights, who chooses slavery, is either insane or treasonous, and therefore by definition incapable of consent—subject to political welfare but not to liberty.[102]

The fate of Pelletier was nothing more than a biopolitical variation on this juridical contradiction. The insane are incapable of consent. Anyone wanting an abortion is insane. Therefore consent is impossible in the context of abortion discourse. At the

99 Reggiani 1996, 744.

100 Pateman 1980, 162-163.

101 I will discuss the implicit collision between autonomy/liberty and integrity/dignity that occurs in this scenario in the next chapter.

102 Vera Bergelson has also commented on the paradox in this interpretation of consent, noting that in the United States context, "from time to time, courts deny the validity of factual consent, arguing that it was irrational or involuntary … [t]he *Samuel's* Court's argument is a perfect example of circular reasoning: a person who consents to X is insane because one has to be insane to consent to X. After the victim's insanity is thus established, the conviction follows automatically because consent of an insane person is invalid." Bergelson *forthcoming*, 25.

same time, however, abortion undermined both sovereign right and the health of the population. In the same way, therefore, that in the classical juridical paradigm an individual who sought to enslave him or herself, who sought deliberately to limit his or her freedom, was committing political or legal suicide, an individual who sought to limit his or her reproductive potential within the biopolitical paradigm, to commit collective race suicide, was likewise in need of institutionalization. In the same way, in other words, that there was no possibility of a choice between being free and being enslaved according to juridical consent theory, there was also no possibility of choice between reproducing and not reproducing in the biopolitical version.[103]

But this does not mean that consent was a meaningless concept in early twentieth century reproductive legislation. Indeed, even as the consenting and the non-consenting collapsed into a single category over these years, this category remained central to the proper functioning of both liberal and fascist sovereign relations. Again, however, this was a consent absent of choice. There was no choice between reproducing or not reproducing—no choice between the womb operating as a public and the womb operating as a private arena. The line between these possibilities was an irrelevant one. Instead, consent served simply, but relentlessly, to define the womb as a space. Twentieth century consent, in other words, was just as much about emphasizing the relationship, and the boundaries of the relationship, between biopolitical sovereign and biopolitical subject as eighteenth century consent had been about emphasizing the relationship, and the boundaries of the relationship, between liberal sovereign and liberal subject. Eighteenth century consent had defined the political borders of, say, the nation state of France—and slavery had become impossible within these

103 For a contemporary take on this issue in the United States context, see Rao 2000, 410-413: "Thirty-three states currently prevent the removal of life-sustaining medical care from an incompetent pregnant woman, regardless of her own wishes previously expressed in a living will or the recommendations of her designated proxy decision-maker. These states deny incompetent pregnant women the bodily autonomy afforded to competent pregnant women and incompetent persons under the right of privacy. Instead, their laws literally 'take' the bodies of incompetent pregnant women, treating them as chattel that may be drafted into service as fetal incubators for the state. In fact, Pennsylvania implicitly acknowledges its 'taking of the incompetent pregnant woman's body by providing 'just compensation' in the form of payment for the expenses associated with continued medical care ... [B]y suspending advance directives to terminate treatment, these laws permit a pregnant woman's life to be prolonged contrary to her express instructions, although they do not necessarily compel this result ... [I]n University Health Services v. Piazzi, a Georgia court granted a hospital's petition to keep a brain-dead pregnant woman on life support until the birth of her fetus, over the objections of her husband and family. The court could have avoided addressing the constitutionality of pregnancy provisions and rendered a decision based upon the specific facts of the case. Donna Piazzi herself had not drafted a living will or other health care directive embodying her intentions in such a situation, and the biological father of the fetus (who was not her husband) favored continuing medical care to save the fetus' life. Nevertheless, relying upon the pregnancy restriction in the Georgia Natural Death Act, the court determined that Donna Piazzi lacked the power to terminate life-sustaining medical treatment during her pregnancy under state law even if she had executed a living will. The court further rejected the argument that Piazzi possessed a constitutional right to refuse treatment and to terminate her pregnancy, concluding that these privacy rights were extinguished when she became brain-dead."

borders. Twentieth century consent defined the political borders of the womb—and abortion became impossible within these.

I want to emphasize, however, that this approach to reproduction was not a product only of interwar *fascist* sovereign relations. As we shall see, when abortion is gradually de-criminalized in a largely neo-liberal context, the womb remains a political space, subject to the same regulation as before. Reproductive behavior still rests on notions of consent—and consent remains a spatial rather than a behavioral concept, the "right to choose" invented for the same common good that the "health of the race" had been before, the womb opened up to women citizens *as a space* in the same way that public schools or open courts had been. The legalization of abortion will thus simply signify the triumph of those who place the abstract notion of "rights" into this space over those who place the abstract notion of the "health of the race" there.

For now, though, I would like to consider some further aspects of the role of consent in the early twentieth century legislation. First of all, when we conceive of consent theory as a theory absent of any choice—operating as a means of delimiting borders rather than of defining behavior—the problems and contradictions that occur when it runs up against "reality" begin to make more sense. When Pateman, for instance, notes that, "consent as an ideology cannot be distinguished from habitual acquiescence, assent, silent dissent, submission, or even enforced submission. Unless refusal of consent or withdrawal of consent are real possibilities, we can no longer speak of "consent" in any genuine sense,"[104] she is clearly understanding consent as something linked to juridical freedom or, more basically, to choice. Likewise, when Agamben, in his discussion of medical experimentation on prisoners in Nazi concentration camps or in United States prisons states that,

> the final criterion, which elicited general agreement, was the necessity of an explicit and voluntary consent on the part of the subject who was to be submitted to the experiment … [T]he obvious hypocrisy of such documents cannot fail to leave one perplexed. To speak of free will and consent in the case of a person sentenced to death or of a detained person who must pay serious penalties is, at the very least, questionable,[105]

he is operating within the same framework. If, however, we understand consent as no more and no less than a means of defining sovereign space—of collapsing political and biological borders and boundaries—the seemingly perverse or at least disingenuous insistence on consent in such situations becomes more reasonable. The question is not whether the individual "really" consented to what is, for all intents and purposes, sexual, social, reproductive, political, biological, or medical enslavement. It is instead the extent to which the consensual relationship has successfully defined both political and biological space. Indeed, we can see in these early approaches to reproduction, experimentation, and execution[106] important precursors to the humane

104 Pateman 1980, 150.

105 Agamben 1998, 157.

106 And I would argue that the three are inextricably linked to one another in the twentieth and twenty-first centuries. To give one example from the Nazi experience, "reading the testimony of VP's who survived, in some cases the testimony of the very subjects

reliance on lethal injection—rather than, say, beheading, hanging, or electrocution—as a means of eliminating criminals in the modern United States. Above all a spectacle of consent, the lethal injection—absent any wound or executioner—plays out first and foremost as a doctor/patient relationship, the physician eliminating the biologically passive, juridically consenting citizen in the end for his own good.[107]

I would in fact like to dwell for a moment on the relationship between absent wounds and the assumption of consent in the twentieth century reproductive legislation. If we compare, for example, the interwar French, Italian, and Turkish laws to the Napoleonic code from a century before, we can see a distinct trend toward a collapse of not just the consenting and the non-consenting, but of the politically active and the biologically passive. I would further argue that this plays out most obviously in the disappearance of violence and, again, wounding from the picture. Whereas the Napoleonic code had associated abortion or sterilization with castration (a presumably violent act), for instance, and had understood all three explicitly as "threats" or "wounds" to the individual, the twentieth century Italian and Turkish codes associate abortion and sterilization with contraception, understanding each as less a violent attack than an irresponsible or negligent undermining of the population. In other words, while in the Napoleonic code, sexuality and an implicit violence were to be regulated or to be punished—criminal behavior associated with threats and wounding—in the twentieth century codes, the focus is on reproduction. There is an emphatic absence of violence. Citizens in the twentieth century legislation have a (consensual) duty to perpetuate the race, and when they fail in that duty, they do so because they are impotent, not because they are violent.

By stressing reproductive diligence rather than sexual passion, the Italian and Turkish passages thus remove any possibility of a wound or a trace of violence that might indicate a lack of consent. They also, however, render meaningless any notion of the sexual or political "active" or "passive." Sexual and reproductive behavior indeed operate in the same universe as the lethal injection—they are medical, consensual, and are undertaken for a greater good. Indeed, one very basic point to note about the twentieth century legislation is that the man's penis disappears

---

described in the extant records, is such an atrocious experience that it is very tempting to consider the experiments as merely sadocriminal acts with no relation to scientific research. But unfortunately this cannot be done. To begin with, some (certainly not all) of the physicians who conducted the experiments were quite well respected by the scientific community for their research. Professor Clauberg, for example, who was responsible for the sterilization program, was the inventor of the 'Clauberg test' on progesterone action, which was commonly used in gynecology until a few years back." Agamben 1998, 156.

107 For another interpretation of the movement away from "violent" forms of capital punishment, see: "the sentimentalized body is also intact one might say perfect, the better to sense as a representation of our own empathy and refinement. The humane versions of capital punishment express their humanity in just this: that they leave the body visibly intact, without dismemberment or marks .... '[B]y taking life without marking the body, reformers retain both literal and figurative control over the story told by the execution. Concealing the violence deprives the body of its ability to speak, and thus opens the door to denial.'"Hyde 1997, 195. For a more nuanced discussion of the issue, see Sarat 2001, *passim*. Especially the chapter "Killing Me Softly: Capital Punishment and the Technologies for Taking Life."

almost completely from it. Whereas in the Napoleonic code, even in its (violent) removal—or especially at that time—the penis remained central to both sexuality and reproduction, in the fascist legislation, it is meaningless. Sexual boundaries are not of interest to twentieth century legislators, nor is the "penetration" of these boundaries.[108] Instead, reproductive boundaries are key, and rather than penetration, trespass is the fear—a creeping infection with syphilis or blennorhagia far more nefarious than any violent act of "passion."

And again, this approach to reproduction, absent any violence or wound, assuming the existence of consent, completely destabilizes any notion of the active or the passive. Just as there is no question of choice on the part of the simultaneously consenting and not-consenting biopolitical subject, there is likewise no question of active or passive citizenship. Indeed, the criminalization of, say, sterilization[109] renders completely irrelevant any scenario in which an active citizen will exert his or her rights in order to retain some "freedom," or in which a state will limit these rights to product collective welfare. This is not a situation in which the active right to behave in x, y, or z way (to kill, to steal, to commit arson) is curtailed for some concept of the greater good. Rather, it is a situation in which the apparently active (and even dangerous) right to be passive (to be sterile, to not-reproduce) is curtailed; it is a situation, in other words, in which the passive becomes actively criminal.

At the same time, I want to emphasize that this legislation is also not *simply* a restatement of political rights having to do with dignity. It does not operate in the same realm as the right, for example, to education—a right which manifests itself most frequently in the criminalization of those who do not invoke it. Such rights, although more seemingly passive than the right, for instance, to speak, also have to do almost solely with defining juridically the *behavior* of the active citizen. The criminalization of non-reproductive behavior is different. It is, again, an attempt first and foremost to turn the citizen into a space—into an area with permeable but defensible boundaries that, *as an area*, must be by definition passive, but *as a citizen*, must be active. Indeed, as Scarry argues, active rights (such as consent and bodily integrity) manifest themselves most obviously, or at least explicitly, when the citizen invoking them is weak, unconscious, or even dead.[110] It is the politically active, physically passive citizen who is key. The reproductive legislation that we

---

108 As Pederson notes in making a different point, "The exhaustive list of prohibited substances included all female methods of contraception but did not include condoms. This indicates that the French legislators' expanded political and medical authority to intervene into family life was extended through the bodies of women." Pedersen 1996, 676-7.

109 Although there is, in a variety of national contexts during this period, a definite attempt to link sterilization and collective welfare. Among many others, for instance, we see in French controlled Syria/Lebanon the following situation: "according to Professor Mahmud Zayid of the American University of Beirut, as early as 1936 Sheikh Ahmad Ibrahim permitted sterilization of carriers of genetic diseases. This was a very daring step, considering the views on sterilization held by most muftis in the second half of the century. Several muftis acquiesce to a temporary sterilization only, if at all. Most of them are against any type of sterilization." Vardit Rispler-Chaim 2003, 86-7.

110 Scarry 1990, 868.

see in France, Italy, and Turkey is therefore simply a hyperbolic variation on this two century long process.

The final collapse of supposedly discrete political categories that we see in the legislation—honor into liberty—is in fact largely a by product of this same confusion over whether the interwar subject is a citizen or a space. "Honor"—and especially familial honor or sexual honor—starts to play a key role in criminal legislation in the early twentieth century precisely because it is central to both the preservation of collective boundaries and the protection of individual ones. Indeed, although the notion of sexual or familial honor has for the most part been regarded as something "traditional," something outside of the realm of the rights-based post-Enlightenment state—best ignored or turned into a non-threatening heritage-on-display—recent work, especially in post-colonial studies, has questioned this approach as well as the progress narrative on which it implicitly relies.[111] Moreover, we can see in both the interwar sexual and reproductive legislation, as well as in its nineteenth century precursor, a situation in which sexual, familial, or reproductive honor was deliberately placed at the center of modern, rights-based French, Italian, Ottoman, and Turkish political structures.

In the Ottoman case, for example, the original liberal formula of "life, honor, and property"[112] that appeared first in the proto-constitutional 1839 edict, reappeared in the criminal codes with a deliberate slippage between "honor" and "chastity" (*ırz ve namus*).[113] Indeed, this political honor, "as sacred and dear to a person as his life," and "among the necessities of patriotism and humanity,"[114] was the same honor that was explicitly attacked during a rape—sexual assaults described in legislation not just as "*fiil-i şeni*" (indecent assault) but, more frequently, as "*hetk-i ırz*" (attack on honor). In the fascist French case, again, it was explicitly "work, family, and fatherland" that were to be protected by new political structures.[115] That the Italian and Turkish

111 Both Parla and Dicle Koğacıoğlu, for example, question the tradition/modernity dichotomy in their work on Republican Turkey. As Parla notes, virginity examinations are "neither throwbacks to tradition, nor protections thereof." Parla 2000, 66. Koğacıoğlu similarly states in her discussion of "honor killing" that tradition has multiple meanings—and that invoking it both reinforces the role of modern institutions in protecting the honor of the state and "signifies multiple things at once. For instance, the signification of tradition by the international news media operates through seemingly timeless binaries of East/West or past/present, while the discourse of Turkish judicial authorities situates tradition as the source of an ultimately temporary resistance to modernization." Koğacıoğlu 2004, 121, 136.

112 The replacement of "liberty" with the more authoritarian "honor" in this formulation might indicate a movement away from liberal ideals. In fact, however, "honor" and "liberty" overlap conceptually in the work of many Enlightenment and post-Enlightenment political theorists, the former shorthand for positive rights (i.e., the right to education) and the latter shorthand for negative rights (i.e., the right not to be coerced). See, for instance, Bartlett 2001, 1-28.

113 Ahmed Lütfi 1888, 128, 132-133.

114 "*Irz ve namus dahi kişinin canı gibi aziz ve muhterem olarak muhafaza ve vikayesi mükteza-yı hamiyet ve mütebegga-yı insaniyetten olup …*", or "Chastity and honor are as sacred and dear to a person as his life, and the safety and protection of these are among the necessities of patriotism and humanity …".

115 Reggiani 1996, 748-750.

discussions of abortion should cite the preservation of sexual and familial honor as a mitigating circumstance in the abortion legislation therefore makes a great deal of sense. It was not just that the future of the nation or race resided in the woman's womb; her womb was also the depository of the collapsed honor and liberty of each individual citizen. This depository, however, had to be pure and, more importantly, public—it had to be circumscribed, in other words, by a theory of consent that disallowed even the possibility of "choice."

Bodily Integrity after the Second World War

After the Second World War, of course, it was choice—or at least a rhetoric thereof—that was held up as a barrier against mistakes made during the 1930s and the 1940s. What this meant in the realm of reproductive legislation was a gradual decriminalization of abortion between the 1950s and the present, and a re-situation of the larger abortion debate within the context of individual rights. By the 1980s, the fetus had reappeared in the arguments of abortion opponents as a citizen in need of protection, supplanting in theory, at least, the besieged nation or race. Three decades before this moment, the woman citizen as a rights-bearing individual had likewise reappeared, her right to bodily integrity at the center of post-war movements to decriminalize abortion and contraception. At the same time, however, consent certainly did not fall by the wayside—indeed, the writing of consent across the body noted by Scarry became if anything more pronounced after the war. Similarly, honor remained central to reproductive legislation—the slippage among sexual honor, family honor, and political honor so prominent in the Ottoman, Turkish, and Italian texts especially replicated in the very post-war vocabulary of bodily *integrity*.

I would in fact like to pause here to consider the meaning of "bodily integrity." Basically, "integrity" means "honor." It is also frequently defined as "honesty," "truth," "veracity," and "reliability." To speak of "bodily integrity," therefore, is to speak of the honor, veracity, and reliability of the body. An undermining of bodily integrity thus does not refer simply to a violation of the boundary between the supposedly external and the supposedly internal; it also refers to a dishonoring of the body, to rendering it somehow untrue or false, to leaving it unreliable or out of control. The "wholeness" implied by bodily integrity is, therefore, not just a physical wholeness with borders intact, it is also an existential wholeness, having to do with reality, truth, and agency. I emphasize these points not because I want to argue that this etymological approach to "bodily integrity" should supplant, or can tell us more than, conventional juridical understandings of the term—indeed, I will turn to these juridical definitions momentarily. I simply want to suggest that the term's more fundamental implications with regard to dichotomies such as whole/not whole, self/not self, intact/disrupted, and real/not real are by no means absent from the legislation that invokes this right, and that they are key to the post-war re-articulation of reproductive space as biopolitical space. Just as consent drew simultaneously reproductive and political boundaries around interwar wombs, in other words, bodily integrity traces the same lines and produces the same overlap.

Likewise, in the same way that discussions of consent theory involve three or four common tropes, discussions of bodily integrity do the same. The usual argument with regard to bodily integrity, for example, tends to revolve around the privileging of one or the other of the dichotomies that I noted above. The question at stake in general is whether the violation of bodily integrity is about physical trespass or whether it is about something else. And if it is something else, is this something a matter of existential identity, political or bodily borders, or political or bodily control? Scarry, for example, begins her discussion of consent and rights with a reference to Judge Cardozo's conclusion in the 1914 case, Schloendorff v Society of New York Hospital, in which Cardozo writes that "in the case at hand the wrong complained of is not merely negligence. It is trespass. Every human being of adult years and sound mind has a right to determine what shall be done with his own body; and a surgeon who performs or operates without his patient's consent commits an assault for which he is liable in damages." In analyzing this passage, Scarry argues that

> the body, in this language, is conceived of as a palpable ground: the body has edges; it has specific boundaries; to cross over these boundaries without the authorization of the person is an act of trespass. Judge Cardozo sets this in a political and philosophical framework by citing the 1905 Illinois Court of Appeals case, *Pratt v. Davis*, in which Justice Brown had asserted "Under a free government at least, the free citizen's first and greatest right, which underlies all others—the right to the inviolability of his person, in other words, his right to himself—is the subject of universal acquiescence." Here, as legal commentators have noticed, the private relations (or what might have been conceived of as merely "the private" relation) between physician and patient is placed within the frame of the "civil rights of citizenship."[116]

The most basic issue raised in both Cardozo's ruling and Scarry's analysis is, then, the issue of space. Bodily boundaries are conflated with civic boundaries. The violation of bodily integrity is not about violence; it is about trespass and the public and private spheres—it is about the duty of a free government to preserve these spheres whole and intact.[117] As Scarry suggests, therefore, if we accept this approach to bodily integrity, and in particular the *right* to bodily integrity, the physical and legal borders of the body and the physical and legal borders of the nation state become in many ways one and the same thing.[118]

---

116 Scarry 1990, 868.

117 Although an issue worth mentioning that is not often raised in discussions of Cardozo's decision is that Mary Schloendorff lost the case against the hospital and that she "had no ordinary tumor, nor was it on her arm. It was a fibroid mass in her uterus and the operation done against her will was a hysterectomy." Lombardo 2005, 795. There are striking similarities, in other words, between this "good" decision on bodily integrity and the "bad decision" a few years later that occurred in *Buck v Bell*. In each, questions about political violations of biological boundaries end with a medico-legal decision—reinforced by the courts—to sterilize unfit women.

118 See also, "though in each instance one is only disposing of a relatively tiny piece of matter—one's own body—in fact by having absolute authority over what can touch, or pass across, the boundaries of one's own person, and conversely, to be able to exercise authority

But Scarry is certainly not the only theorist to point out this relationship between rights rhetoric and bodily integrity or between bodily borders and the articulation of political space. As Alan Hyde has noted in his *Bodies of Law*, for instance, "the 'private body' is a *right*, conceptualized as *space*, *weighed* against other interests and therefore not absolute; it is, therefore, public and social … [R]ights are often visualized with spatial metaphors; in *Roe v. Wade*, typically they are 'areas or zones.'" [italics in original][119]

Scholars such as Catharine MacKinnon and Jean L. Cohen, arguing on separate sides of the US abortion-rights-as-privacy-rights debate, have likewise suggested the inherently spatial dimensions of the rhetoric surrounding bodily integrity—even if they have not effectively problematized these dimensions in the way that Scarry and Hyde have.[120] In another context, Luise White has critiqued the neo-colonial implications "lurking behind western notions of bodily integrity," arguing that "stories of body parts, hearts, doctors and border crossings are not only a debate about the vulnerability of African bodies, but about the vulnerability of African borders, and about the language of individual rights that protects bodies and undermines borders."[121] Like so many other aspects of the "global" rights rhetoric that reinforces the borders surrounding European and North American political space, in other words, the right to bodily integrity likewise produces a porous, permeable boundary around nation states in the rest of the world.[122]

The point to be made here, however, is simply that the linkage between modern notions of bodily integrity and modern notions of political space—be it the space enclosed by sovereign, national boundaries, the "public sphere," the arena of the "private," or colonized space constantly in flux—is one that has been developing over a number of years. Crimes against bodily integrity are about a physically defined political trespass. They involve a biological undermining of sovereign boundaries, the public sphere, or the domain of the private.

At the same time, not all contemporary discussions of bodily integrity fall so obviously into the paradigm of overlapping biological and civic or national rights. Nadine Taub, for instance, begins her analysis of bodily integrity and reproduction by arguing that it is central to debates about abortion and contraception first and foremost because of "the tremendous impact pregnancy and childbearing have on a woman's body."[123] Here, in other words, the basic issue at stake is an actual physical change (addition, subtraction, transplant, or removal) that occurs in an individual's body, and how this change might affect that individual's sense of "personhood." Taub further links reproduction related discussions of bodily integrity to similar discussions in the realm of medical experimentation and treatment, and she concludes

over the world space in which one places or displaces oneself, one has just gained absolute authority vis à vis the world." Scarry 1990, 880.

119 Hyde 1997, 82.

120 Cohen 2002, 62 and MacKinnon 1989, 187.

121 White 1997, 332, 326.

122 A subject to which I will return in the last chapter of the book.

123 Taub 1999, 455.

that "this right of bodily integrity has been clearly articulated constitutionally."[124] Rather than protecting the liberal notion of an intact civic relationship occurring in protected public space, therefore, bodily integrity here is protecting the broader notion of "personhood" as it is expressed in physical wholeness.

Drucilla Cornell addresses the question of bodily integrity, personhood, and the legal protection of both in a related way, arguing that,

> the right to abortion should not be understood as the right to choose an abortion but as the right to realize the legitimacy of the individual woman's projection of her own bodily integrity, consistent with her imagination of herself at the time that she chooses to terminate her pregnancy.[125]

Here, in other words, personhood and bodily integrity are not about physical wholeness but about psychological or existential wholeness—the relationship between an intact body and a sense of self. A woman's identity (political and otherwise) is based on the projection of her physical and psychological self, and a legal system must protect a woman citizen's ability (and "right") to maintain this identity. As Taub notes, although "far more sophisticated" than many other approaches, Cornell's analysis is also based both implicitly and explicitly upon a Lacanian interpretation of the mirroring process.[126] Taub further argues that if we do not accept Lacanian analysis, Cornell's argument becomes problematic.[127] I would respond, however, that psychological projections of the self based on bodily integrity are not any more constructed (or "false") than physical projections of the same, and that Cornell's approach is therefore useful regardless of whether or not we accept the details of Lacanian analysis.[128] Indeed, both the more "basic" approach and the more "sophisticated" approach appear to get at the same issue—the linkage

124 Ibid, 455.

125 Cornell 1995, 82.

126 Taub 1999, 456.

127 Ibid, 456.

128 Although a second critique of Cornell's analysis might be elaborated via a reading of Lesley Caldwell's discussion of abortion in Italy: "because [abortion as contraception] does not imply the forethought that most methods of contraception demand, it more readily accommodates women not thinking of themselves as active sexual persons; this is a refusal that closely aligns with dominant ideas of masculinity and femininity." Caldwell 1981, 59. Here, in other words, we have women using the right to bodily integrity and their right to abortion to project themselves (psychologically—if not according to strict Lacanian analysis) as participants in patriarchal gender relations. Women's right to bodily integrity in this context reinforces notions of women's sexual passivity. At the same time, I should emphasize that my point is not to argue that abortion rights always, or even often, lead to a re-inscription of patriarchal power structures. Nor do I want to argue that Cornell's approach to bodily integrity is somehow flawed. Instead, I want to caution that the late twentieth century rhetoric of bodily integrity, like the early twentieth century rhetoric of consent, is a complicated one—by no means leading us inexorably to a changed or altered relationship between politics and reproduction. Indeed, as we shall see, the late twentieth century decriminalization of abortion, with its invocation of bodily integrity, defined in far more uncompromising terms women's bodies as incubators for future political subjects.

of personhood or the self to the ideal of wholeness, and the need for legal structures or rights rhetoric to protect this connection.

Each of these approaches to bodily integrity, in other words, highlights an aspect of physical, political, or psychological wholeness as well as an aspect of physical, political, or biological space. In Cardozo and Cohen, the issue at stake is defining spheres (the public as well as the private) and the civic or political relationships that are mediated in these spheres. In Taub and Cornell, the issue at stake is physical and psychological personhood, how each relates to political identity, and how attacks on each need to be prevented using a rhetoric of rights and duties. All four thus in a basic way see bodily integrity as central to defining the self, to defining "reality," and to defining political space. As I will suggest over the following pages, it is this understanding of the right to bodily integrity precisely and in particular that reinforces—in a far more relentless and effective way than even the right to consent did in the early twentieth century—the articulation of women's wombs as biopolitical space. Bodily integrity—physical, psychological, and political—has been constructed for distinctly political reasons, having to do with distinctly political notions of reality, identity, and personhood.

I would like to turn now to a brief doctrinal history of abortion legislation in Turkey, Italy, and France after the Second World War. In Turkey, government officials continued into the 1950s to support the pro-natalist policy enshrined in the Rocco Code. By 1958 and 1959, however, citing "high infant, child, and maternal mortality," "high urban population growth," and "employment problems," attitudes toward the regulation of reproduction had already begun to change, and throughout the early 1960s, more and more advocates of anti-natalist population policies began to declare themselves.[129] In 1962, the Turkish Parliament officially adopted an anti-natalist position for "social reasons," in 1965 it passed the "Population Planning Act," and in the same year abortion was partially decriminalized if a continued pregnancy endangered "the health of the offspring or the health of the woman."[130] By the early 1960s, in other words, connections were already being forged between threats to "the population" (in this case the threat of growth, rather than the threat of decline), "social problems," and "the health of the woman and her offspring." Various dangers to the collective provoked an alteration of government attitudes toward reproduction, that is, but the vocabulary in which this alteration was couched was a vocabulary of the individual woman's or child's "right to health."

This overlap between a woman's right to health and collective politics was further accentuated in the "liberalization" of abortion legislation that occurred in the 1983 revision of the criminal code—although I should note that even prior to this decriminalization, abortion was widely available to the Turkish population, with estimates that over one-third of the women in the country had terminated their pregnancies in the 1960s and 1970s.[131] In 1983, therefore, Turkish legislators moved abortion into the "crimes against the person" chapter of the code and drew up a separate section to address it. In this section, abortion is allowed up through the

129 İçduygu 1996, 132.
130 Tezcan 1980, 5, 9.
131 Senlet, Curtis, Mathis, and Ragges 2001, 42, 45.

tenth week of pregnancy, and after the tenth week for medical reasons. The question of consent or choice remains a key one for criminal abortions following the tenth week, and the articles on abortion are followed by one on sterilization of "either sex." Finally, the last article of the section notes that if any of the preceding crimes, aside from sterilization, are committed for the sake of personal or family honor, the punishments will be reduced by a half or a third.[132] Here, in other words, reproductive health and reproductive legislation are moved into a more straightforward liberal context of individual rights, individual health, and the tension between the two.

In Italy, the pro-natalist approach to reproduction likewise remained in effect after the war—gradually replaced in the 1970s by a likewise self-consciously "liberal" interpretation of abortion legislation. Just as in Turkey, in Italy as well, abortion was certainly not unknown prior to the 1970s, and indeed "the extreme discrepancy between the previous law on abortion and the reality of women's lives (estimates of three million illegal abortions a year were common)," were primary motivations in "the campaign to change the law."[133] In 1975, therefore, Italian Parliament passed a law allowing therapeutic abortions if woman's health was in danger, basing its decision on "the priority of *diritto alla salute* (right to health) of the mother, who is a born person, over that of the fetus."[134] In 1978, abortion was further decriminalized, "and legally recognized by law no. 194, titled 'Norme per la Tutela Sociale della Maternità e sull'Interruzione Volontaria della Gravidanza' (Norms for the Social Protection of Motherhood and about the Voluntary Interruption of Pregnancy)"[135]—the individual's "right to health" thus likewise conflated in Italy with collective notions of "social protection" and "motherhood." As Calloni notes, the law allows for a situation in which,

> a woman can be administered a voluntary interruption of pregnancy in the first 90 days of her pregnancy, when circumstances can prevent the continuation of her pregnancy, [when] birth [or] mothering/motherhood put in serious danger her physical or mental health, in relation to her health state, economical/social/family conditions, circumstances in which the conception has happened, [and when there are] expectations of anomalies or malformations by the conceived. The woman can turn to a public consulting structure, a socio-medical structure, fully licensed by the region, or to a physician in attendance.[136]

This last aspect of the law has provoked criticism from abortion advocates in that physicians and nurses can refuse to perform an abortion for "reasons of conscience."[137]

Finally, in France, immediately following the end of the war, the *Tribunal d'état* was abolished, as was the Vichy regime's "300 Law." In 1947, a new medical (but

132 *Türk ceza kanunu* 1994, Art. 468-472.

133 Caldwell 1981, 49-50.

134 Calloni 2001, 186.

135 "Note that legal abortion is referred to in Italian as Interruzione Volontaria della Gravidanza (IVG)." Calloni 2001, 182.

136 Art. 4, Law no. 194 as cited in Calloni 2001, 186.

137 I will discuss this issue in more detail below.

not criminal[138]) code allowed for abortion for therapeutic reasons, "but required the signed certificates of three doctors instead of two."[139] In 1955, the criminal code was likewise modified, allowing (but still not decriminalizing) therapeutic abortion when pregnancy threatened the life of the woman.[140] Eventually, in 1965, the French president formed a committee within the Ministry of Health to look into the introduction of birth control pills,[141] and in 1967, the Neuwirth law legalized contraception, while the Veil law "provided for legal abortion in the first ten weeks of pregnancy but did not erase the criminalization of abortion under other circumstances."[142] In 1979, the Pelletier law further "liberalized" French abortion legislation, but, as Robinson notes,

> with significant new requirements. Doctors were required to inform patients of the consequences of abortion on the national demographic situation, and of every person's national obligations … [T]he conservatives succeeded in framing the debate in their own terms and sought to discourage abortions by requiring doctors to inform their patients of the "grave biological risks they were taking by intervening in pregnancy."[143]

In France, in other words, even in 1979, the "biological risk" that abortion posed to an individual woman—in this scenario both having an abortion and not having an abortion were apparently considered attacks on bodily integrity—was directly linked to the still present *pro-natalist* fear of a national population decline. Also, as in Italy, abortions could be performed only by a doctor and only in a hospital, while physicians and nurses could refuse to operate for "reasons of conscience."[144]

In 1981, feminist movements in France turned their attention more overtly to the issue of reproductive legislation, invoking explicitly not just "the right to health" but the "freedom to control one's body" in their discussions.[145] The 1982, 1992, and 1993 laws thus further loosened restrictions on abortion and were each deliberately couched in a rhetoric of bodily integrity and the duty of a modern state to protect this right.[146] In France, therefore, as well as in Turkey and Italy, the abstract concept, "health," as well as the collective entity in need of protection, "the population," were eventually placed under the larger rubric, "bodily integrity," with all of the implications about political and biological selfness and wholeness that this rubric entailed.

138 Meaning that even therapeutic abortions remained technically "crimes." See also MacKinnon's discussion of the decriminalization of abortion in the United States: "Women were granted the abortion right as a private privilege not as a public right … [A]bortion was not so much decriminalized as it was legalized." MacKinnon 1989, 192.

139 Watson 1952, 268-9.

140 Robinson 2001, 87.

141 Terrade 2001.

142 Robinson 2001, 87.

143 Ibid, 93. See also, Terrade 2001.

144 Terrade 2001.

145 Robinson 2001, 95.

146 Terrade 2001.

In Turkey, Italy, and France, therefore, a woman's right to health/right to control her body gradually moved to the center of the post-war abortion legislation. As I will suggest over the remainder of this section, however, given the ways in which bodily integrity has been interpreted, this decriminalization of abortion in fact inscribed political space onto reproductive space with far more success than the criminalization of abortion had done before. To the extent that abortion was linked even more explicitly, first, to contraception and, second, to sterilization, for example, the concept of reproductive space was privileged over the concept of the reproducing individual. Put another way, when contraception and sterilization are understood within the same rhetorical framework as abortion, it is not the product of reproduction (which may or may not exist)—or the person doing the reproducing (who may or may not be active)—that is at issue. Instead it is, again, the arena in which this process may or may not be happening. Likewise, to the extent that criminalizing abortion is seen as an attack on bodily integrity in this rhetoric, it reinforces the importance of first, delimiting, and then, of protecting, this same biopolitical space.

If we look, for example, at the gradual decriminalization of abortion in Turkey, we see first of all an increasingly explicit connection between reproduction on the one hand and sterilization or contraception on the other. We likewise see an increasingly overt attempt to understand "modern" reproductive space as a space in opposition to something called "traditional" reproductive space. The former is defined as an area with boundaries that get transgressed. The latter is defined as an area with barriers that get penetrated. The former is linked securely to notions of "self" and "not self." The latter is largely unrelated to such concepts. Most basically, for instance, although removed from any explicit association with the race or the national collective, abortion and sterilization in the 1983 law continue to operate within much the same rhetorical framework that they did before. Contained within a single, short chapter, the articles on abortion and sterilization rely on the same vocabulary of health, hygiene, and the post-Enlightenment honor/liberty that had been so prominent during the interwar period. The two, in other words, remain inextricable in the new law, just as they had in the earlier legislation.

At the same time, however, it is worth pointing out that whereas the attempt to protect honor does mitigate the crime that is abortion, it does not mitigate the crime that is sterilization—a difference that would seem to place sterilization into a different analytical category than that occupied by abortion. If we think more carefully about the implications of this caveat, though, we can see that in fact what is happening is, again, a further delimiting of the womb as pre-eminent political or biopolitical space: an abortion that is performed for the sake of sexual/political honor is less criminal than a sterilization performed for the same purposes. Pregnancy is thus something that affects honor (and must therefore be stopped), whereas the inability to conceive is something quite different. Just as the interest in castration so prominent in the Napoleonic code gradually waned in the early twentieth century, in other words, so too is the interest in actual procreation, so prominent in the early twentieth century, disappearing in this late twentieth century code. "Honor"—with all of its political, sexual, "modern," and "traditional" connotations—remains resident in the womb; it continues to define a *space*. But it ceases to have anything obvious to do with actual procreation—with functional or not functional testicles or ovaries. It has become quite irrelevant to *behavior*—linked *only* to reproductive space and to the political area that this space has come to represent.

Indeed, if we consider the role of bodily integrity in this formula—the notion that the right to have an abortion rests upon the right to bodily integrity, just as the right *not* to be sterilized rests upon the same ideal—we can see the growing importance of reproductive space in defining the boundaries of the late twentieth century self and not-self. First of all, for instance, it is only when conflated with "honor" or with "health" that the right to bodily integrity can trump, in this law at least, the basically criminal nature of abortions performed after the tenth week of pregnancy. It is only a citizen *already* defined as politically whole (possessing an individual or collective honor that might be undermined) or medically whole (possessing a "health" that might be undermined), in other words, who can invoke "the right to bodily integrity"—otherwise such a right is irrelevant, or at best severely circumscribed. The selfness and the wholeness implied by bodily integrity, therefore, rest squarely upon an *already* relentlessly defined liberal or neo-liberal notion of political or medical identity. An individual without honor, whose womb is not effectively politicized, cannot invoke bodily integrity—nor can an individual without health. Sterilization is thus in this sense immaterial, except as a means of further defining reproductive space.[147] Indeed, the notion of sterilizing an individual for the sake of collective or individual honor is meaningless; it affects, again, "traditional" *behavior* rather than "modern" *space*, and is thus irrelevant to the late twentieth century citizen.

The importance of space as opposed to behavior in nineteenth and twentieth century interpretations of abortion legislation in fact becomes overt in many analyses of the Turkish law. As one scholar has noted in the midst of a discussion of contraception and abortion in Turkey, for example, "although overall contraceptive use has been stagnant [between 1988 and 1998] … a gradual shift has occurred from use of traditional to modern contraceptive methods … [i]n 1978, the practice of withdrawal made up half of all contraceptive use."[148] The notion of withdrawal as a

147 For a discussion of sterilization by scholars of Islamic Law in modern Turkey (who do not have a great deal of overt influence over government legislators, but who are certainly influential in other realms), see, for instance: "Dr Huseyn Atay, Professor of (Islamic) Theology at the Faculty of Theology, Turkey, researched the legality of family planning. He considered the issue of multitude and concluded that Islam prefers the multitude of quality. He added that the Muslim world today is not suffering from a lack of people, but from a lack of great industrious Muslims … [i]n considering abortion and stages of fetal development, he introduced an intriguing concept. Al-azl [contraception], in Arabic, as already indicated, means a separation. In seeking to extend the meaning beyond its customary use, he drew an analogy between the act of separating sperm from ovum (al-azl) and the act of preventing the early 'product' of contraception from ever reaching the stage of ensoulment … [h]e then turned to sterilization and tried to differentiate between it and castration. Castration is forbidden and entails the destruction of the power of getting children. Sterilization, on the other hand, allows the individual to resume his natural functions. He suggested that the issue of sterilization should, at least, be discussed." In this (modern) context as well, in other words, the focus ceases to be on the penis or behavior, and becomes instead the womb or space. In Omran 1992, 235.

148 Senlet, Curtis, Mathis, and Ragges 2001, 41.

"traditional" form of contraception is one that we see in a number of studies.[149] Its implications with regard to the politicization of the womb and the increasing focus on space, however, are worth emphasizing. Basically, withdrawal is considered "traditional" because, as a form of contraception, it focuses, first, on behavior, and second on the penis. Withdrawal, in other words, is a form of contraception that inevitably evokes the Napoleonic code's fascination with castration. "Modern" contraception, contrarily, is different. Its focus is space rather than behavior—the womb, and various means of protecting it. Modern contraception, in other words, is interested in preventing a transgression of the boundaries of female reproductive space—indeed, in preserving female bodily integrity.

At the same time, however, as Jessica van Kammen has argued, this approach to modern contraception has also redefined the modern female body (but not the modern male body) as necessarily a body under constant attack, with boundaries constantly on the verge of dissolving—in need, therefore, of a likewise constant protection or regulation. As she notes with regard to the intellectual framework in which twentieth century anti-fertility products were developed, for instance,

> sperm was obviously foreign to a woman, and its transient presence was predominantly restricted to her reproductive tract … [T]herefore, only anti-sperm and anti-placental antigens in women were acceptable to the immunologists, since they could be categorized as non-self and thus fit into the existing immunological paradigm … [B]ody boundaries were interpreted as being permeable and allowing in a non-self, thus permitting immunocontraceptive intervention.[150]

This approach to modern contraception indeed has remained the dominant model despite the fact that "spermatozoa could be considered foreign to the male immune system because their production starts at puberty." But such an approach to reproductive behavior has become impossible. Fundamentally, as van Kammen concludes, "male users [are] inconceivable."[151] I would further argue, however, that male users were and are inconceivable in part because space has so effectively overtaken behavior as the politically relevant aspect of reproduction; a focus on the male body at this point would be seen as quite literally backward, traditional, and contrary to modern rights. As reproduction, abortion, and abortion rights became linked not only to contraception and sterilization, but also to the post-Second World War ideal of bodily integrity, in other words, the womb became a space, ironically, far *more* open to regulation than it had ever been before. This regulation, however, was occurring now in the name of protecting a woman's political, sexual, social, and civilizational self, rather than in the name of the health or integrity of the race. By the late 1970s, in fact, the Council of Europe was arguing that this approach to reproduction was an eminently public, *national* concern—"the activities of private

149 And one that leads inevitably to "more" abortions—see also Tezcan 1980, 46.

150 van Kammen 1999, 312-313.

151 Ibid, 314-315.

family planning associations … supported as complements of, not substitutes for, vigorous national programs."[152]

But it was not just the politicization of reproductive space—or the mapping of the public onto the womb—that occurred with the entry of bodily integrity into discussions of reproductive law. It was also that the public sphere was likewise transformed into an arena for expressing sexual, reproductive, and therefore biopolitical identities. The conflation of bodily borders and national borders explicitly noted by White[153] and implicitly suggested by philosophers such as Locke[154] thus became increasingly overt as the twentieth century progressed. Indeed, bodily integrity, far more than consent, became *the* means of defining the biopolitical subject, politicizing not just the womb, for instance, but the hospital in which the abortion would be performed—inscribing the nation onto a reproductive space now defined explicitly as a container for both the consenting patient and the non-consenting citizen.

In France, for example, one of the most "symbolic moments in the history of feminist movement," was the 1971 "Manifesto of the 343" published in *Le Nouvel Observateur*—a letter signed by 343 women declaring that they had undergone illegal abortions. Described as key to the gradual decriminalization of abortion precisely because it both brought the "sphere of the intimate" into the open and "lifted a taboo on affirming a violation of the law,"[155] it is in a very straightforward way a deliberate conflation of bodily and national identities. It is not just that "the 343" are attacking the liberal notion of the public/private distinction—declaring, as it were, that the personal is political. Although this is certainly an important aspect of their "disobedience." It is also—and perhaps more so—that they are constructing a new, biologically defined collective and that they are then situating this collective within each, individual body. "The 343" is a whole—it is a collection of liberal citizens operating in the public sphere. But it is a whole defined emphatically by the biological—a collective solely because bodily integrity is situated above the law.

152 "Council of Europe: 'Make Birth Control Available" 1976, 16. See also, in the same article, "sterilization should be made available as a medical service, the Council advises, provided that those who want to be sterilized realize that this procedure is 'generally irreversible.'" "Council of Europe" 1976, 16.

153 Again, "this paper suggests that these stories of body parts, hearts, doctors, and border crossings are not only a debate about the vulnerability of African bodies, but about the vulnerability of African borders, and about the language of individual rights that protects bodies and undermines borders." White 1997, 326.

154 "Locke, for example, uses the verb 'injure' both when the object is the material reality of the body and when the object is freedom, just as he speaks of 'invading' another's body, invading another's property (the 'annexed body'), or instead invading another's rights. When Locke uses the idiom of 'invasion' for a nonphysical object, he often immediately follows it by the word 'rapine,' in order to restore the physical referent." Scarry 1990, 874.

155 Terrade 2001. See also, "in 1971, 343 prominent women, including Catherine Deneuve, Simone de Beauvoir, Françoise Sagen, Giselle Halimi, and Yvette Roudy, earned the sobriquet of 'whores' (*salopes*) for issuing a manifesto, published in *Le Nouvel Observateur* (1971), affirming that they had undergone illegal abortions." Robinson 2001, 87.

Indeed, law must be violated in order to preserve the body.[156] The clear message is that national identity—liberal citizenship even—has nothing to do with juridical boundaries and everything to do with biological ones.

This message becomes even more overt in Turkey of the 1990s, when the right to bodily integrity is invoked as a means of halting state-sponsored virginity examinations. I will discuss these examinations in more detail in the next chapter, but for now I would simply like to consider the implications of one of the more common slogans of the campaign against the procedure—"No to Virginity Tests! This is My Body!" ("*Bekaret Kontrolüne hayır*! *Bedenimiz Bizimdir*!"). As Ayşe Gül Altınay states in an endnote to an essay discussing the campaign, "it is hard to find an appropriate translation for 'Bedenimiz bizimdir,' which means 'these are our bodies' or 'our bodies belong to us.' It is problematic to translate it as the singular 'this is my body,' but I could not find anything that was more appropriate."[157] The basic problem with translating the slogan, in other words, is that *beden* refers to a singular "body," but it is attached to a plural possessive. The most literal translation of the phrase would therefore be "this is our body" or "our body belongs to us." As Altınay notes, such a translation would undercut the broader purpose of the slogan, and is therefore inappropriate in an essay lauding the campaign.

At the same time, however, it is worth considering the implications of both the slogan's singular and the slogan's plural, given the connection between reproduction and law that I have been suggesting in the formulation of biopolitical identity. As Foucault has argued with regard to biopolitics in general,

> what we are dealing with in this new technology of power is not exactly society (or at least not the social body, as defined by the jurists), nor is it the individual-as-body. It is a new body, a multiple body with so many heads that, while they might not be infinity in number, cannot necessarily be counted. Biopolitics deals with the population.[158]

The biopolitical focus on population, in other words, is a focus that produces precisely a collection of protesting, juridically defined citizens claiming the public sphere as a means of protecting "their" (plural) biologically defined "body" (singular). The invocation of bodily integrity, therefore, quite overtly turns not just reproductive space into political space, but political space into reproductive space—reducing legal, political, and biological bodies as well as borders to one and the same thing.

Indeed, one of the more basic effects of thinking of citizenship in terms of bodily integrity is that the "public sphere" gradually ceases to be defined as the "arena in which consent is formed" and comes instead to be understood as a place in which bodies are defined and reproductive space established. In the case of reproductive legislation, we see an attempt to turn the places (the hospital here as well as the womb) where abortions are performed into simultaneously modern space and political space. In Turkey, for instance, in addition to the trope of "traditional" contraception, there is also the trope of abortions performed in "traditional" or "rural" settings—abortions

156 I will elaborate on this point in my discussion of rape legislation in the next chapter.

157 Altınay 2000, 404, 411.

158 Foucault 2003, 245.

understood to be both more widespread and less appropriate than those performed in "urban" settings by "trained" personnel.[159] Likewise, in all three states, there is a concerted effort to restrict "legal" abortions to certified hospitals or clinics.[160] This effort to confine abortions to legally defined, modern arenas—to vilify the "backstreet abortion" alongside the "untrained midwife"—is not, however, simply a continuation of the nineteenth century process of linking the medical to the legal and of criminalizing unregulated medical practitioners. More so, I would argue, it is part of a new, late twentieth century process of aligning reproductive space, political space, and now medical space as well.

One of the strongest criticisms of the laws restricting abortion in Italy and France, for example, has been the existence of the "conscience clause," allowing for physicians and nurses to refuse to perform an abortion for reasons of personal conscience. Activists and scholars in both countries have argued that "the extremely restricted application of the law does not begin to answer the needs of women,"[161] and, more basically, that it has prevented women from "exercising their rights."[162] But both the existence of the conscience clause and the debate surrounding it also emphasize the importance of reproductive space as well as the role of bodily integrity in describing this space. There is, first of all, an age old collision in these discussions between consent (in this case on the part of the physicians), and rights, freedom, or necessity (on the part of women seeking abortions). On one level, therefore, the hospital has indeed become a part of the juridical public sphere—a space where consent is formed and rights are articulated. As Scarry has noted in reference to judge Cardozo's statement that,

> a hospital opens its doors without discrimination to all who seek its aid. It gathers in its wards a company of skilled physicians and trained nurses, and places their services at the call of the afflicted, without scrutiny of the character or wealth of those who appeal to it, looking at nothing and caring for nothing beyond the fact of their affliction,

"the hospital becomes in this regard a miniature nation-state. Judge Cardozo's statement about the hospital reads almost like a poem by Emma Lazarus (the stone edifice of the hospital becoming like the ingathering skirts of Lady Liberty)."[163] The hospital as well as the body in the hospital are thus above all politically defined entities—inscribed irreversibly into the liberal, juridical structure.

At the same time, however, when we consider what right exactly is being articulated in the case of abortion legislation, and what role precisely the consent of the physician is playing in this articulation, the hospital becomes a nation-state linked far more overtly to biopolitics than to juridical sovereignty. Fundamentally,

159 See, for example, "although Turkey has conditionally restrictive abortion laws, induced abortions are available for private gynecologists in urban areas and are performed by untrained local midwives or the pregnant women themselves, particularly in rural areas." Tezcan and Omran 1981, 262.

160 Robinson 2001, 90.

161 Caldwell 1981 62-3.

162 Terrade 2001.

163 Scarry 1990, 871.

bodily integrity cannot exist in this formulation (in either the clause or in the rhetoric criticizing this clause) without physicians' consent. It is, in other words, the consenting/non-consenting physician/citizen, acting within the "miniature nation-state," who alone produces whole bodies endowed with a sense of self. To the extent that the hospital has become the public sphere, therefore, it is not consent that is formed there, but intact bodies—or, more basically, bodily integrity. Bodily integrity cannot exist on its own, that is—it must be mediated through this newly defined public sphere. Without a consenting/non-consenting physician, therefore, ("consenting" if the clause remains in effect, "non-consenting" if its critics successfully remove it—but linked to the citizen in either case), an abortion cannot be performed, and the right to bodily integrity will remain un-invoked. As a result, the borders and boundaries once more collapse into one another, reproductive space, political space, biological space, and medical space all, quite literally, defined as one.

Conclusion

I would like to conclude this chapter by returning to the late nineteenth century fear of race suicide with which I started. Race suicide as a concept is a complicated one. And it gets at two of the major themes of this chapter—collectivity and life. The notion of a politically and biologically defined collective depriving itself of life—with all of the hints of voluntarism, consent, and irrationality that this act implies—immediately raises the further question of where exactly such an event could occur. Against what backdrop, or within the confines of what boundaries, does a race kill itself? Legislators in the late nineteenth and early twentieth century seem to have developed a relatively confident answer to this question: races kill themselves in reproductive space.[164] Thus, abortion became explicitly linked to citizenship over the final decades of the nineteenth century, and reproduction became a central concern of parliaments and politicians in the early twentieth. At the same time, however, this linkage drew upon a tradition already 150 years in the making, and set the foundation for a rhetoric that would likewise be articulated over the next hundred years. And it is this tradition and this rhetoric that have been the subject of the preceding pages.

Indeed, the moment that reproduction—or more specifically, abortion—became the link between the biological and the political, first, *space* began to replace *behavior* as the politically relevant issue, and second, all other political categories began to collapse into one another. The reproduction-related sections of Napoleonic criminal code and its Ottoman counterpart, for example, were primarily about defining and delimiting this newly crucial arena—most obviously by marginalizing or rendering invisible the fetus-as-individual as well as the woman-as-individual. The fact that Ottoman legislators likewise reinterpreted *diyet* through the lens of this newly liberal approach to political belonging simply reinforces its biopolitical implications—the relentlessly "universal" nature of the biologically defined modern sovereign/subject.

164 Whereas, of course, races are killed (i.e., genocide is committed) in the camp.

By the early twentieth century, therefore, as consent in particular began to play a key (if perhaps unexpected) role in the fascist reinterpretation of this space, a vocabulary for describing it was already in place. The shift from understanding consent as something that defines behavior or that is based in choice to understanding consent as something irrelevant to choice, and solely about defining space indeed becomes inevitable given this earlier framework. Likewise, the means by which the invocation of consent collapses categories such as active and passive (as well as liberal and fascist)—this collapse implicitly or explicitly at the heart of most contemporary critiques of consent theory—could only have been elaborated given this tradition.

Finally, the return to individual rights, and in particular to the right of bodily integrity that we see in the late twentieth century is arguably more a continuation of this process of defining space and collapsing categories than a departure from it. To the extent that bodily integrity is about issues of wholeness, selfness, and even reality—and to the extent that the right to bodily integrity is understood, as Scarry argues, in terms of trespass (rather than, say, violent penetration), the rhetoric surrounding it inscribes this whole self onto simultaneously political and reproductive space. The issue at stake is the conflation of reproductive, biological, and political boundaries, and whether or when these boundaries might be transgressed. In the meantime, behavior—like withdrawal as a form of contraception—is relegated to the realm of the traditional.

Race suicide thus becomes central to the redefinition of sovereign right—especially to the extent that this sovereign right has been articulated through a vocabulary of appropriate, politically responsible reproductive behavior. As we shall see in the next chapter, however, it is also, if less overtly, linked to the sexual aspects of modern sovereign relations—sexual violence such as rape, for instance, is resituated politically and legally within the same biopolitical arena as the suicidal, aborted national collective.

Chapter 3

Sexuality and Citizenship Formation

Introduction

In 1977, in response to a question posed by a commission out to reform French criminal law, Michel Foucault suggested a new approach to rape legislation. Situating his reply within a larger analysis of sexuality and power, he argued that:

> there are problems [if we are to say that rape is more serious than a punch in the face], because what we're saying amounts to this: sexuality as such, in the body, has a preponderant place, the sexual organ isn't like a hand, hair, or nose. It therefore has to be protected, surrounded, invested in any case with legislation that isn't that pertaining to the rest of the body … [I]t isn't a matter of sexuality, it's the physical violence that would be punished, without bringing in the fact that sexuality was involved.[1]

This re-interpretation of rape-as-crime has received much attention since Foucault proposed it in the late 1970s. Throughout the 1990s, for example, the journal *Hypatia* ran a series of articles criticizing Foucault's position, while nonetheless taking into account both the value of his broader analysis of sexuality, and the similarities between his argument and that of feminist theorists such as Susan Brownmiller[2] who, a number of years before Foucault, "were seeking to purge rape of its sexual content in order to render moot the legal question of victim (i.e. female) culpability."[3] Scholars such as Ann Cahill argued that attempts to disassociate rape from sexuality ignored the role of rape in enforcing "a systematic … sexualized control of women."[4] Laura Hengehold likewise questioned the "recklessness" of "male theorists [choosing] rape law as the initial battleground for their counter deployment of power/knowledge on behalf of an (apparently) genderless society," given that rape was by no means "unconstructed … prior to its insertion in the juridico-discursive apparatus."[5]

Other feminist legal scholars in the late 1980s and 1990s also questioned the trend toward understanding rape as violence rather than as sex. Contextualizing her analysis within a criticism of the consent theory[6] that buttressed what she called a "male supremacist" reality, and responding more to Brownmiller than to Foucault, for example, Catharine MacKinnon argued that "rape is not less sexual for being violent. To the extent that coercion has become integral to male sexuality, rape

1 As cited in Cahill 2000, 43.
2 See Brownmiller 1975, *passim*.
3 Cahill 2000, 43.
4 Ibid, 44.
5 Hengehold 1994, 90-91.
6 To which I will return in more detail below.

may even be sexual to the degree that, and because, it is violent."[7] It was not only that a supposedly gender-neutral approach to rape ignored the reality of women's subordination in the social and political order, in other words, it was that the conflation of sex and violence, or the construction of sex as violence, had made a separation of the two impossible. MacKinnon continued by suggesting that this rhetorical overlap of sex and violence had inappropriately privileged the penis and vaginal penetration in discussions of rape law. Making a case for female subjectivity and bodily integrity as the appropriate subject of sex legislation, she asserted that,

> the law to protect women's sexuality from forcible violation and expropriation defines that protection in male genital terms. Women do resent forced penetration. But penile invasion of the vagina may be less pivotal to women's sexuality, pleasure, or violation than it is to male sexuality. This definitive element of rape centers upon a male-defined loss. It also centers upon one way men define loss of exclusive access. In this light, rape, as legally defined, appears more a crime against female monogamy (exclusive access by one man) than against women's sexual dignity or intimate integrity.[8]

In quite different ways, in other words, Cahill, Hengehold, and MacKinnon were all implicitly or explicitly advocating, first, an understanding of rape that addressed both the reality and the rhetoric of women's sexuality, and, second, a more critical approach to crimes committed against this sexuality. To the extent that—constructed or not—sexual identity intersected with social, political, or national identity, rape needed to be understood as an attack on subjectivity as much as it was understood as a physical assault. To the extent that the centrality of the penis (counter intuitively) highlighted the violent as opposed to the sexual nature of rape, the male penis needed to be downplayed in favor of female bodily integrity. All three of these theorists, in other words, were understanding rape in terms of "trespass" rather than in terms of "penetration." To draw on the vocabulary of the last chapter, identity was trumping violence.

All three of these theorists were also, however, writing in the late 1980s and 1990s. By the first years of the twenty-first century, both international law[9] and European law had changed. Indeed, by 2005, various international legislative commissions had started defining rape in precisely the terms advanced by Cahill, Hengehold, and MacKinnon. Meanwhile, French, Italian, Turkish and other nation-state based jurists were coming to understand rape explicitly as an issue of bodily integrity, identity, and dignity—highlighting the victim's subjectivity, and marginalizing or in some cases eliminating completely the role of violence, penetration, or the penis. If we are operating in a progress narrative, therefore, we seem to be on the right track. In fact, if we look further back in time, past the 1977 conversation with Foucault, we can see a distinctly progressive transformation—from a "traditional" approach to rape, in which a woman's sexuality, or more specifically her virginity, was the property

7 MacKinnon 1989, 173.

8 Ibid, 172.

9 Which I will address in more detail in the next chapter.

of her family, her father, or her husband,[10] to a late nineteenth/early twentieth century moment during which women were understood as (liberal) political actors theoretically (if not actually) capable of consent, to, finally, this late twentieth/early twenty-first century point at which women became embodied subjects, political actors to the extent that their bodily integrity remained intact.

My purpose in this chapter is to destabilize this narrative. I will not be arguing that bodily integrity is an inappropriate lens through which to view rape legislation or that violence should be privileged over sex in discussions of rape. But I do think it is important to examine the implications of understanding "integrity" or even "humanity" as the object of attack in rape. I will thus be suggesting in this chapter that just as the shifting focus of reproductive legislation turned the womb into public space, this same shifting focus in sex legislation has turned women's bodies writ large into public space. Furthermore, just as the history of reproductive legislation involved not so much a progression from the traditional to the liberal to the post liberal as it did a collapse of all three into one another, so too will I understand contemporary sex legislation as the product of simultaneously liberal, authoritarian, and fascist trends. Indeed, approaches to rape from the nineteenth century onward have not so much progressed, I will argue, as repeatedly folded into one another.

One might in fact ask why—in a chapter devoted to rape *and* adultery—I have focused thus far only on rape legislation. The two do not seem immediately related to one another, except under the most "traditional" of circumstances. I will be suggesting, however, that the two are unquestionably the same, interchangeable even—and that this is the case precisely because of modern and contemporary liberal and authoritarian politics. Indeed, I will try to demonstrate over the following pages that the overlap between rape and adultery, far from being the product of "traditional" approaches to sex or radical reinterpretations of tradition, is and has been at the foundation of all modern and contemporary legislation on sexuality. If in the sixteenth century rape and adultery were one and the same thing because each was an identical attack on religious or communal honor, by the twenty-first century they were likewise the same thing, each an identical attack on biopolitical honor. The only difference between the legislation of the two periods, I will assert, is in their assumptions about the nature of political space—and just as modern abortion law gradually turned the womb into biopolitical space, so too has modern rape law turned women's bodies into biopolitical space.

Historical Context

Adultery (*zina*) receives a great deal of attention in discussions of so-called classical Islamic law as well as in discussions of contemporary radical (often dubbed "traditional") re-interpretations of Islamic law in countries like Sudan, Nigeria, or Afghanistan. One reason for this is that adultery is a *hadd* crime, one of the seven most serious crimes against God in the Islamic legal system—the others being

10 Most discussions of the history of rape/seduction legislation start at this "traditional" point. MacKinnon disagrees that there was ever a moment at which women were property, however, arguing that "to be property would be an improvement." MacKinnon 1989, 172.

apostasy, highway robbery, rebellion, drinking alcohol, theft, and false accusation of adultery (qadhf).[11] All of these crimes are mentioned specifically in the Quran, as are the evidentiary requirements needed to prove them and the requisite punishments should these evidentiary requirements be met—usually dismemberment, lashing, or death. When trying a *hadd* case, a judge's only role is, first, to decide whether the crime does indeed conform to the definition (or interpretations of the definition[12]) of the crime in the Quran, and, second, to evaluate the character of the witnesses testifying.

At the same time, a convincing argument has been made that the evidentiary requirements needed to prove *hadd* crimes are so nearly impossible to meet (four male witnesses of "good character" who witnessed a couple in the actual act of adultery, for example), that the verses in the Quran referring to them are intended more descriptively than they are normatively.[13] But the fact nonetheless remains that analyses of these *hadd* crimes, and in particular analyses and interpretations of adultery, have become a trope in discussions of Islamic "authenticity" from a variety of perspectives, especially in the modern period. Adultery—and legislation on adultery—has indeed been seen by both modern jurists and modern critics as somehow central to or ineradicable from Islamic legal and political identity.[14]

In this section, I want to discuss the development of Islamic and early Ottoman jurisprudence on adultery without paying undue attention to these more recent developments. In particular, I would like first to examine the ways in which medieval and early modern jurists defined and re-defined adultery as both a *hadd* crime and as a *tazir* crime (a crime against the state/society, rather than against God). Second, I want to look at the extent to which lines were drawn and the extent to which they were blurred between *zina* as adultery and *zina* as rape. Third, I will turn to the relationship between adultery and religious/political identity in the medieval and early modern Islamic and Ottoman legal systems. And finally, I want to suggest that the interpretations and re-interpretations of rape and adultery law that we see in the medieval and early modern Islamic context—especially in the Ottoman Empire—are in many ways identical to similar interpretations in the Catholic context—especially in France and Italy. I will further suggest that these early modern interpretations have played a key role in modern approaches to sex law.

With that in mind, I would like to start with Abdel Salam Sidahmed's translation of Ibn Rushd's general but influential definition of *zina*/adultery: "any copulation [between a man and a woman] without a valid marriage contract, a suspected

11 Modern commentators of various political stances have tended to downplay the importance of *qadhf* as a *hadd* crime. As Judith Tucker notes, however, it was taken as seriously as—if not more seriously than—*zina* in the medieval and early modern period: "most of the fatwas dealing with *zina* focused, indeed, on the pitfalls associated with bringing an accusation." Tucker 1998, 165.

12 Which I will discuss in more detail below.

13 Faizan 1993, 31. Peters 1994, 251.

14 This obsession with sexuality and Islamic authenticity is of course not surprising given the colonial context in which it developed. For more on this subject, see Said 1979, 78.

matrimonial relationship, or lawful concubinage."[15] In elaborating on this definition, Sidahmed argues that "a *zina* penalty would be inflicted on any Muslim—male or female—with full age and understanding who intentionally commits fornication with the full knowledge that it is illicit," but that sexual activity that excludes intercourse might also be punished at the discretion of a judge (i.e., as a *tazir* crime).[16] Finally, on the subject of evidence, Sidahmed notes that prior to the modern period, only one of the four major Sunni schools of law—the Maliki school—considered the pregnancy of a married or unmarried woman as proof of adultery or premarital fornication. Jurists in the other four schools—the Hanafi, Hanbali, and Shafi'i schools—disregarded pregnancy as evidence, given that "one of the problems associated with the presumption of *zina* on grounds of pregnancy of an unmarried woman is that it overlooks the possibility of rape or compulsion as a cause of pregnancy."[17]

In this medieval approach to *zina* as adultery, therefore, three issues are paramount. First of all, there is the differentiation between Muslims and non-Muslims. Only a Muslim male or female with full understanding (that is, an individual with a full, if not modern, legal or political identity) can commit the *hadd* crime that is adultery. Second, whereas the question of the contract between the individuals having sex—marriage, suspected marriage, or concubinage—is central to the definition of adultery, the definition of actual "copulation" itself is left relatively vague. And finally, there is the dismissal of pregnancy or reproduction as evidence of adultery in all but the Maliki school. As Sidahmed argues, this last position is the result of an assumed line between adultery and rape. *Zina*/adultery can happen only in the absence of "compulsion," whereas *zina*/rape implies "force." The further implication of this analysis is that jurists in the early Hanafi, Hanbali, and Shafi'i schools considered rape and adultery to be relatively separate issues.

Sidahmed's analysis of this legislation is convincing, but I would nonetheless like to propose one alternative interpretation of the Hanafi, Hanbali, and Shafi'i position on pregnancy. Rather than, or in addition to, separating adultery from rape, I want to suggest, medieval Muslim jurists were also separating sexuality from reproduction in their approach to the crime. *Zina* had to do with sex. Pregnancy—made explicitly irrelevant to sex in these interpretations—had to do with reproduction. Sexual behavior was thus legally meaningful, whereas reproductive space was far less so. Put another way, by not citing pregnancy as evidence of adultery, jurists were downplaying the position of womb as a site of jurisprudence and emphasizing the activity of the penis. Understanding reproductive space as juridical space, in other words, was a move that jurists of the twelfth and thirteenth centuries were not going to make, even if the Maliki position allowed at least for a conversation on the subject.

As I will argue below, however, this "Maliki"[18] approach is precisely the one eventually advocated by nineteenth century jurists. Rather than an increasingly modern *separation* of sex and reproduction, therefore, we will see instead an increasingly

15 As cited and translated in Sidahmed 2001, 190.

16 Ibid, 190.

17 Ibid, 197.

18 I do not mean here that modern jurists necessarily looked to the Maliki school for precedent.

modern *conflation* of the two. In the earlier period, it is clear that sexuality is largely what is at stake, and that sexuality is a largely masculine affair. Yes, sexual behavior is seen as central to the definition of all "good Muslims," male or female. But in all but the Maliki school, "women's" reproduction is to a great extent subordinated to "men's" sexuality. And it is this separation that sets the foundation for medieval and early modern interpretations of *zina*-as-rape. Indeed, as Amira Sonbol argues in her discussion of Egyptian *zina*/rape law,[19]

> [t]he definition of rape shares further differences among the four schools of Sunni jurisprudence. Malikis define *zina* as "sexual intercourse by a legally capable Muslim of a vagina (*faraj*) to which he had no right (*mulk*)," and Hanafis define *zina* as "sexual intercourse committed by a man in the genitals (*al-qibal*) in other than his property (*mulk*)." This means that both Malikis and Hanafis refer to sexual rights as property. It should be remembered, however, that both men and women who commit *zina* were subject to *hudud* ....[20] [T]he other schools define rape differently from Malik and Abu Hanifa. Shafi'is defined rape as "forcing the male organ or part of it into forbidden (*muharram*) genitals (front or back) of a male or female. While Hanbalis define it as "committing forbidden fornication" ... [S]hafi'is clearly defined the rape of a male as *zina* while Hanafis see no harm in the act because it does not involve *nasab* (lineage), therefore they consider it *ta'zir* ... rather than *hudud* and recommend throwing the offender in prison until he repents or dies.[21]

We have, therefore, the typical "traditional" interpretation of rape here, in which the crime that is committed is a crime against a passive woman-as-property—in which the right that is undermined is the right to property (*mulk*).

At the same time, however, it is important to pause for a moment to consider the implications of both this "traditional" approach, in which women are associated with property rights, and the movement away from it, in which women as newly defined political actors come to be associated with political rights.[22] One aspect of the legislation on *zina*-as-rape that we see above, for instance, is that the discussion

19 Sonbol's focus is on the nineteenth and twentieth centuries—the following passage is a legal/historical contextualization of her main argument.

20 Plural of *hadd*.

21 Sonbol 2000, 312.

22 Indeed, even the more basic, "traditional" notion of [women's] bodies as property is more complicated than one might at first imagine. As Hyde notes with regard to the "ungendered" body-as-property model, "the body may be property in order to explain or justify human domination, in either or both of two somewhat different ways. In the first, a human may be dominated because, after all, its body is just property. Aristotle derives a justification for the government of some over others from the domination of the slave by the master. Leibniz justifies domination over animals by analogizing them to machines: 'if we are compelled to view the animal as being more than a machine, we would have to become Pythagorians and renounce our domination of animals.' If people are property or machines, they may be dominated too. A counter tradition, however, constitutes the body as property to emphasize autonomy. John Locke moves from the claim that 'every man has a property in his own person' to a general theory of the institution of private property." Hyde 1997, 54. I should note that Hyde continues this discussion by critiquing Locke's rhetorical move in this interpretation.

revolves much more explicitly around the copulation part of the story than it does around the contract part of the story. Whereas analyses of adultery assumed copulation and then spent some time discussing various licit and illicit relationships or contracts, analyses of rape assumed a contract (or breach of contract) and instead spent time going into detail about various licit and illicit forms of copulation. Does *zina* involve a penetration of just the vagina, or does the anus count as well? Can *zina* involve two male actors or must the possibility of "lineage" come into play? Whatever the answer, all four of the schools are clearly focusing on the question of sexual behavior (defined via the role of the penis) far more than on the question of the contracted relationship. Discussions of *zina*-as-rape, in other words, even more so than discussions of *zina*-as-adultery, privilege male sexuality, male activity, and female passivity.

At the same time, as we shall see when we get into the modern period, the movement away from this paradigm—the elimination of this "traditional" emphasis on property—by no means rendered women somehow more active than they were in the medieval period. All that happens in the nineteenth century is that the contract comes to be privileged over the copulation in discussions of rape as well. Granted, this modern contract is more political and more public than the property-based and *quasi* private[23] contract of the medieval period. But the results are largely the same—indeed, in many ways they are more pronounced: first, the medieval and early modern dichotomy between *zina*-as-adultery (with its focus on the contract) and *zina*-as-rape (with its focus on the copulation) breaks down in the modern period, as the contract comes to define both. The *zina* "confusion" between rape and adultery, in other words, becomes *more* pronounced, not less so, in the nineteenth century. And second, to the extent that this focus on the contract implies the possibility and then produces the actuality of women as political space—of the womb as a site of jurisprudence—women become if anything *more* passive, more obviously *settings* than they were before. Again, the sole difference between the "traditional" and the modern is thus arguably that women's bodies have become increasingly political, public space, rather than private, economic space, since the eighteenth century.[24]

But before discussing this eighteenth and nineteenth century transformation in detail, I would like to turn to early modern Ottoman interpretations of *zina* as both adultery and rape. Again, although Ottoman legislation was without question a legacy of earlier Islamic jurisprudence, it also departed from these interpretations in various ways. Indeed, the usual starting point for analyses of pre-Tanzimat era Ottoman law is the Sultan Süleyman's early sixteenth century compilation or codification (kanunname) of both *hadd* and *tazir* crime—a codification that in and of itself was something of an innovation, given that just Muslim rulers were supposed to maintain a hands off approach to *hadd* (if not *tazir*) jurisprudence.[25] Süleyman,

23 To the extent that the private exists prior to the modern period.

24 One could in fact argue that the story of late twentieth and early twenty-first century feminist theory and in particular feminist critiques of rape legislation has been an ongoing one of the (futile) attempt to separate the political contract implied by bodily integrity from the public/private paradigm.

25 Gerber 1994, 76.

however, did just the opposite, and started a tradition among Ottoman legislators of attempting to reconcile *hadd* and *tazir* such that each might serve as a pillar of the new, relatively centralized state structure. One of the most important areas in which this new approach to law played out was in the realm of sexual crime.

Sixteenth and seventeenth century Ottoman legislation on adultery and rape, for example, stipulated the frequent use of fines, moving away from the earlier emphasis on corporal punishment.[26] The *hadd* penalty of flogging or death for sexual crime (or even less severe *tazir* variations on this punishment) was for the most part replaced in this period by a scale of fines that depended on an individual's marital, religious, and economic status.[27] This did not mean, however, that *hadd* punishments disappeared completely. As Leslie Peirce notes, the punishments articulated in the codes are "qualified … with the brief statement 'provided the sharia punishment is not applied.'"[28] Nonetheless, the basic assumption was that "the fine for adultery imposed on a rich Muslim was six times greater than that imposed on a poor Muslim and twelve times that imposed on a poor non-Muslim or a slave."[29] Fines tied to both economic and political/religious status, in other words, replaced universal physical punishments applicable to everyone in the Muslim community.

At the same time, I should also emphasize that corporal punishment continued to play a role in the jurisprudence of the early modern period. As Judith Tucker notes in her analysis of seventeenth and eighteenth century legal structures in Ottoman Syria, for example, the shifting line between adultery and rape led many jurists to develop completely new types of physical punishment to respond to sexual crime. While noting that most judges did not make use of these prescriptions in their actual adjudications, Tucker observes that,

> [t]he various evolving Ottoman criminal codes (*kanun*) authorized the Islamic judge to fine a perpetrator of simple *zina*' in lieu of applying the *hadd* penalty of the shari'a, but in the case of forced abduction and rape, whether of a woman, a girl, or a boy, the criminal code prescribed castration of the guilty.[30]

In this interpretation, in other words, *zina* as rape led to a severe, corporal *tazir* punishment that bore very little relationship to *hadd* adjudications. At the same time, however, it was not just *zina* as rape, but rape along with abduction—the movement of a perpetrator and his victim across space—that merited this particularly formidable response. The crime, that is, was conceived of as one that struck not just at sexual morality, but also at emerging notions of public and private space. And indeed, a second moment at which corporal punishment continued to be invoked was one that also revolved around questions of space. In this situation, however, the issue at stake was the respectability of the woman involved in the case. As Peirce argues,

26 See, for instance, Peirce 2003, 331, and Tucker 1998, 162.
27 Tucker 1998, 164, and Peirce 1999, 150.
28 Peirce 2003, 331.
29 Peirce 1999, 150 (paraphrasing Heyd 1973, 102-3).
30 Tucker 1998, 162.

> [i]f the mufti gave the category muhaddere [respectable] a definition, imperial law endowed it with material consequences. According to the statute books issued by the sultans, penalties for illegal behavior might differ according to whether a woman was muhaddere or not ... [i]n other words, the non-muhaddere woman might suffer a severe flogging and a substantial fine, while the parallel punishment for the muhaddere woman was the public humiliation of her husband and the imposition of a comparatively lesser fine.[31]

By translating *muhaddere* as "respectable," Peirce provides the literal translation (veiled, modest, concealed)[32] with a significant social and legal meaning. At the same time, however, by choosing the word "respectable" in particular, she likewise gets at nascent modern notions of, of course, "respectability," of the spaces in which respectable women travel, of where exactly women of what type move.[33] Along with this new, sliding scale of fines linked to social status linked to corporal punishment,[34] therefore, we can also see by the seventeenth and eighteenth centuries an interest on the part of the Ottoman government in defining not just the contract and copulation as they relate to sexual crime, but the sexual, moral, marital, economic, and political status of the individuals involved in them—especially to the extent that this status was manifested in movement across space.

This interest becomes even more overt in explicit discussions of rape and abduction. Peirce notes, for example, that early modern Ottoman rape/abduction law focused primarily on preventing attacks against married women or young men, while paying very little attention to unmarried women or girls:

> numerous fetvas and court cases addressing the issue of physical mobility in this period suggest that young girls moved about their villages or their city neighborhoods less guardedly than did their married older sisters ... [w]hen Sultanic legislation addressed the issue of who required protection from *levends* and other disorderly males, it was the married woman and the young boy who were specified, not the young girl.[35]

Peirce attributes this focus in turn to jurists' concern for lineage and to their interest in preventing the "social disruption" that would be caused by a married woman's adultery. The illegitimate pregnancy of an unmarried woman, she argues, did not

---

31 Peirce 1999, 142. In another study, Peirce also asks us to "consider the section on sexual offenses, where Süleyman's law book featured two clauses regarding the female adulterer: the first prescribed that she herself pay the fine, the second that her husband be fined for her offense." Peirce 2003, 331.

32 At the risk of giving too much weight to these etymological arguments, the masculine, *muhadder*, also means "benumbed," and the root is likewise the root of "narcotic."

33 In a manuscript nearing completion, Woodruff Smith has developed a convincing argument that "respectability" by the eighteenth century can be conceived of precisely as a "map."

34 Peirce especially links the two, arguing with regard to the former, that "the apparent rational for these wide gaps was that the well-off, free, married Muslim enjoyed the greatest blessing possible in life and that the failure to honor this blessing should, therefore, suffer correspondingly high penal sanction." For this, she cites al-Marghinani 1840, 2:5. Peirce 1999, 150.

35 Peirce 1997, 184.

threaten family lineage in the way that a similar pregnancy on the part of a married woman would.[36] This analysis, however, does not get at the question of why then young boys should also be considered vulnerable. Similarly, it does not address explicitly the role that space or movement seems to be playing in this legislation (young girls moved about less guardedly than married women). Indeed, there appears to be a direct connection being forged in the legislation between sexual vulnerability on the one hand and public space on the other. As Peirce notes in another piece, although court records indicate that sexual assault or rape could in practice happen equally well "at home and on the street," *in theory*, "rape was envisioned as occurring together with breaking into a house, not as an assault in a public or semi-public place."[37]

Obviously, the rhetoric of the public/private distinction that would underlie modern political behavior had not been constructed in the Ottoman Empire in the sixteenth and seventeenth centuries. There does, however, appear to be a starting point set for an eventual movement in that direction. A hierarchy of sexual vulnerability (married women to young boys to unmarried women to adult men) is being formulated here and then linked to notions of physical mobility and space. Those who are more sexually vulnerable cannot venture out into public space; those who are less so can cross the public/private divide with more confidence. Likewise, those who are a threat are primarily defined as such because they are capable of carrying those who are threatened across spatial lines. And indeed, theoretically, at least, the crime that was rape occurred only as a result of a violation of these assumptions about space.[38] Finally, for women but not for men,[39] it was the precise act of entering into a contract (marriage, concubinage) that redefined both sexual vulnerability and physical mobility. It was indeed the contract above all that defined sexualized political space ("the public") and politicized sexual space ("the private").

One can, of course, make an argument that the practical purpose of this contract was to prevent the social disruption that Peirce mentions above, and to ensure the proper lineage of children. But I want to emphasize that an additional effect of

36 Ibid.

37 Peirce 2003, 7, 354.

38 Another area in which this issue of political/sexual space seems to play a determining role is in the question of adultery and "honor killing." As Tucker notes, "in denying family members, specifically a husband or brother, any defined role in the punishment of women for sexual crimes, the muftis were adhering to the doctrine that unlawful intercourse was, as we have seen, a crime against religion, not an offense against one's relatives." Tucker 1998, 166. At the same time, however, if the sexual crime occurred in private or domestic space, the issue of who would be punished became more ambiguous. Relatives were certainly not encouraged to kill their female relatives but—as in the later Napoleonic code—the prohibitions against homicide were lifted if a husband or father killed his wife or daughter as a result of 1) seeing either engaged in adultery or fornication in private space, and 2) bringing the public together to witness this violation of the space. Avcı 2005, 21-22.

39 While it is true that a ceremony marked a boy's transition from youth to adulthood, this ceremony did not have the legal (or arguably the political) meaning that the marriage ceremony/contract had. The sexual status or sexual vulnerability of a 14-year-old boy was not functionally different from that of a 13-year-old boy. The sexual status of a married woman was in every way different from that of an unmarried woman.

the contract was to define women as early modern political subjects and to set a foundation for understanding them as modern citizens. In the same way that the traditional approach to women-as-property did not differ in any obvious way from the modern approach to woman-as-political-space, in other words, the traditional approach to public and private here is leading us directly to its modern counterpart. Understanding early modern sexual legislation as legislation having to do with overlapping sexual, political, and contractual identity—rather than, or in addition to, understanding it as necessarily about lineage—can indeed help us to understand some of the seemingly illogical or contradictory ways in which seventeenth and eighteenth century jurists put it into practice.

One such practice, for instance, was the acceptance of claims of *shubba* in seventeenth and eighteenth century rape trials. In such trials, as Tucker notes in an extensive analysis of the phenomenon,

> the perpetrator would be given the opportunity to claim *shubba*, that is, to argue that the act he committed resembled a lawful one so closely that he had, in fact, acted in good faith. The claim of *shubba* in this instance could be based only on the notion that the accused thought he had contracted a legal marriage with his victim and had acted on that assumption … [S]uch a use of *shubba* was not altogether an innovation. Hanafi jurisprudence had long held that certain kinds of unlawful sexual intercourse "resembled" licit relations closely enough that *hadd* punishment was not appropriate. If a man had sexual relations with a slave owned by his wife, mother, or father, for example, or with a woman he thought he had married legally even though the marriage was not valid, some Hanafi jurists had ruled that he could escape *hadd* punishment … [T]he concept of *shubba* allowed the muftis to convert the usually draconian punishment for rape into the relatively mild requirement of an indemnity. In the various cases they considered—most involving the willful abduction and rape of minor or virgin girls—the muftis strain credibility by repeatedly accepting the claim of *shubba*, despite the fact that the actions of the accused are clearly described as "abduction" and intercourse with the use of "force." Rape was clearly a criminal act, but punishment was routinely muted by the legal fiction of *shubba*. We cannot know with certainty why the muftis allowed virtually every rape case they considered as a matter of indemnifying the victim.[40]

Above, we saw that in theory a violation of spatial boundaries—abduction—merited severe corporal punishment. Here we see that in practice, such punishment was rarely meted out. The question is why this should be. Tucker discusses a number of possible explanations in the analysis that follows this passage.[41] One additional way of approaching this issue, however—and one that arguably allows the muftis to preserve their credibility—is to understand the early modern contract in the same way that we understand modern consent: as a question of space.

Just as consent is less about an actual choice than it is about defining the political sphere, it seems that the contract here is less about an actual relationship than it is about defining this same sphere. And indeed, with that in mind, the "fiction" of *shubba* makes a great deal of sense. Unmarried women ("minor or virgin girls") could be attacked but not legally raped, not—in the words of MacKinnon—because they

---

40 Tucker 1998, 161

41 Ibid.

were by definition "fuckable."[42] They could be attacked but not raped because they were contractible. They carried public space around with them in a way that married women and young boys did not. Rape thus had less to do with sexuality than it had to do with political identity. In fact, as we shall see, this relationship—and the extent to which it played out across women's bodies—became even more pronounced in the modern period, as consent and then integrity/autonomy eventually replaced the early modern contract.

In medieval and early modern Islamic legislation on *zina*, therefore, a number of issues collide with one another, setting the foundation for eventual modern reinterpretations. Most fundamentally, sex law is intimately connected in this jurisprudence—as it is in the modern period—to both political identity and political space. At the same time, however, although there is a definite overlap between rape and adultery under the larger rubric of *zina*, the two remain relatively distinct—rape having to do with inappropriate copulation and adultery having to do with violating a contract. Likewise, for the most part sexuality and reproduction are emphatically separate—pregnancy irrelevant to adultery legislation and (male) sexual behavior the issue at stake in determining sexual crime.[43]

Nonetheless, there is also a starting point set here for an eventual conflation of rape and adultery as well as an eventual conflation of sexuality and reproduction. Indeed, by the time the early modern Ottoman codifications were being promulgated, these lines had been effectively blurred. Sexuality and reproduction remained to some extent separate, but with the collapse of *hadd* and *tazir*, sex crime became increasingly political and increasingly central to state structures. Likewise, sex crime became far more closely linked to emerging notions of the public and the private spheres—the primary difference between the seventeenth century and the nineteenth century being the seventeenth century emphasis on *quasi* private contracts and the nineteenth century emphasis on the emphatically public social contract.

Moreover, these issues play almost the same role in medieval and early modern Catholic, French, and Italian law. There is, for example, a definite overlap in medieval France and Italy between rape and adultery—rape "defined as any sexual act outside of marriage and in particular applied to sexual intercourse with virgins, regardless of the aspect of violence."[44] At the same time, however, the punishment for adultery/rape—death and/or the obligation to settle a dowry on a deflowered virgin[45]—sets up distinctions between the two that should at this point be familiar. The emphasis on the marriage contract, for example, once again creates a situation

42 MacKinnon 1989, 175.

43 With the exception, again, of the Maliki school.

44 Lombardi 1994, 152.

45 Additionally, however, "violence was an ambiguous term: according to some jurists, like Giovan Stefano Menochio, even persuasion, seduction, and deceit were lines of conduct that could be assimilated to violence, and hence they were punishable by the death penalty. The Jesuit Francesco Toledo did not differentiate between violent rape and rape by deceit or seduction, as far as the punishment was concerned: the obligation to marry or settle a dowry on the deflowered virgin applied in both cases. On the other hand, no penalty was laid down in the case of consensual rape, that is, if there was no violence or any form of persuasion." Lombardi 1994, 152.

in which the punishment for raping a woman capable being contracted in marriage (i.e., a virgin) is far less severe than the punishment for raping a woman who could not be contracted in marriage (i.e., a married woman).

As Nicholas Davidson notes, there is likewise a growing emphasis in medieval Italy on the illicit crossing of spatial boundaries and on ways of rendering this movement licit. "The term *raptus*," he states,

> could … be used for any abduction, whether sexual intercourse followed or not … [I]n the fourteenth century, cities such as Ceneda and Mantua merely required rapists to marry or dower their victims—nothing more … than the obligation normally imposed on men who had deflowered a virgin *with* her consent.[46]

Just as we saw in the medieval Islamic and Ottoman interpretations of *zina*, in other words, we see here in this medieval Catholic and Italian approach to sexual crime an interest above all in two issues: first, in the movement of women across space, and second, in the type of contract that could be invoked to normalize this movement. The question at stake was whether a woman had left the *quasi* private sphere, whether she could be contracted into marriage as a result this movement, the nature of the marriage contract itself, and in turn the spaces—public, private, politicized, or sexualized—that the contract would delimit.

Indeed, just as Süleyman's sixteenth century codifications drew on medieval interpretations while nonetheless setting a foundation for the modern collapse of rape into adultery, early modern interpretations of sex crime in Europe, particularly after the 1563 Council of Trent, produced similar results in France and Italy. As Daniela Lombardi paraphrasing John Bossy notes, the Council of Trent "represented a watershed,"

> "because it transformed marriage from a social process which the Church granted to an ecclesiastical process which it administered." Until then, Canon law and doctrine had considered the consent of the couple *per verba de praesenti* sufficient for the marriage contract to be valid; so much so that the mere promise of matrimony (*sponsalia per verba de futuro*) followed by copulation was commonly held to be marriage, thus making it difficult to distinguish between wedding (*sponsalia de praesenti*) and betrothal (*sponsalia de futuro*).[47]

With the Council of Trent, however, the marriage contract—and the contract alone—began to underwrite both political and religious identity in Catholic states. An individual's stated intention no longer mattered—all that mattered was the sanctioned religious/legal process that rendered sexual behavior respectable. The marriage contract thus began at this point to differentiate explicitly the public and the private. A "clandestine marriage" or a "private" promise of marriage was no longer legitimate. And, as Lombardi continues, the increasing "regulation of the crime of non-violent rape" (i.e., adultery-as-rape or fornication-as-rape) over the

46 Davidson 1994, 84.
47 Lombardi 1994, 143.

sixteenth century was an indirect result of this shift.[48] Just as occurred in the sixteenth century Ottoman Empire, in other words, here as well, we have a movement toward a modern overlap of political and sexual identity, toward a modern division of public and private space, and toward a therefore *modern* conflation of adultery and rape.

Moreover, all of this was happening at precisely the same time that we see an increasingly secure link being formed between political crime and sexual crime in European states. It was happening as, in France for instance, there was the repeated promulgation of edicts that "openly charged women with potential wreckage of the family and, by analogy, the state, through adultery (an act of treason)."[49] It was likewise happening as the foundation was being set for the writings of Montesquieu, Pothier, and Rousseau, who argued that "the marital contract justly subjected wife to husband on grounds of presumptive blame: potential adultery became possible treason."[50] And it was happening as the antecedents for Napoleon's 1804 Civil Code and 1810 Criminal Code were being developed—as the stage was being set for the nineteenth century transformations that will be the subject of the next section of this chapter.

Defining Nineteenth Century Sexual Space

The laws on adultery and rape that we see in the 1810 Napoleonic code and in its mid century Ottoman counterpart, that is to say, did not develop in a vacuum. They were the product not just of liberal revolution and authoritarian reform, but also of medieval and early modern interpretations of sexual crime. They owed their existence to a constantly evolving understanding of threat and to a constantly re-imagined notion of bodies as property and bodies as contractible rights that had antecedents in centuries of prior legislation. But by the nineteenth century, the ground had been prepared in both the Ottoman Empire and in France for turning this legislation on rape and adultery into legislation that would define the modern political subject—for transforming women's bodies into public and then biopolitical space, and for collapsing rape and adultery into a single, indivisible and, again, modern category.

Sexual crime first appears in modern Ottoman legislation, for example, in 1851. The 1851 Ottoman criminal code, inclusive of the 13 articles that made up the 1840 code along with 10 years of rulings by the judicial council, describes rape/

48 "We find intermediate stages in the early sixteenth century in the threat of punishment, such as disinheritance for those who contracted marriage clandestinely, and in more indirect forms of control such as the regulation of the crime of non-violent rape." Lombardi 1994, 142.

49 Hanley 1997, 32.

50 Ibid, 43-44. Hanley continues that "it is also evident that, from the 1750s, the ideology upholding the system of marital-regime governance (rhetorically expressed in household-state analogies) no longer held fast." Ibid, 46. I will argue that although the metaphor may have disappeared to the extent that it rested on a vocabulary of contracts and property, it re-emerged with some violence when political rhetoric collided with biological rhetoric in the nineteenth century.

abduction (literally "making off with a girl")[51] as a crime against the family, the family's reputation, and the nascent notion of public civil status. Incorporated into the chapter on crimes against honor,[52] the article states that anyone who abducts a girl and takes her to a court in another district cannot marry her because the judge may not know whether or not the couple is socially and legally equal (*kefaet*).[53] Although this article appears for the most part to be operating in the realm of early modern or even medieval jurisprudence, it thus nonetheless also forms a bridge between the earlier legislation and that which was to come. The fundamental issue at stake is the crossing of spatial boundaries—what it means when "unknown" individuals enter public space, how honor (but not property) broadly defined might be threatened in such a situation.

In 1851, such a question was easily answered—when the individual was unknown, public space could not exist, and political or legal contracts could not be formulated. Being known was a political and a legal state that was a necessary foundation for political or legal interactions. Less than a decade later, however, as we shall see, the question posed in the 1851 code was being answered in a very different way. Rather than assuming an individual's (and in particular a woman's) identity to be known or unknown and proceeding from there, legislation on sexual crime instead sought to render all women known—to render, that is, all women contractible. Women indeed were soon conceived of as public space in and of themselves—as open settings against which both political and sexual relationships could be played out. Rather than criminalizing abduction because an inappropriate marriage might result from it, in other words, abduction instead became criminal because it undermined the very notion of the known public citizen—because it, like abortion, implied a trespassing of political boundaries.

The 1859 Ottoman adaptation of the Napoleonic Code, for example, overtly reconfigured women's bodies as public space. In this law, sexual crime—at this point rape, seduction, adultery, transvestitism, and public indecency—operated under a single chapter heading, "attacks on morality."[54] The articles in this chapter (197 through 201) transition into one another almost seamlessly, discussing, variously, the punishments for an "attack on the modesty" of a child under the age of 11, "violent attacks on modesty" that may or may not be consummated, the rape of unmarried girls, the inciting of youth to debauchery, and adultery. There is particular mention in these passages of guardians, educators, and those in authority who attack the modesty of their charges (and the relatively harsher penalty they incur), the extra fine for those who rape specifically unmarried girls, and the separate punishment for seducing girls with false promises of marriage.[55]

51 The word used is *kız kaçırmak* rather than *zina*.

52 As opposed to one of the other two chapters—on "crimes against life" and "crimes against property."

53 Social inequality being an impediment to marriage. The article continues that the two should be apprehended by the civil authorities and sent to a court in their own district. Ahmed Lütfi 1888, Art. 6.

54 "*Attentats aux moeurs*."

55 "Code pénal ottoman" 1905-6, Chap. 3, Art. 197-201.

In a second chapter, not on "moral crime," but on "illegal arrests, sequestering of persons, theft of children and adolescents, and kidnapping of girls," there is an elaboration on the abduction theme. Article 206, for example, notes that anyone who kidnaps a child who has not reached puberty will be imprisoned, that if the kidnapped person is a *girl* who has not reached puberty the punishment will be forced labor, that an attack on the modesty of said girl will be liable to the maximum penalty, and that if the kidnapper intended to marry the kidnapped girl the case will be decided according to the "disposition prescribed in that regard by Islamic law." Finally, if the kidnapped girl has reached puberty, the punishment will be the same, and if the victim is already married, the punishment will include forced labor.[56]

I should also emphasize that the final article (201) of the first chapter addresses the corruption of youth *together* with adultery, producing an unexpected correlation between the debauchers of young people and adulterous women. It states, first, that anyone who facilitates the debauchery or corruption of children of either sex will be imprisoned, and that if the debauchery or corruption is facilitated by mothers, fathers, or guardians, the punishment will be more severe. It then immediately switches gears and continues that only the husband or, in default of him, the guardian can accuse [a wife] of adultery. Furthermore, a wife who has committed adultery will be imprisoned, and the husband will remain her jailor if agreeing to take her back, while her accomplice will also be imprisoned and fined. As for proof, only directly witnessing the act, evidence of the wife's presence in a Muslim's harem, or written evidence is acceptable. Finally, a husband who maintains an adulterous relationship in his own house and who is convicted of it on the complaint of his wife will be punished by a fine.[57] A separate article in the chapter on homicide notes that anyone who surprises his wife or "one of the women of his home"[58] in the midst of committing adultery is excused from killing her or her accomplice.[59]

The Napoleonic Code from which these articles were adapted is similar, integrating rape, statutory rape, public obscenity, debauchery of youth, and adultery under a single chapter heading—prescribing harsher penalties for guardians and those in authority, and including an article under a separate heading on the abduction of minors. The primary differences between the two texts are that the French code focuses more on the public nature of various crimes, it designates functionaries and religious leaders along with guardians and educators as subject to particularly harsh penalties, it specifically refers to rape victims of either sex, and it discusses the possibility of a kidnapped girl having consented to her abduction.[60] Also, adultery is addressed in four separate articles apart from those on the corruption of youth, evidence of having been in someone else's harem is not mentioned as proof of adultery, the husband's "entering into an adulterous commerce in the conjugal domicile"[61] is changed to

56 Ibid, Chap. 4, Art. 206.

57 Ibid, Chap. 3, Art. 201.

58 "*une des femmes de sa maison.*"

59 "Code pénal ottoman" 1905-6, Art. 188.

60 "Code pénal Napoléon" 1849, Section 4, Art. 330-333 and Section 6, Art. 355-357.

61 "*Le mari qui entretiendra un commerce adultérin dans la maison conjugale.*"

"maintaining a concubine in the conjugal domicile,"[62] and a concluding article states that anyone who contracts a marriage without having dissolved a previous marriage will be punished with forced labor, as will any public official who performs the marriage, knowing of the existing one.[63] The article excusing the husband who kills his adulterous wife and accomplice is the same except that it excludes mention of "one of the women of [the husband's] home" and it is followed by another which similarly excuses castration, or death that specifically results from castration, if it is provoked by a violent attack on modesty (*pudeur*).[64]

The most basic point to note about these articles is that jurists were clearly still understanding rape and adultery as related, overlapping crimes—as crimes that attacked or undermined the same ideal, even if this ideal was now reconstructed into something called "public morality." At the same time, however, I think that the way in which rape and adultery intersect with one another in these nineteenth century codes is very much the product of eighteenth and nineteenth century notions of citizenship, public space, and political behavior, and not simply holdover of "traditional" attitudes. Indeed, what I would like to do over the remainder of this section is to discuss a number of questions that arise from these self-consciously modern codes, and to consider the ways in which they point to the transformation of women's bodies into political space. For example, why are educators, guardians, authority figures and—in the French code—functionaries and religious leaders subject to harsher penalties when they commit sexual crime? Why is the *rape* of unmarried women punished more harshly (as an attack on morality), whereas the *abduction* of married women is punished more harshly (as an illegal arrest)? Why in the Ottoman code is adultery nearly synonymous with debauching the youth? Why is adultery gendered in the particular way that it is in both Ottoman and French law? And finally, why is an adulterous woman deprived of her right to life (specifically via the invalidation of the article protecting this right in the chapter on homicide), and—in the French code—why is a man who "assaults a woman's modesty" deprived of his right to a penis (specifically via the invalidation of the article protecting this right in the chapter on wounding)?

With regard to the first question, it seems to rest in particular on the type of authority represented by educators, guardians, French functionaries, and French religious leaders. Educators, guardians, functionaries, and—to the extent that the religious establishment had been transformed into a pillar of the laicist (but never secular) French state—religious leaders all represent modern, or in Foucault's terminology, disciplinary[65] and totalizing authority. They are each in a different way involved in the production of modern truth and knowledge as well as in the production of

62 "Le mari qui aura entretenu une concubine dans la maison conjugale."

63 "Code pénal Napoléon" 1849, Art. 336-340.

64 Ibid, Art. 324-325

65 Especially to the extent that disciplines "in fact have their own discourse. They do, for the reasons I was telling you about a moment ago, create apparatuses of knowledge, knowledges and multiple fields of expertise. They are extraordinarily inventive when it comes to creating apparatuses to shape knowledge and expertise, and they do support a discourse, but it is a discourse that cannot be the discourse of right or a juridical discourse." Foucault 2003, 38.

modern populations.[66] At the same time, in a classical juridical framework, educators, guardians, and functionaries are all likewise involved in contracts, and especially in contracts having to do with rights. They mimic or reproduce the political relationship that operates at the heart of sovereign power, suggesting a consent to rule on the one hand in the name of civilization on the other.[67] In the French and the Ottoman codes, these authority figures thus occupy a paradoxical space, representing both discipline *and* juridical rule, the two types of power that Foucault argued were to a large extent unrelated to one another.[68]

If we consider the way in which these two seemingly unrelated discourses interact with one another, however, we can also see that it is precisely at the point of their contact that the biopolitical potential of nineteenth century sexual legislation is realized. Indeed, the incorporation of disciplinary authority figures into juridically defined sexual legislation—as particularly culpable actors at that—is a distinctly concrete manifestation of what Agamben has called the "hidden point of intersection between the juridico-institutional and the biopolitical models of power."[69] Educators, guardians and the like are all involved in *quasi* or actual political contracts that represent the classical sovereign relationship. They are particularly culpable in sexual crime, therefore, not because they are abusing some sort of institutional position or personal power, but because they are distorting the sovereign relationship and undermining the *sovereign* right to regulate biology and, more specifically, sexuality. Likewise, educators, guardians and the like are integral elements of disciplinary, totalizing power networks. They are thus also particularly culpable in sexual crime not, again, because an individual might be harmed, but because the regulatory power of these networks might be weakened. These crimes, after all, are understood specifically as attacks on morality rather than as attacks on the individual—and on a

66 Foucault brings together his theory of disciplinary power and his theory of biopolitics later on in *Society Must Be Defended*. In paraphrasing the relationship between the two, Agamben notes that "in one of his last writings, Foucault argues that the modern Western state has integrated techniques of subjective individualization with procedures of objective totalization to an unprecedented degree, and he speaks of a real 'political "double bind,"' constituted by individualization and the simultaneous totalization of structures of modern power" (*Dits et écrits*, 4: 229-32)." Agamben 1998, 5.

67 As Foucault also notes, "in the case of the classic juridical theory of power, power is regarded as a right which can be possessed in the way one possesses commodity, and which can therefore be transferred or alienated, either completely or partly, through a juridical act or an act that founds a right—it does not matter which, for the moment—thanks to the surrender of something or thanks to a contract. Power is the concrete power that any individual can hold, and which he can surrender, either as a whole or in part, so as to constitute a power or a political sovereignty. In the body of theory to which I am referring, the constitution of political power is therefore constituted by this series, or is modeled on a juridical operation similar to an exchange of contracts." Foucault 2003, 13.

68 Ibid, 38.

69 He continues that "the two analyses cannot be separated and that the inclusion of bare life in the political realm constitutes the original—if concealed—nucleus of sovereign power. *It can be said that the production of a biopolitical body is the original activity of sovereign power*." Agamben 1998, 6.

morality embedded simultaneously in sovereign right *and* disciplinary power, in the modern political duty to regulate each citizen's sexual and biological existence.

Moreover, what becomes apparent when we consider the second question that I posed above is that the citizen in this formulation is implicitly a *female* one, defined and bounded spatially as well as politically. In both the Ottoman and the French codes, it is the abduction of *married women* that is conceived of as one of the most serious types of "illegal arrest" and it is the rape of *unmarried women* that is conceived of as one of the most serious types of "attacks on morality." It is true that at first glance, these articles seem to refer back solely to medieval and early modern legislation: married women could not travel in space or be carried across spatial boundaries because the ostensible purpose of travel or abduction (i.e., marriage) was unachievable. Unmarried women could travel and be abducted, but rape itself was problematic because it involved sexual activity prior to the compensatory marriage or dower. But I want to suggest that, more than this, each of these articles is also repositioning rape/abduction law within a biopolitical framework, and positing the bodies of female citizens as the particular settings against which modern sovereign relations would be played out.

The abduction of married women, for example, is understood in these nineteenth century codes fundamentally as an "illegal arrest." It is addressed, in other words, as no more and no less than an assault on that pillar of democracy and the rule of law—and, as Agamben has argued, that fundamentally biopolitical pillar of democracy and the rule of law—*habeas corpus*.[70] Considered doctrinally, *habeas corpus* protects citizens first and foremost from, precisely, "illegal arrest." Considered theoretically, it is the principle by which juridical law acquires a biopolitical body. In this particular context—although it is true that the abduction of children and unmarried women is also understood as "illegal arrest"—it is the abduction of married women *especially* that is an assault on both principles, and that merits therefore the harshest punishment. It is the abduction of married women, therefore, that represents a coming together of early modern and modern notions of sexual and political identity. In the early modern period, carrying a married woman across spatial boundaries was an attack on nascent notions of the public and the private. In the nineteenth century, this interpretation remained valid—married women effectively represented domestic space, and exhibiting the domestic in public was in and of itself unnatural.[71] But more so, married women represented political space—it was in their bodies *in particular* that the political right to *habeas corpus* was embedded. It was within their

70 "[I]f it is true that law needs a body in order to be in force, and if one can speak, in this sense, of 'law's desire to have a body,' democracy responds to this desire by compelling law to assume the care of this body. This ambiguous (or polar) character of democracy appears even more clearly in the *habeas corpus* if one considers the fact that the same legal procedure that was originally intended to assure the presence of the accused at the trial and, therefore, to keep the accused from avoiding judgment, turns—in its new and definitive form—into a grounds for the sheriff to detain and exhibit the body of the accused. *Corpus* is a two faced being, the bearer of both subject to sovereign power and of individual liberties." Agamben 1998, 123-4.

71 See below for an elaboration of this theme.

silent, private, bodily borders specifically, in other words, that biopolitical sovereign relations were articulated.

But what about the attack on morality manifested in the rape of unmarried women? Again, first of all, there is in this article a continuation to some extent of early modern interpretations of sexual crime: the harsher penalty represented by the extra fine is arguably a rephrasing of the early modern standpoint that marrying or dowering a rape victim canceled out the crime inherent in sexual assault. Just as married women, by virtue of being non-contractible, continued in the modern period to carry a now politicized domestic space around with them, unmarried women, always contractible, continued to carry around the public. Once more, however, the nature of the potential contract (always conflated with the potential assault) that was constantly hovering over unmarried women shifted meaning in the nineteenth century. It was not just that rape undermined a private contract and that marriage could thus justify it; it was that rape undermined both a private and a, or *the*, political contract—the political contract embodied in public morality. The punishment for the rape of an unmarried woman was thus a strangely mismatched combination of the fine-as-dower[72] that would rectify the breach of the private contract and the imprisonment that would rectify the assault on the sovereign relationship. Just as rape/abduction law positioned *married* women as the backdrop for biopolitical sovereignty manifested in the right to *habeas corpus*, therefore, it likewise positioned *unmarried* women as the backdrop for an identical sovereign relationship manifested in the right to a sexual/social contract.

Indeed, the extent to which this sexual legislation, first, reifies these basic political and biopolitical relationships, and, second, articulates them against women's bodies-as-settings becomes particularly clear in the articles on adultery. The juxtaposition of adultery and the debauching of youth in the Ottoman code,[73] for example, the particular ways in which the definition and punishment for adultery is gendered in both codes, and the way in which sexual crime limits a woman's right to life but a man's right to a penis all suggest the hyperbolically political and then biopolitical nature of the legislation.

---

72 Or as *diyet*: "as part of their normal duties, *Shari'ah* courts in Ottoman Egypt looked into cases brought by rape victims or their guardians who demanded the punishment of the offender, and the payment of compensation (*diya*). Courts treated rape as an issue of 'rights' whereby a person's right to dispense of his or her own body was violated and was therefore due compensation … [T]hus, redress had to be sought by the 'property' owner; the rape of a person, or the 'robbery' of virginity, was equated with a sense of personal property right. Notwithstanding, how dishonorable or psychologically harmful rape may have been, it was not that which was paramount in the mind of the court as much as how the victim was to be compensated for the harm that had befallen him/her. A *diya* had to be paid, just as it did for the loss of a life (*nafs*), the loss of a limb or body part, or any other physical injury, such as severe wife beating." Sonbol 2000, 313-316.

73 This plays out in a different, but related, way in French legislation, where "the articles dealing with private life in the civil code of 1804 and the penal code of 1810 remained almost unchanged, apart from minor rectifications. The law established a discriminatory statute for women, and more specifically for married women, who upon their marriage became legal minors." in Sohn 1995, 469.

By placing adultery and the debauching of youth into the same article, for instance, Ottoman legislators were getting at one of the most fundamental aspects of modern sexuality. Sexual relationships according to this modernist interpretation could occur only among individuals with complete, active political identities, and only among individuals whose political identities as such were manifested in a liberal social contract. Adultery and inducing children to debauchery, therefore, each in a different way involved an undermining of the contract. In the case of the adulterers, the political nature of the crime was relatively straightforward. By the nineteenth century, the marital contract was a public contract and sex outside of marriage was thus a betrayal of both public and private relationships. Although the case might be brought by one or the other spouse, the particular victim of the crime was a collective thing called "public morality," and sex within the contract did not undermine it in the way that the same behavior outside of the contract did.

As for the sexual activity of children, the political aspects of the crime are not quite as overt, but they are nonetheless revealing. As we saw in the discussion of educators and guardians above, children were incorporated into the social or political contract specifically as incomplete, passive citizens. Inducing them to sexual activity was thus particularly criminal not because children *qua* children should not have sex, but because incomplete, passive citizens should not play the part of complete, active citizens. Both adultery and the debauching of youth, therefore, had become by the nineteenth century far more about modern politics than they were about medieval or early modern sex.

The extent to which each also had to do with biopolitics, and especially with a biopolitics embedded in women's bodies, becomes evident in the ways in which the articles are gendered. That they are gendered at all is obvious. It is the wife, not the husband, who runs the risk of imprisonment upon committing adultery. It is the wife, not the husband, who forfeits her "right to life," or at least political protection of that right, upon transgressing collective sexual norms. I want to emphasize again, however, that these passages are not simple restatements of "traditional" moral postures. First of all, both the condemnation and, in the case of the wife, the imprisonment for adultery happen in a self-consciously "private" arena—separate from the "public" realm of the police in which the corruption of youth, for example, would be punished.[74] The early modern Ottoman, French, and Italian movement toward a separation of spheres, toward a separation of the public from the private, had thus reached its logical conclusion by the nineteenth century—the "traditional" attitude that adultery was a crime and a sin no matter where it happened largely forgotten.

Indeed, with this invention of privacy, this creation of domesticity, and this construction of the public, politically active citizen, adultery became first and foremost something that women could do anywhere, but that men could do only in their own homes. Whereas women were adulterers, men kept concubines in the next room. It was therefore above all *women's* political activity that was conflated with their sexual activity—above all the public space surrounding the *woman* citizen that was saturated with the sexual and the biological. Male political actors were, if anything, detached from their sexuality. If they had a sexual identity at all, it was

74 "Code pénal ottoman" 1905-6, Art. 201.

only in the small, contained domestic space that in their case *was* confined to the home and the conjugal relationship. The result was thus an unexpected inversion of the public/private distinction so fundamental to liberal notions of appropriate governance. Women—idealized as the overseers of private, domestic space—ceased to have any but a public role, with every private, sexual, and biological aspect of their lives displayed and regulated for the sake of the common good. Men—idealized as public actors—were reduced to a private role, their sexuality politically non-existent except in specifically defined and extreme circumstances.

That this structure possessed an explicitly biopolitical potential becomes clear in turn in the articles on honor killing and castration. In these articles, an adulterous woman loses political protection of her right to life, while—in the French code—a male rapist[75] loses political protection of his right to a penis. This distinction immediately suggests two questions: first, why associate adultery with women and rape with men; and second, why deprive a woman of her right to life and a man of his right to a penis? I think the answer to both of these questions is embedded in the construction of the explicitly female biopolitical citizen that I sketched above. Indeed, I would argue that these two articles in particular are above all constructing women as the central, prototypical biopolitical citizen, are placing women's sexuality at the heart of modern political identity, and are therefore linking women's biological and political existence to their sexual existence in a way that men's biological and political existence is not. By suggesting that a woman who transgressed sexual norms should be deprived of her right to life and that a man who transgressed sexual norms should be deprived of his right to a penis, French and Ottoman legislators were saying quite basically that a man's sexuality was situated in (and only in) his sexual organ whereas a woman's sexuality was situated in her very life—in her biological *as well as* in her political existence.

And I want to emphasize again that this is not a simple restatement of the medieval or early modern positions on honor killing and castration. First of all, before the nineteenth century, men and women were in theory at least equally culpable—equally subject to death or corporal punishment—in cases of adultery. Second, the castration stipulated in the early modern Ottoman legislation and noted by Tucker was for the most part a variation on the notion of retribution—the penis behaved badly, and so the penis must be removed. In the nineteenth century, contrarily, we have a very different situation, in which both men and women are citizens and in which both men and women have certain rights—provided they adhere to the social contract. Each has the right to life. In France, men likewise have the right to a sexual organ. It is therefore not that corporal punishment will be meted out for various sexual crimes. Rather, it is that the state withdraws its protection of certain rights (life in the case of women, a penis in the case of men) given certain inappropriate sexual behaviors. The message is thus *not* that certain criminal sexual acts get punished by various physical penalties. It is that certain criminal sexual acts 1) undermine the political or social contract and 2) lead in turn to a retraction of the protection of the political rights enshrined in this contract. It is, in other words, not that adulterous women and

75 I am interpreting the relatively vague "attack on modesty" narrowly here as "rape." It could also refer to a sexual assault that did not conform to the specific definition of "rape."

male rapists will be penalized by death or castration—it is that adulterous women and male rapists will become incomplete citizens, unprotected, vulnerable to death or castration, and occupants of explicitly lawless space.[76]

That it is the *woman* who loses her right to life—and particularly upon committing adultery—simply plays up the extent to which it is women's bodies that are the backdrop for this newly articulated political identity. It is adultery—that hyperbolically contract-oriented sexual crime—that serves as a framework for the linkage between sexual and political identity. It is the violation of the marital contract, in other words, that is specifically conceived of as a violation of the social contract, seen as a grounds for placing women into lawless space, and considered a rationale for legally depriving them of their legal rights. It is likewise life—not the sexual organ, as in the case of men—that is linked to a woman's sexual behavior. It is thus life, basic biological identity, that is connected to both sex and politics here. Like the legislation on rape, adultery, debauchery, statutory rape, abduction, and indecency, therefore, the nineteenth century French and Ottoman legislation on so-called honor killing explicitly transforms women's bodies into settings against which modern biopolitical sovereign relationships can be carved out.

Consent and Interwar Sexuality

By the early twentieth century, this articulation of women's bodies as biopolitical space had become far more pronounced—expressed throughout the 1920s and 1930s in particular in a language of consent. The talk of contracts, and especially the reinterpretation of the medieval private contract as a nineteenth century social contract,[77] had led above all to an interwar fascination on the part of jurists with the biologically defined citizen and how consent theory specifically might regulate this citizen's sexuality. Italian fascist legislators, for example, began to imagine rape as both a crime against public morality *and* a crime against something called "sexual liberty," [78] the latter operating as a subset of the former. What exactly was meant by "sexual liberty" and why fascist legislators found it meaningful will be the questions that drive this section.

76 One might even analyze this process by understanding the adulterous woman as a variation on Agamben's *homo sacer*—deprived of her right to life, but operating in a legally defined space, she can be killed but not sacrificed.

77 Bergelson likewise discusses the role played by consent in the transformation of private contracts into public contracts in the seventeenth and eighteenth centuries. She notes that whereas in the early modern period, consent was a catch all defense in penal legislation, "changes in the power of an individual to consent to personal harm came in the seventeenth century. They were a natural consequence of the monopolization of the system of punishment by the state. While in the early ages of criminal justice the victim was the central figure in the prosecution and settlement of any non-public offense, in the normative and centralized juridical structure the victim became almost entirely excluded from the criminal process." She continues by noting that the right to consent was thus constrained, as the victims of crime became abstract concepts such as "public peace" or sovereignty. Bergelson, *forthcoming*, 9-10.

78 See below, *Penal Code of the Kingdom of Italy* 1931, Part 9, Chap. 1.

I will indeed suggest over the next few pages that "sexual liberty" was a right that could be possessed only by biopolitically defined citizens, and that the consent on which this right was founded was likewise a biopolitical one—that paradoxically, as Vera Bergelson puts it, "valid consent eliminate[d] [the possibility of a] violation of rights."[79] I will therefore also suggest that consent played the same role in interwar sexual legislation that it had in interwar reproductive legislation. First and foremost a means of transforming women's bodies into space, it had little or nothing to do with "choice" or "freedom" *per se*, and placed women, not men, at the center of the public sphere.

As I argued in the last chapter, Scarry's notion that consent as a political concept is meaningful only given a passive or threatened body leads likewise to the notion that the liberal citizen's political autonomy, his or her ability to consent or to invoke political power, is inversely proportional to his or her bodily or biological autonomy. It is important to reiterate, in fact, that Scarry's reading of consent theory brings us directly to a spatial rather than a behavioral understanding of political activity. If the ideal, politically active, consenting citizen is a physically incapacitated or immobile one, consent necessarily has to do with boundaries rather than behavior. I examined the reproductive implications of this reading in the last chapter. What I would like to do now is to discuss its implications in terms of sexual legislation—to ask especially what happens when consent describes sexual and political space, and when the act of consent is in and of itself a waiver of rights.[80]

---

79 Bergelson *forthcoming*, 72. One major theme that runs throughout Bergelson's article is this tension between the ability to consent, which "is recognized in moral philosophy as a central manifestation of personhood and individual autonomy," and the act of consent, which is "a waiver of rights." Bergelson *forthcoming*, 5,7.

80 That consent has almost nothing to do with choice and everything to do with an unabashedly authoritarian understanding of political space in which rights are assumed to be waived can be seen in the actual outcome of the case in which Scarry contextualizes her analysis. As Paul A. Lombardo has observed, "it is rarely clear in most discussions of the Cardozo opinion that Mary Schloendorff lost her case. That result is not only startling because of the way Cardozo ignored the absence of consent for dangerous and unwanted surgery, but also for its extraordinary deference to charitable immunity of hospitals, employing questionable arguments and contorted interpretations of the facts to reach a conclusion that would allow the case to be dismissed. The very Court that Cardozo sat on—New York's Court of Appeals—criticized the reasoning on charitable immunity in the Schloendorff case as 'logically weak' only ten years after it was decided, and it was completely overruled in 1957 when the shield of non-profit status was discarded in New York as 'out of tune with life about us.' Yet we still celebrate the case as a salute to patient autonomy." Lombardo continues by pointing out that the specific unwanted surgery performed on Mary Schloendorff was a hysterectomy to rid her of a "phantom tumor." Lombardo 2005, 792. John T. Parry has addressed this paradox—the extent to which contemporary rights are assumed to be enforced only by the act of waiving them—as well, noting in his analysis of the 2002 case *USA v Drayton*: "Justice Kennedy closed with the following comments on citizenship, police conduct, and the rule of law: 'In a society based on law, the concept of agreement and consent should be given a weight and dignity of its own. Police officers act in full accord with the law when they ask citizens for consent. It reinforces the rule of law for the citizen to advise the police of his or her wishes [whether or not he or she actually knows what his or her rights are, as the Court had just

A number of feminist theorists have already addressed these issues, particularly to the extent that they are linked to the liberal public/private distinction. Pateman, for example, has stated unambiguously that "women's bodies represent the private, they represent all that is excluded from the public sphere," and continues by arguing that according to patriarchal political theory, "women lack the capacities necessary for political life," most notably the ability to consent.[81] Brown makes a similar point, suggesting that the "liberal subject" who "moves freely between family and civil society," is plainly male, given that "his enjoyment of his civil rights is buttressed rather than limited by his relations in the private sphere while the opposite is the case for women."[82] Cahill notes the emphatically embodied nature of this spatial divide, positing not just "a constant state of danger for the feminine body," but indeed the "source of danger within the feminine body itself."[83] Finally, MacKinnon addresses the question of consent, the public, and the private within the context of rape law specifically. Noting the redundancy of legislation that defines rape as intercourse "with force and without consent,"[84] she first posits the absurdity of such an approach by comparing it to a definition of violent assault that could be "consented to," and then argues that such an understanding of force and consent[85] "rationalizes

---

held] and for the police to act on that understanding. When this exchange takes place, it dispels inferences of coercion' … *[D]rayton* indicates that the reasonable innocent person best asserts his rights, whether or not he knows what they are, by refusing to invoke them and instead cooperating with state authority. Indeed, to the extent state authority is represented by the armed and uniformed police officer, the *Drayton* Court asserts that people are likely to feel increasingly 'assured' and 'safe,' with the implication that cooperation and refusal to assert rights in these circumstances becomes more voluntary and more consistent with good citizenship, not less." Parry *forthcoming*, 42-3.

81 Pateman 1989, 4.

82 Brown 1992, 18.

83 Cahill 2000, 54.

84 MacKinnon 1989, 172.

85 Bergelson's analysis is an implicit critique of this approach. Rather than seeing the use of force and consent as the same thing, Bergelson develops a more sophisticated definition of the latter, in which consent operates in some cases as an inculpatory factor and in some cases as an exculpatory factor. Taking up the comparison between rape and assault specifically, she states that "an unavoidable question for anyone contemplating the boundaries of consent in criminal law is: why the victim's consent to sex renders the defendant not guilty of rape, whereas the victim's consent to injury has no similar effect?" She continues, "if consent is an element of the charged offense … the very presence of consent negates an element required for conviction. For example, consensual sex is not rape, even if one of the partners is not aware of the other's consent. However, when consent is a defense, the knowledge of a justifying circumstance is essential … [C]onsider offenses of rape, kidnapping, theft, and trespass, to name just a few. In all of them, the *act itself* does not violate a prohibitory norm. Having sex, transporting someone to a different location, taking other people's property, or entering someone's home is not bad *per se*. It becomes bad *only* due to the attendant circumstance, namely the lack of consent: i.e., unless consent is missing, the conduct is outside the boundaries of criminal law … [c]onsent alone is sufficient to make theft or rape impossible. Significantly more is required to justify killing or maiming." Bergelson *forthcoming*, 45, 50, 57, 60.

force."[86] Consent in this model becomes "more a metaphysical quality of a woman's being than a choice she makes and communicates."[87] Moreover, she asserts more broadly that,

> to complain in public of inequality within the private contradicts the liberal definition of the private … [I]njuries arise through violation of the private sphere, not within and by and because of it. In private, consent tends to be presumed. Showing coercion is supposed to void this presumption. But the problem is getting anything private to be perceived as coercion … [W]hy a person would "allow" force in private (the "why doesn't she leave" question raised to battered women) is a question given its insult by the social meaning of the private sphere as a sphere of choice."[88]

Each of these theorists, in other words, links the failure of neutral or equal citizenship to the creation of the private sphere, to the placement of women into this sphere, and to the indeed dangerous way in which women's bodies personify it. Consent—a public, political act—becomes meaningless in such a framework.[89] Indeed, as MacKinnon argues with reference to rape law, consent is simply assumed in the private, that "arena of choice;" it is a metaphysical quality rather than a political act. Women carry the private around with them. And it is as a result of their emphatically private nature that consent theory cannot serve them as citizens in the end.

My purpose over the next few pages will be to challenge this analysis. More specifically, I will try to demonstrate that to the extent that sexual legislation—and more basically, sexual identity—became central to political identity over the first few decades of the twentieth century, women, sexualized, increasingly became actors within the rhetorical public, rather than within the rhetorical private. Indeed, rape and adultery law rendered women essential, prototypical, biopolitical subjects, their bodies representative of a new, relentless concept of the political.[90] Moreover, I will argue that it was the rhetoric of consent in particular that transformed women citizens in this way. Far from meaningless or irrelevant, consent instead served as a foundation for an interwar reinterpretation of both sexual and political identity. The paradox of both the biologically passive, politically active consenting individual

---

86 "Usually assault is not consented to in law; either it cannot be consented to, or consensual assault remains assault. Yet sexual assault consented to is intercourse, no matter how much force was used." MacKinnon 1989, 174.

87 Ibid, 175.

88 Ibid, 190-191.

89 See also, for example, "the relationship between rape laws, democratic theories of consent, and patriarchy has been a matter of concern to feminist political theorists for some time. These feminists have exposed the 'double speak' of social contract consent theory … [T]hey have detailed the ways in which the emphasis on consent relies on a masculine concept of the self as an autonomous, independent being. They have examined the ways in which this concept of self runs counter women's experiences of the self as a relational being with responsibility to/for others … [I]t prompts us to argue for the rule of consent in the context of *a theory of justice* where vulnerability rather than autonomy defines the integrity of the political subject." Bergoffen 2003, 126.

90 I am deliberately invoking Carl Schmitt here—and will return to his analysis in the next chapter.

described by Scarry, and Bergelson's autonomous, rights-bearing citizen whose act of consent waives the rights that he or she bears is, I will argue, resolved in interwar (fascist) sexual legislation.

Put another way, just as the absurd notion of an individual consenting to enslavement in Pateman's analysis[91] ceased to be absurd in the context of interwar abortion legislation, the absurd notion of an individual consenting to "forced sex" or any other violation of bodily integrity in MacKinnon's likewise becomes entirely reasonable—and indeed, politically necessary. Moreover, this seeming contradiction, I will argue, was not (just) a product of patriarchal blindness or sadomasochistic interpretations of sexual intercourse. It was fundamental to the construction of the twentieth century biopolitical citizen—and it was a foundation for the eventual twenty-first century reinterpretation of rape as a crime against bodily integrity.

That sexual legislation was at the heart of twentieth century Ottoman/Turkish political practice had become apparent by the Young Turk revolution of 1908. Between 1908 and 1918, the Young Turks enacted a vast array of decrees regulating marriage, divorce, adultery, and sexual assault that bolstered and in some cases replaced the stipulations of the 1859 criminal code. For now, I just want to mention three of these that get at the heart of a new sexual/biological/political identity—a series of laws from 1913 and 1914 having to do with wartime amnesties granted by the Sultan. The first of these decrees states simply that those who commit rape (*hetk-i irz*) or indecent assault (*fiil-i şeni*) cannot be pardoned or given commuted sentences.[92] The second contains a more detailed discussion of convicts who have been called upon to go to war. In it, any convict who wants to go to the front, will be allowed to do so, except for those who have committed rape or indecent assault.[93] Finally, the third law states that all convicts will be granted a general amnesty by the Sultan except those who have been sentenced to death and hard labor or those who have committed rape or indecent assault.[94] In this wartime situation, in other words—a period during which any and every citizen was increasingly capable of reintegration back into the national collective—it was sexual criminals who were the exception. Murderers, thieves, and brigands could be called upon to defend the nation against attack. Political criminals and corrupt officials could be pardoned by the Sultan and become functioning members of society. Sexual criminals, however, could not. And indeed, the single defining characteristic of those who would be excluded from the political structure—and implicitly, the single defining of characteristic of those who would be included within it—was sexual in nature. Sexual identity was, in other words, absolutely central to political identity.

The 1926 and 1938 Turkish criminal codes picked up on this theme and developed it. In the 1926 text, the articles on adultery and rape are contained in a chapter entitled

91 Enslavement in Pateman's analysis made analogous to a marriage that rendered an individual economically dependent and a legal minor. See above.

92 *Düstur* [1332], vol. 7, no. 9, 76. (20/12/1332).

93 Ibid, no. 110, 407. (17/4/1333).

94 Ibid, no. 262, 631. (18/8/1333).

"crimes against public morality and the constitution of the family,"[95] in subsections on "adultery," "rape, excitation of minors to debauchery, and outrages on modesty," and "the rape of girls, women, and men." The articles in the first of these subsections are similar to those adapted from the Napoleonic code, with "an adulterous wife" and "a husband who keeps a concubine in his conjugal domicile" punished for the same crime. The difference is that if the husband's acts are "notorious," he can be prosecuted as well. The other articles lighten the punishment if the couple is legally separated and reiterate that the complaint must come from the husband or wife, while necessarily also implicating what is now called the "co-perpetrator" rather than the "accomplice" of the wife.[96] The 1938 code retains these passages,[97] adding a sentence to the end of art. 441, stating that a woman who knows a man to be married and "makes herself accomplice to the act [of adultery]" will be punished in the same way as the others.[98]

The articles on sexual assault begin with a discussion of statutory rape, the definition of which fluctuated throughout the 1930s between sexual intercourse with children and sexual intercourse with "children, the insane, and the mentally disabled."[99] After statutory rape, the text turns to "violent attacks on modesty," where "violence" is expanded to include "threats" or "any other means that paralyze resistance." Likewise, the notion of "guardianship" is broadened to include not just parental guardians and educators, but "anyone with authority over [the female victim]," as well as "multiple people" writ large. Gang rape is in this way equated with rape committed by an authority figure. Finally, the question of injury or death caused during rape is extended to "the communication of an illness," "a serious undermining of health," and the production of "an infirmity or defect (*tare/mayubiyet*) in the victim."[100] Two other articles in this section, separated from the above by passages addressing public obscenity and transvestitism, state first, that anyone who "seduces and deflowers" a girl of at least 15 years with a promise of marriage will be imprisoned, that the marriage itself will cancel the penalty, but that a divorce by repudiation[101] will bring it back into force. Second, the court can impose an additional fine according to the situation, the social position of the victim, and the

95 "*Des délits contre les bonne moeurs et contre la constitution de la famille*"/"*Adabı umumiye ve nizamı aile aleyhinde cürümler*." The French "*bonne moeurs*" is not an exact translation of the Turkish "*Adabı umumiye*," the former meaning "good morals" and the later meaning "public morality," "general morality," or more colloquially, "common decency." I am relying on the Turkish version of the text.

96 "Code pénal Turc" 1927, Art. 440-444.

97 Meaning that the government did not adopt wholesale those from the 1930 Italian fascist code.

98 "Code pénal Turc" 1938, Art. 441.

99 It is restricted to children again in 1936. "Code pénal Turc" 1938, Title 8, Chap. 1, Art. 414-415.

100 Ibid, Art. 416-418.

101 A footnote in the text of the code notes that this final phrase of the article would not have had effect, given that "repudiation" was changed to "divorce without good reason" following the adoption of the 1926 Swiss Civil Code. "Code pénal Turc" 1938, Art. 423, footnote.

nature of the attack.[102] The last two articles in the chapter address pornography and singing indecent songs in public.

The final subsection begins with an article on kidnapping. In the 1926 version of the text, the article states that anyone who violently, with threats, or by fraud kidnaps a person will be punished. By 1937, the stipulation had become "anyone who violently, with threats, or by a ruse kidnaps a mature woman or a woman declared to be mature, as well as anyone who imprisons her in an enclosed space (*l'aura enfermée dans un endroit/[onu] bir yerde alıkor*) with the purpose of satisfying a carnal passion or marrying her," will be punished.[103] Similarly, the 1926 version of the next article addresses the kidnapping of boys under fifteen, girls, or women, as well as situations in which the kidnapped person, "male or female," undergoes "an act of libertinage." The revised version of the article addresses first, the kidnapping of children[104] with the aim of satisfying a passion or taking them in marriage, and second, the kidnapping of married women for the sole purpose of "carnal passion."[105]

The final four articles of the section reinforce the notion of marriage as a mitigating circumstance—repeating the harsh stipulation for kidnapping *married* women, the lighter penalty if the victim is returned to his or her family, and the cancellation of the penalty altogether if an appropriate marriage ceremony with the consent of the victim, her family, or a judge is performed.[106] These chapters are followed by a third on prostitution and a concluding one, stating that the rights of guardianship will end if a guardian is involved in any of these behaviors, that the penalties will be reduced by two-thirds if the victim is a woman employed as a prostitute, and that if the victim is wounded or killed, the penalty will be more severe.[107]

Although these articles are for the most part taken from the Italian fascist legislation, in some ways they depart from it. Like the Turkish code, the Italian code places the subsection on rape ("crimes against sexual liberty") into a broader section entitled "crimes against public morality and decency." Adultery falls into a separate broad section on "crimes against the family." The former begins with an article on "carnal violence," punishing anyone who uses "violence or threats" to "compel" another person to have carnal intercourse. It stipulates the same punishment for those who engage in non-violent "carnal intercourse" with anyone under fourteen, with anyone "mentally deranged or … not able to resist by reason of conditions of mental or physical inferiority," or with anyone under 16 "when the guilty person is the ascendant or the guardian, or another person to whom the minor is entrusted for the purpose of treatment, education, instruction, supervision or custody." "Carnal intercourse" itself is not defined, although the pronoun used for the victim is feminine, and that for the perpetrator masculine.

The next article expands on the theme of intercourse, this time alongside abusing one's "capacity as a public official." There is specific mention in this article of

102 Ibid, Art. 423-424.
103 Ibid, Art. 429.
104 Without the explicit "male or female."
105 "Code pénal Turc" 1938, Art. 430.
106 Ibid, Art. 431-434.
107 Ibid, Art. 437-439.

an official who has sex with someone arrested or detained under his observation. The third article discusses "acts of lust" apart from intercourse—defined as "compel[ling] or induc[ing] anyone to commit acts of lust on himself, on the body of the guilty person, or on others." The next two articles discuss and differentiate "rape with the object of marriage," and "rape for the purpose of lust," with "rape" defined as "abduction" by "violence, threat or deceit," and with the second variation punished more severely than the first—particularly if the victim is under 18 or a married woman. The final articles cover rape (i.e., abduction) of individuals under 14 or "of unsound mind … [or] not in any manner capable of resistance by reason of conditions of physical or mental inferiority," and seduction with a promise of marriage committed by a married person.[108]

The stipulations on adultery state that an adulterous wife and her accomplice will be punished with penal servitude for 1 year, which can be extended to 2 years "in the case of an adulterine relationship." The case, however, must be brought by the husband. A second article on "concubinage"—but not on "adultery"—specifies a 2 year sentence of penal servitude for "a husband who keeps a concubine in the conjugal home, or notoriously elsewhere," as well as for the concubine. The wife must initiate the case. Three further articles mitigate or eliminate the punishments if a husband induces his wife to commit prostitution or if he profits from it, if the married people are legally separated or "unjustly deserted," if the marriage is annulled, or if the injured spouse dies.[109]

In France, the Napoleonic code continued to influence legislation on sexual crime throughout the 1920s, although reforms of the divorce law in the 1880s and the 1890s necessarily affected approaches to adultery in particular. As Theresa McBride has noted, the 1810 Napoleonic Code had actually "reinvented" adultery as a crime—and as a distinctly gendered crime—after "revolutionary penal legislation had suppressed [it]."[110] By the third republic (1870–1940), the legislation on adultery in both the criminal and the civil codes was distinctly dated, and so eventually,

> the senate abandoned the distinction between male and female adultery [in the civil code] by the narrow margin of 87 to 82. The version of article 230 which was agreed upon read simply that "a wife may sue for a divorce on account of the husband's adultery," and did not require that this act of adultery be committed in the conjugal domicile. This decision prepared the way for the resolution of the situation that placed the adulterous wife in double jeopardy, because she could be condemned to prison for the crime of adultery by the same civil judgment that granted divorce (art. 298). The husband who was successful in a divorce suit for adultery could thus have his wife automatically imprisoned as a result of his civil suit for divorce. On the narrower issue, the legislators agreed that the Civil Code should not dictate criminal penalties in civil actions, and this section of article 298 was also replaced.[111]

108 "Penal Code of the Kingdom of Italy" 1931, Part 9, Chap. 1, Art. 519-526.

109 Ibid, Art. 559-563.

110 McBride 1992, 762.

111 Ibid, 763.

With regard to criminal sanctions in the late nineteenth and early twentieth centuries, the fine for adulterous husbands and mistresses,

> was initially very high, fixed between 24,000 and 480,000 francs, but … was during the Third Republic reduced to between 100 and 2000 francs … [f]rom 1871 to 1921, the number of criminal proceedings increased by a factor of ten, from 210 to 2,241, but the sharp break took place between 1871 and 1890, during which time the amount of litigation concerning adultery multiplied four-fold.[112]

With regard to legislation on adultery, sexuality, and the family in general, French politicians and jurists followed a line similar to that which they were simultaneously following on abortion and reproductive legislation. Gustave Rivet, for example, "a left-radical deputy for Grenoble," defended his advocacy for paternity suits and for a reform of family and criminal law writ large in 1912 by stating that such reforms would bolster the strength of the French nation state.[113] As one scholar notes, by doing so Rivet aligned "himself with a strong national interest in having the state take measures to prevent infant mortality and depopulation [and] he buttressed his proposal with data linking infant mortality rates to the marital state of the mother. He showed that out-of-wedlock children had a mortality rate almost twice that of those born of a married couple."[114]

In Turkey, Italy, and France, in other words, the link between sexual legislation and a fascist or *quasi* fascist public morality/national interest was just as strong as the link between reproductive legislation and the health or integrity of the race/nation. In France, this was explicit, with a low infant mortality rate associated with appropriate, legally sanctioned marital unions. Less overt, but perhaps more significant, in Turkish, Italian, *and* French legislation, the running theme of consent, of marital consent, of consensual sex, and of the relationship between all three and political space appears in nearly every article. Moreover, the role played by consent in these articles is above all to trace the spatial boundaries of biopolitical citizenship and to inscribe these boundaries across the bodies of women citizens. Sexual legislation in all three states held up women citizens as the superlative representatives, first, of Scarry's politically active, physically[115] passive consenting citizen and, second, of Bergelson's autonomous, rights bearing citizen, defined according to his or her ability to consent, but waiving these rights upon the actual act of consent.

Indeed, the questions that arise upon reading these articles all point toward a mobilization of consent for precisely the transformation of women citizens into biopolitical space. Why in the Italian and Turkish legislation is the woman citizen capable of committing adultery anywhere, but the male citizen capable only of keeping a concubine in his own house? Why is the only exception to the latter the husband's specifically "notorious" extra-marital sex outside of the home? And why is a concubine punished as an accomplice precisely if she knows her partner to be

112 Sohn 1995, 470.

113 Fuchs 2000, 957.

114 Ibid. One result was an increase throughout the third republic in "court decisions awarding mothers damages for seduction." Ibid, 960.

115 And biologically and sexually.

married? In the chapters on rape, why does statutory rape become suddenly central, and why is there a tension between defining children and defining the insane or the mentally incapable as its victims? Why does the definition of "violence" expand to include not just coercion but threats and anything that "paralyzes resistance." Why does the definition of sexual injury expand to include causing an illness, an undermining of health, or a "defect"? Why does inappropriate sex with or by authority figures now include not just guardians or educators, but a countless array of others, including, in the Italian legislation, public officials who have specifically detained or arrested their victims? Why the now almost hyperbolic insistence that the very worst kind of abduction is the abduction of married women, and why the emphasis on enclosing married women in confined spaces? And finally, why is there such a focus in the Italian code on the relationship between "compelling" sexual intercourse and individuals "incapable of resistance because of physical or mental inferiority"?

Arguably, the answer to each of these questions has to do with the production of political space. In some cases, this is overt. Adultery, for example, is defined first by gender and second by space. Adultery is something that women do, and it is something that they do in a broad, public arena (defined as "anywhere" even if it happens to occur in the domicile). Keeping a concubine is something that men do. And it is something that they do in a constrained, private arena—unless, of course, the concubinage is "notorious"/"*notoire*" or "such that everyone knows"/"*herkesçe bilinecek surete*." In such a situation, the juxtaposition of space (anywhere v. in private) gives way to a juxtaposition of state (known by anyone v. known by everyone). And it is this slippage between space and state that plays up the centrality of women citizens as biopolitical actors in this legislation. For women citizens, criminal behavior could occur anywhere and it could be known by anyone. For men citizens, criminal behavior had to be in the domicile or it had to be known by everyone. It was women citizens, in other words, whose sexual, biological and political identities overlapped, and whose biopolitical identity saturated public space. It was women citizens, more basically, who were by definition "known." Men at this point still had to make a concerted effort, an act of will, to consent, as it were, to be known. As such they were unquestionably secondary to the new political structure.

Indeed, if we compare the approach in these passages to the approach taken, for example, to abduction in the 1851 Ottoman code, the extent to which women had eclipsed men as public, political actors becomes clear. In the 1851 code, an abducted woman could not be married in a court outside of her own district because, first, she was not known and, second, the equality of the couple could not therefore be established. It required, in other words, a distinct act of will to make a woman "known" in the mid-nineteenth century Ottoman Empire. The default position was that she was not—even if the man who abducted her was. Here, in the early twentieth century, the opposite is the case. It is women who are known. Men are explicitly not. Here, it takes the same act of will—indeed, more than an act of will, the establishment of an "everyone"—to make a male citizen known. Indeed, a valid defense even for the concubine is that her (male) partner's status was not in fact "known."

Such a defense does not hold for the wife's accomplice because a woman is by definition known and public. Her sexual behavior is simultaneously political behavior.[116] And this situation leads to a number of consequences. First, being known means, again, necessarily being contracted or contractible. In the 1851 Ottoman code, an individual could be contracted into marriage upon being known. In a more broadly defined social or political contract, an individual who is politically known is one who has consented in some form to the sovereign relationship. The fact, therefore, that the default position of early twentieth century women is that they are known, whereas the default position of early twentieth century men is that they are not implies that it is women—but not men—who are contracted and who have consented. It is women citizens, therefore, far more than men citizens, who take Bergelson's understanding of consent to its logical conclusion. They are public and political rights bearing citizens because they are capable of consent. But they are likewise known—already consenting—and therefore have waived their rights and entered biopolitical space.[117] Men citizens fulfill only half of the definition. They are capable of consent, they are capable of being known, but it takes an effort of will to turn them into individuals who are actually consenting.[118]

The chapter and article headings under which these stipulations on adultery operate highlight this situation—highlight the public, biopolitical nature of women citizens. The fact, for example, that women are adulterers, whereas men keep concubines implies more than just a gendered approach to sex law. It also reinforces the space/behavior divide that we saw in the abortion laws. Keeping a concubine is decidedly a behavior—it is something that an individual does. Being an adulteress—as it is called in the legislation—is a state of being. While it is true that one can also *commit* adultery, the emphasis remains on the state of the individual who does so—and even in the Turkish code, where the designation is "a woman who commits adultery," rather than "an adulteress," the extent to which it is a state rather than an

---

116 For an analysis of adultery as a political act, see, for instance, Laura Kipris: "if adultery summons the shaming language of bad citizenship, this also indicates the extent to which marriage is meant to function as a boot camp for citizenship instruction, a training ground for resignation to the *a priori*." Kipris 1998, 294-5.

117 My point here is similar to, but not identical to, MacKinnon's that "all women are divided into parallel provinces, their actual consent counting to the degree that they diverge from the paradigm case in their category. Virtuous women, like young girls, are unconsenting, virginal, rapable. Unvirtuous women, like wives and prostitutes, are consenting, whores, unrapable. The age line under which girls are presumed disabled from consenting to sex, whatever they say, rationalizes a condition of sexual coercion which women never outgrow." MacKinnon 1989, 175. MacKinnon continues to operate within a liberal paradigm, even as she criticizes it. The problem with consent, she argues, is that women must consent given that they are relegated to private space. By operating in a biopolitical paradigm, I am making a very different point: women instead must consent because they are relegated to—or synonymous with—public space.

118 Another area in which the question of being "known" became particularly relevant was when a woman was a "known prostitute," thus unprotected by Turkish rape law, and more overtly subject to adultery law. See, for example, Avcı 2005, 3.

act is played up by the torturous language in which a man who engages in extra-marital sex is defined.[119]

Similarly, the change in the chapter headings, from adultery as an "attack on morality" in the Napoleonic Code and its Ottoman counterpart to adultery as a "crime against public morality and the constitution of the family"[120] in the Turkish[121] likewise indicates a divide between women citizens defined by their biopolitical state and men citizens defined by a relatively dated liberal notion of behavior. Indeed, the addition of "the family" as victim to "morality" as victim in the Turkish law arguably resulted not in an overlap between the two, but in distinct categories. Adulterous women, by virtue of their state, had committed and continued to commit crimes against morality. Men who kept concubines, by virtue of their behavior, committed crimes against the family. Adulterous women were public and political. Men who kept concubines were private and domestic. The former operated in a realm where the sexual, the biological, and the political were constantly meeting—where a newly defined biopolitical identity was what mattered. The latter operated in a realm where the sexual and the political were separate, where the modern family unit so central to liberal politics preserved the notion of *behavior* as politically relevant, and hid any evidence of *identity*.

Moreover, to the extent that women were defined by a state of being rather than by a behavior, they also possessed an almost hyperbolic political presence, conforming to the paradigm of the consenting citizen outlined by Scarry. They did not act. They were explicitly passive. Unlike men, their behavior was irrelevant. But they had a political identity, they were protected by political structures, and were in fact classified according to their status in social, political, and marital contracts.[122] Physically passive and politically active, they operated as paradigmatic consenting sovereign subjects, just as they had in the abortion legislation.

Indeed, the chapters on sexual assault, and rape in particular, are overtly indebted to consent theory. By emphasizing statutory rape especially, these articles necessarily raise the question of how exactly sexual behavior and consent are going to interact with one another in defining the modern, twentieth century citizen. In fact, the tension between defining statutory rape narrowly as sexual intercourse with children, and defining it broadly as sexual intercourse with children, the insane, or the mentally disabled is arguably a tension about how exactly political subjects are going to become biopolitical subjects. The basic question is not *whether* declarations of rights will inscribe an individual's biology and sexuality into political structures;

119 "*karısı ile birlikte ikamet etmekte olduğu evde yahut herkesçe bilinecek surete başka yerde karı koca gibi geçinmek için başkası ile evli olmıyan bir kadını tutmakta olan koca.*" ("a husband who keeps a woman not his wife together with his wife in their domicile, or who lives as man and wife in another place with this woman, such that everyone knows about it.")

120 Another point to note about this transformation is that "the family," like sexual honor, had become more, not less, central as modern criminal law had developed. It is, in other words, a product of modern nationalism and not some sort of "traditionalism."

121 But not in the Italian, where they are separate chapters.

122 See below, for example, on the importance of women's but not men's marital status in rape law.

it is whether declarations of rights will do so because of an individual's age and mental capacity or whether they will do so because of an individual's act of consent. The relationship between rights rhetoric and biopolitical sovereignty has already been established—sexual behavior has become political behavior, and discussions of liberty and autonomy serve solely as a means of regulating it. The question, in other words, is simply what role consent will play in bringing the two together.

Indeed, when MacKinnon criticizes statutory rape legislation by arguing that it makes a mockery of consent theory—that,

> the law takes the most aggravated case of female powerlessness based on gender and age combined and, by formally prohibiting all sex as rape, makes consent irrelevant on the basis of an assumption of powerlessness. This defines those [women] above the age line as powerful, whether they actually have power to consent or not,[123]

I think she misinterprets the role played by consent in both statutory and non-statutory rape legislation. The purpose of the law (whether or not it is actually achieved) is not to produce a situation in which women above the age line, by virtue of their ability to consent, are likewise able to make a choice about engaging in sexual behavior. It is not—as MacKinnon implies—that the theory of consent is irrelevant, meaningless, or dangerous because the "reality" of women's situation is different or contrary to the theory, that they have no "real" power to consent that matches their theoretical power. It is that the power to consent—in reality *as well as* in theory—has nothing to do with making a choice. It has to do with defining a space. The question that gets asked and answered in legislation on statutory rape is not who is capable of making a decision about engaging in sexual behavior. It is whose body might be effectively delimited as biopolitical space. Criticizing the divide between theory and reality in statutory rape legislation, or in rape legislation in general, is thus an empty gesture—the point of the theory never was to posit some women as able to make a choice and others as not.

Indeed, this situation becomes absolutely explicit in the ways in which notions of "violence," "injury," and "guardianship" expand in the early twentieth century Turkish and Italian laws. It is mature women, above the age of consent, who are increasingly subject not just to physical violence, but to threats, and to anything that might "paralyze resistance." It is likewise mature women, above the age of consent, who might suffer not just wounds, but illnesses and defects upon being raped. The most obvious result of this transformation is that the act of consent becomes something that occurs in an increasingly constrained space. Just as expanding the definition of statutory rape limits the number of people capable of consent, in other words, expanding the various methods by which violence might replace consent likewise limits the arena in which consent is relevant.

As statutory rape was defined as intercourse with children, and then as intercourse with the insane, and then as intercourse with the mentally disabled,[124] the number

123 MacKinnon 1989, 175.

124 Keeping in mind that throughout the 1920s and 1930s "insane" and "mentally disabled" likewise became expanding, catch-all categories in a variety of different fascist and ostensibly non-fascist national contexts.

of individuals with whom intercourse was not, by definition, criminal shrank. Likewise, as violence was defined as physical coercion, and then as threats, and then as "any means that might paralyze resistance," the definition of non-violent sex also narrowed. But my point here, I should emphasize, is not that physical coercion is the only means employed by rapists, and that therefore rape legislation should not consider threats or other types of violence in developing a definition of the crime. My point is simply that as both the definition of statutory rape and the definition of violence became increasingly broad, the definition of non-criminal, consensual sex became increasingly narrow.

Similarly, we can see in the expanding definition of "injury" the gradual disappearance of *non*-injurious sex as a category. Understanding not just wounds, but illnesses, and indeed "defects" as criminal injuries that might arise from non-consensual sex indeed eliminates the possibility of intercourse without injury, especially when we consider the implications of the notion of "defect." The word for defect used in the Turkish law, for example, *mayubiyet*, refers explicitly to any "shameful" mark on the body that might, in early modern and medieval law, have voided a marriage or engagement contract. For women, one of the most straightforward of such marks or defects was evidence of prior sexual intercourse. Positing this sort of defect as an injury that might arise from nonconsensual sex therefore suggests that *any* physical evidence of intercourse is simultaneously injurious. "Injury" thus becomes in this interpretation, at least, essentially synonymous with "sex."

At the same time, by articulating the notion of defect through this modern vocabulary of rights and injury, the legislation also played up the emphatically embodied nature of rape. It is not just that rape had to do with the political act of consent or the lack thereof; it is that these political acts likewise defined spaces—they were in fact physically inscribed on the bodies of women citizens in the form of injuries and defects. Indeed, my purpose in discussing the increasingly circumscribed space in which consent was possible and the dwindling category of non-criminal, non-injurious intercourse is not to argue that—criminal and injurious—all sex was prohibited. Obviously it was not. My argument is instead that—criminal and injurious—all sex came to be articulated and regulated through a particularly biopolitical language of rights and consent. Children, the insane, and the mentally disabled were incapable of consent. They were in this way defined *politically* as physically, biologically, and sexually passive. They were hyperbolic, active citizens who had by definition waived all of their biological rights. Mature women likewise—given the ever expanding definition of "violence" in the law—were incapable of consent. They too were defined *politically* as physically, biologically, and sexually passive. They too became hyperbolic, active citizens who had by definition waived all of their biological rights.

That married women played the same role in rape/abduction legislation as children ("girls" and "boys under fifteen") is thus not solely a result of the eighteenth century liberal marital contract that rendered women legal minors upon their entering into the "conjugal union."[125] There is also a biopolitical tone to these passages. Married women were necessarily above the age of consent—they had consented, if nothing

125 Pateman 1988, 119.

else, to marriage. By defining them in the same way as children when it came to sex, however, by positioning them as subject almost by definition to violence and threat, by seeing them as incapable of consenting to intercourse, by playing up the sexual connotations of enclosing them in small spaces, the legislation was also linking women, and in particular mature women, inextricably to political space. Women citizens were capable of consent, but they could not consent. Their bodies were simultaneously political and apolitical, sexual and asexual. They thus represented once again the logical conclusion to Bergelson's consenting citizen—defined politically as capable of consent, but deprived of any (biological or sexual) rights the moment they invoked this (political) identity.

And indeed, this necessarily biopolitical role played by women citizens in early twentieth century rape legislation becomes most overt in the expanded notion of guardianship and its betrayal in the Turkish and the Italian codes. In each, the "guardian" or "educator" of the Napoleonic law came to be defined as anyone "in authority," "multiple people," or in the Italian code any public official responsible for a victim detained or under arrest. Just as it was in the Napoleonic code, the severity with which individuals who betrayed the guardian relationship were punished is arguably more about liberal notions of contractual obligations than it is about assault. It is about mocking the give and take of variations on the social contract.

At the same time, however, there is something more going on in this early twentieth century legislation on guardianship than there had been 100 years before. First of all, there is the focus in the Italian legislation on the public official abusing his position as a jailor or an interrogator. There is a focus, in other words, once more on *habeas corpus*. But whereas before, the abduction of the married woman as an "illegal arrest" *implied* a sexualized violation of this right, here the sexual nature of the violation is explicit. The "guardian" who has intercourse with his charge in this scenario is violating not just public morality, but the "rule of law" broadly defined and represented by the right of *habeas corpus*. He is replacing the political possession of the body with a personal possession of the body, and by doing so he is upsetting liberal as well as fascist notions of democracy.

Likewise, the entry of the seemingly unrelated "multiple people" into the text, the association of gang rape with rape by a guardian, is arguably about the now ineradicable relationship between twentieth century democracy and twentieth century sexual crime. The assumption upon which the insertion of "multiple people" into the text rests is that these multiple people are in the same position of authority over a woman citizen as a guardian, educator, or jailor is. The gang is in this way both let into the social contract and implicated in the jailor's violation of the right of *habeas corpus*. Gang rape is transformed into an emphatically political crime—not just against public morality, certainly not against an individual, but against legitimate sovereignty and (waived) rights. As Ellen Kennedy has noted, interwar fascists[126] were fascinated by the political potential of the gang or the crowd. Unlike liberal theorists, who mistrusted the threat to rational structures posed by what had come to be termed "crowd psychology," fascist theorists such as Carl Schmitt saw the

126 She is discussing the work of Carl Schmitt specifically.

crowd as "something that [could] be transformed into the Volk of public law."[127] In this sense, therefore, the conflation of gang rape with rape by public officials is a reasonable—and indeed necessary—one within the context of the new mass democracy.[128]

I noted at the beginning of this section that the underlying question driving my investigation of interwar legislation was why fascists especially should find the notion of "sexual liberty" useful or meaningful. Most scholars have argued that liberty was irrelevant to fascist political theory, and that the consent theory and rights rhetoric that operate in support of it are the product of purely liberal structures. Given the paradoxical relationship between consent as a right and consent as a waiver of rights, however, the fascist insistence on this particular sort of liberty begins to make some

---

127 Kennedy's analysis of this point runs as follows: "If a liberal public is rational and individual, the alternative conception in contemporary thought was neither. Research into 'crowd psychology' had presented a very different social reality than that of classical liberalism by the time Schmitt wrote *Der Begriff des Politischen*. Attention to the behavior of men in groups encouraged social science to focus on mass society as a profoundly irrational phenomenon. In *Psychologie des Foules* (1895) Gustav Le Bon had asserted that 'The substitution of the unconscious action of crowds for the conscious activity of individuals is one of the principal characteristics of the present age.' Liberal philosophers such as Locke and Bentham, and the men of the Enlightenment had presented the individual as a rational, perfectible being but Le Bon emphasized the way 'unconscious qualities obtain the upper hand.' In a crowd the individual loses his inhibitions, experiencing a feeling of power he would not have normally. There is a 'contagion' among the members of a crowd resulting from their high level of 'suggestibility,' a phenomenon Le Bon compares to that of the hypnotized individual. In a crowd 'the individual differs essentially from himself' and is capable of great heroism or barbarity. The First World War and the revolutions which followed further stimulated the study of crowd psychology. Sigmund Freud's *Massenpsychologie und Ich-Analyse* (1921) accepted much of Le Bon's argument, while noting that a crowd intensifies affect and inhibits intellect. In Freud's argument, irrational characteristics of the mind enable the psychology of the crowd through suggestion and libido. These bind the individual to the leader and the crowd, allowing the primitive to emerge within civilization. The work of 'elite theorists' such as Gataeno Mosca, Vilfredo Pareto and Robert Michels developed the argument that crowds subordinate reason to the irrational influence of the leader and the group. They all stressed the weakness of rationality in politics, arguing that subconscious suggestion dominates politics in mass society. Rousseau saw democracy as a means of human perfection in which governed and governing are identical. When Max Weber redefined it as a method of leadership selection, this 'demystified' democracy. For the elite theorists, democracy as an ideal and as a method were equally misleading myths that clothed the structures of power with comforting notions of participation. The people never rule, these sociologists argued; elites rule … [L]astly, *Der Begriff des Politischen* suggests Schmitt's awareness of political facts used by the elite theorists and crowd psychology, but this theme works its way through the text more as an intrigue than a statement. There is only one reference to that literature (Pareto) and no discussion of the political movements of the day. The underlying urgency of the text, however, conveys a sense of the political as irrational and unpredictable. While the elite theorists saw only the fact of the crowd, Schmitt sees it as something that can be transformed into the Volk of public law while recognizing (as they did) its volatility." Kennedy 1997, 45-7.

128 I will discuss the ways in which this paradigm is shifted to the realm of international law in the next chapter.

sense. It was indeed specifically the right to consent hovering over early twentieth century sexual legislation that rendered women citizens emphatically incapable of actually doing so. The ever expanding definitions of statutory rape, threat and injury (along with the ever expanding categories of "insane" or "mentally disabled" that we likewise see in the 1920s and 1930s) in turn transformed "consensual sex" into nothing more than a backdrop against which all sex could be reinterpreted as criminal, and against which women's bodies would offer up physical testimony of this criminality. It was thus specifically via consent theory that adultery and rape became political acts, became a means of defining citizens—and in particular women citizens—as passive, biopolitical settings in which the interaction between "acts of lust" and individuals "incapable of resistance because of physical or mental inferiority" was an ever present one.

Bodily Integrity after the Second World War

Legislation having to do with sexuality, however, like legislation having to do with reproduction, underwent a change after the Second World War. Consent gradually played less of a role in most national criminal codes, and by the 1990s especially, the right to bodily integrity or bodily autonomy became the underpinning of both rape law and adultery law.[129] At the same time, it is important to keep in mind that consent and bodily integrity were by no means separate issues—that, as Scarry notes, consent is invariably written across the body, while bodily integrity comes to the fore only as consent defines biopolitical boundaries. Moreover, the emphasis on bodily integrity *and* bodily autonomy—often used interchangeably or synonymously—is a particularly problematic one, especially given their relationship to consent theory. As a number of scholars have argued, the two are by no means the same and indeed often contradict one another—the "dignity" implied by integrity clashing with the "liberty" implied by autonomy when an individual consents, for example, to what is politically perceived of as a degrading abuse of his or her body.[130]

Broadly, therefore, my purpose in this section is to look at the ways in which Turkish, French, and Italian legislators have dealt with these contradictions and overlaps. My basic position will be once again that even as the late twentieth century rhetoric of bodily integrity replaced the early twentieth century rhetoric of consent, the resulting articulation of women's bodies as biopolitical space remained the same. Similarly, just as the gradual decriminalization of abortion in the late twentieth century turned women's wombs increasingly into public space, the simultaneous rearticulation of the crime that was rape likewise turned women's bodies into a public arena. Indeed, if anything, their bodies became subject to more extensive searches and to further regulation as bodily integrity became the central right to protect—the

---

129 To the extent that the latter remained in force.

130 Bergelson, for example, discusses this issue specifically in the context of a German individual who consented in 2003 to being cannibalized. When German courts maintained that even with his consent, cannibalism was a crime, they were essentially undermining his bodily autonomy in favor of his bodily integrity. (Although the case was tried long after the individual had in fact been eaten.) Bergelson *forthcoming*, 66.

(mute) biological testimony of women's bodies central to contemporary notions of legitimate governance and democratic process.

Before moving to a specific discussion of this legislation, however, I would like to spend some time contextualizing it—describing the various ways in which theories of bodily integrity have become integral to theories of late twentieth and early twenty-first century "rule of law" writ large. I will thus briefly examine analyses of rape in contemporary international law, and I will likewise address the right to, or the rhetoric of, bodily integrity in discussions only tangentially related to rape law *per se*—in debates concerning, for example, the legitimacy of state sponsored virginity examinations in Turkey, and in the lack of debates concerning the legitimacy of search warrants for women's vaginas in the United States. Only then will I turn to specific Turkish, French, and Italian rape and adultery law.

To begin with, however, I want to return to eighteenth century France. Rachel Fuchs describes an interesting phenomenon surrounding paternity suits in France at this time, observing that jurists of the period "believed that during the pains of childbirth, as in torture, a woman would reveal the truth [about the paternity of her child] and her word at that time should be accepted (*creditur virgini* ….)."[131] By the early nineteenth century, she continues, such attitudes toward extra-marital sex, pregnancy, and labor had disappeared, and,

> rather than follow the eighteenth century maxim of *creditur virgini*, or the interpretation of natural law voiced by several men in 1792 that all children, including natural children, had the right to a family, the majority of men who framed the 1804 Code appealed to an opposing "law of nature." They declared that all children were fatherless at birth and only a marriage marks a father.[132]

Finally, by the late nineteenth and early twentieth centuries, "the rhetoric shifted from the eighteenth century maxim of *creditur virgini* to the … idea that one should not believe a single mother without proof, because she would likely lie and name a man in bad faith."[133] Although paternity suits are not central to my analysis, I think that the progression that we see here concerning the role of a woman's body in establishing "truth" is nonetheless a good starting point for an examination of late twentieth century bodily integrity broadly defined.

In addition to the basic correlation here with Foucault's periodization of punishment and testimony—of the movement from an early modern reliance on torture to a modern reliance on discipline[134]—we can likewise see in all three approaches to

131 Fuchs 2000, 949.

132 Ibid, 953. [art. 340 forbade paternity searches, as reinforcement, art. 341 allowed *recherché de la maternité*.]

133 Ibid, 962.

134 "If torture was so strongly embedded in legal practice, it was because it revealed truth and showed the operation of power. It assured the articulation of the written on the oral, the secret on the public, the procedure of investigation on the operation of the confession; it made it possible to reproduce the crime on the visible body of the criminal; in the same horror, the crime had to be manifested and annulled. It also made the body of the condemned man the place where the vengeance of the sovereign was applied, the anchoring point for a

paternity an effort to endow women with a subjectivity directly proportional to their bodily integrity. In the seventeenth and eighteenth centuries, women's bodies were unprotected. They were permeable, penetrable texts that might be read, analyzed, and exposed. Women by their very (sexual and reproductive) nature indeed *could not* possess a coherent subjectivity, given that torture and labor played identical roles in destabilizing it. Just as torture simultaneously marked and revealed the truth of a crime on a broken, objectified individual's body, in other words, so too did labor mark and reveal the same on a similarly objectified woman's body. By the late nineteenth and twentieth centuries, however—largely in the name of creating a legally defined, uniform citizenry, where the concept "natural," even, was linked to the marriage contract—women's bodies became unbroken, and unbreakable. Even in labor, women maintained their subjectivity. They were indeed so intellectually collected, so capable of producing their own narratives, that they could deliberately obscure or hide a "truth" that in the eighteenth century would have appeared on their pain racked bodies regardless of their volition.

At the same time, however, I want to suggest that this taking for granted of women's bodily integrity (linked to their subjectivity)—which eventually became the taking for granted of their *right* to bodily integrity (linked to their subjectivity)—did not by any means render women's bodies less spatially defined than they had been before. The only difference was that rather than serving as political space, they began to serve as biopolitical space. Just as occurred at the beginning of the twentieth century with the mobilization of consent theory, in other words, here with the mobilization of bodily integrity, we have, first of all, the rendering of all sex criminal by its very nature—subject to regulation by national and international structures. Second, there is the replacement of torture by forensic medicine—each search for testimony reading women's bodies as passive objects, the only obvious difference between the two being forensic medicine's reliance on consent theory. And finally, we have the at this point exaggerated overlap between bodily boundaries and political boundaries—the mobilization of the right to bodily integrity turning violations of a woman's biological barriers into acts of treason.

Whereas in the early twentieth century the criminalization of sex happened via an expansion of the categories of statutory rape and coercion, however, in the late twentieth century, it was a result of the overlap between consent and bodily integrity—the conflation of "autonomy" (or rights) and "integrity" (or dignity). Approaches to rape in contemporary international law, especially since the Bosnian genocide, for example, have relied heavily upon a new understanding of the relationship between consent and bodily integrity.[135] As Debra Bergoffen argues, the International Criminal Tribunal for the former Yugoslavia (ICTY) ruling in the *Kunarac* rape trial of February 22, 2001 affirmed "the principle of embodied

manifestation of power, an opportunity of affirming the dissymmetry of forces. We shall see later that the truth-power relation remains at the heart of all mechanisms of punishment and that it is still to be found in contemporary penal practice—but in a quite different form and with very different effects." Foucault 1995, 55.

135 I will discuss this relationship in more detail in the next chapter.

subjectivity," and set a foundation for further reforms to international rape law. Before this ruling, she asserts,

> the standard against which evidence for or against the charge of a crime against humanity was the normative "neutral" body. Using this body as a measure, torture, understood through the criteria of physical pain, was identified as a crime against humanity … [T]he court took a different position. It identified an act as rape, a crime against humanity, whether or not there was evidence of violence or physical pain and injury. It decoupled the idea of forced entry from the idea of painful entry.[136]

She suggests furthermore that by "drawing on the principle of consent, the court refused to define rape as an act of sexual penetration accompanied by coercion or force or threat of force," and concludes that "in dismissing the apparent consent defense and in insisting on proof of genuine consent, the court determined that the situation of the woman, her capacity to give consent, not the quota of violence inflicted on her body determines whether or not rape occurred."[137]

Put another way, by bringing together consent and bodily integrity, the court was eradicating any political understanding of sex and reinforcing a new, biopolitical understanding of it. Rather than interpreting sex as a non-criminal act that only in certain circumstances (namely in the absence of consent) became criminal, the court instead interpreted sex as a criminal act that only in certain circumstances (the presence of consent) became acceptable.[138] This may seem like a minor, or indeed

---

136 Bergoffen 2003, 118.

137 Ibid, 118. She also argues that "in focusing on the matter of consent and in using criteria of consent, rather than criteria of violence or pain, for determining whether or not a crime against humanity occurred, the court took note of the relationship between a woman's humanity and her sexual integrity." Ibid, 119. This argument is similar to Kirsten Campbell's analysis of the international law of rape, where she notes that "following this consideration, it [the Tribunal] defines the crime of rape in terms of the conventional legal categories of the *actus reus*—the criminal act—and the *mens rea*—the criminal intent: ' … the *actus reus* of the crime of rape in international law is constituted by the sexual penetration, however slight: (a) of the vagina or anus of the victim by the penis of the perpetrator; or (b) of the mouth of the victim by the penis of the perpetrator; when such sexual penetration occurs without the consent of the victim. Consent for this purpose must be given voluntarily, as a result of the victim's free will, assessed in the context of the surrounding circumstances. The *mens rea* is the intention to effect this sexual penetration, and the knowledge that it occurs without the consent of the victim.'" Campbell 2003, 508.

138 Karen Engle notes a similar trend in the *Kunarac* trial that I will address more fully in the next chapter. For now, it is sufficient to note the following: "In some ways, the ICTY's development of the doctrine of consent in the rape cases reflects a tension about the extent to which women could be *presumed* to have been rape victims … [W]hen the Tribunal made factual findings that the witnesses had engaged in sexual intercourse with the accused it severely limited the possibility of a consent defense. The consent defense was most restricted in the appeals decision in *Kunarac* … [The *Kunarac*] decision's discussion of consent, torture, and armed conflict combine, I argue, to reinforce an understanding that Bosnian Muslim women had little, if any, sexual agency during the war … [B]ecause the appeals chamber found that the circumstances in Foča were inherently coercive, it did not require the prosecution to prove lack of consent for each of the rapes, concluding that the

nonexistent, difference. But in fact it indicates a complete transformation in the role of political structures in incorporating, defining, and regulating sexual and biological behavior. As Bergelson has argued with regard to consent and rape law in the liberal context, for example,

> we need two sets of consent rules—one for cases in which consent plays the inculpatory role; and the other for cases in which its role is exculpatory. Instances of bodily harm all fit into the second category, which explains why analogies of consensual killing with consensual "theft" or "rape" do not work: the latter examples belong to the first category of consent. Consent alone is sufficient to make theft or rape impossible. Significantly more is required to justify killing or maiming … [T]o conclude, it is important to distinguish between offenses, in which the act becomes wrongful due to the lack of consent, from offenses, in which the very conduct constitutes a prima facie norm violation. All offenses involving injury or death belong to the second group; therefore, with respect to those offenses, the victim's consent may play only an exculpatory role.[139]

Here in the February 22, 2001 ruling, however, the link forged between consent and bodily integrity—indeed, the overlap of the two as each defines women's subjectivity—brings rape very much into Bergelson's second category. Sex is an act of bodily harm. It is conceived of as a violation of bodily integrity. It undermines an individual's (biopolitical) dignity, whether there is consent or not. Consent merely serves to mitigate the crime. It is therefore emphatically not, as Bergelson states elsewhere, that "consensual sex is not rape, even if one of the partners is not aware of the other's consent."[140] The burden of proof in the context of the February 22, 2001 rape trial was explicitly on the defendant—to show that consent occurred.

In the very process of reinforcing women's subjectivity, therefore—in the very process of eliminating the humiliating effects of considering consent alone in rape legislation (namely, the effects of placing the burden of proof on the victim to show that she did not in fact "want it")—contemporary international law is also effectively criminalizing all sex. Whereas it is true that rape is not like torture to the extent that pain *per se* is not the issue, in other words, it is exactly like torture in that regardless of consent it is a crime against bodily integrity, autonomy, and therefore humanity.

---

notion of consent was meaningless in such circumstances … [B]y presuming coercion, the ICTY's jurisprudence essentially makes consensual relationships legally impossible, in some sets of circumstances, which would include those around Foča … [T]his broad reading of 'armed conflict' suggests that all sexual relationships between Bosnian Muslim civilians and Serbian soldiers in Bosnia and Herzegovina could be seen as nonconsensual, expanding the reach of *Kunarac* well beyond Foča." Engle 2005, 803-806.

139 She also states, "consider offenses of rape, kidnapping, theft, and trespass, to name just a few. In all of them, the *act itself* does not violate a prohibitory norm. Having sex, transporting someone to a different location, taking other people's property, or entering someone's home is not bad *per se*. It becomes bad *only* due to the attendant circumstances, namely the lack of consent: i.e., unless consent is missing, the conduct is outside the boundaries of law … killing or hurting another is bad *per se*. The fact that a person may be legally justified in, say, killing of another in self-defense does not make the killing as morally neutral as borrowing a book; it is still regrettable." Bergelson *forthcoming*, 57-62.

140 Ibid, 50.

Rape is a crime not because there is an absence of consent, but because sex is an assault on politically defined biological boundaries. The role of *proving* consent is thus, again, simply to mitigate the original crime. Far more so than early twentieth century fascist and *quasi*-fascist legislature, contemporary international law has thus mobilized the "right" implied by integrity/autonomy to turn sex into something in need of constant regulation.

And indeed, to the extent that both integrity and autonomy play interchangeable roles in the contemporary legislation, the passive, spatial nature of women's bodies is highlighted. In Kirsten Campbell's description of the ICTY's approach to rape law, for instance, we learn that,

> the Tribunal's conception of the crime of rape rests upon notions of integrity of the body and of the self of the survivor of sexual violence … [T]his model of rape as a crime against humanity thus rests upon a conception of the material integrity of the body, and of the crime as a trauma to it … [I]n *Kunarac* the crime consists not only of a breach of bodily integrity but also of sexual autonomy … [T]his model of rape reflects the more liberal model of rape, which "now understands the crime as a violation of autonomy, as a failure to recognize the victim's civil rights of self determination" and assumes that "personhood is intricately tied to self-determination and autonomy."[141]

In a very different context, Alan Hyde has argued that,

> bodies may indeed be experienced as autonomous, but, when this is so, this is because of their social, discursive construction as autonomous. Body autonomy is really social, public, and conventional … [I]t follows that the body is not the best but the worst standpoint for defining legal subjects, particularly subjects' autonomy against public intrusion (the aim of those who would replace the right of privacy with a right to bodily integrity or autonomy).[142]

Hyde's analysis is more critically informed than Campbell's is—working from the notion that the autonomous body is a political construct rather than some pre-existent, natural reality. But each in a different way accepts unquestionably the slippage between the "autonomy" associated with the liberal right to do with one's body as one wishes, and the "integrity" associated with the authoritarian insistence that the body is inviolable and deserving of respect. In Campbell's discussion, we have first a conflation of the "self" and bodily integrity, followed by a characterization of rape as a simultaneous assault on bodily integrity and sexual autonomy. The passage concludes with a conflation this time of "personhood," "self-determination," and "autonomy." Hyde's discussion is almost a mirror image. We start with bodily *autonomy*, and then move on to the strange assertion that autonomy (rather than integrity) serves as a barrier "against public intrusion." We then conclude with integrity *or* autonomy replacing the notion of privacy.

If integrity and autonomy—and the right to both—were the same thing, then these discussions would be entirely reasonable. Without question, however, they are not. The "*self*" that is projected onto Campbell's inviolate body, possessed of

141 Campbell 2003, 508-9.

142 Hyde 1997, 11.

integrity, is an embodied self—a self with biological borders that must be preserved intact. The "*person*" who would disappear in the absence of *autonomy* is a purely political being, a being who must be free from coercion, but who can do with the physical self as he or she pleases. The notion of "autonomy against public intrusion" is therefore a strange amalgamation of the two—especially when we consider the autonomous political *person* who wants to disrespect the inviolate, physical *self* (the masochist, say, who consents to being cannibalized[143]), or the inviolate physical *self* who violates the autonomy of the political *person* (the same masochist who commits him or herself to an institution to prevent the possibility of consenting to being cannibalized). At the same time, however, the conflation of autonomy and integrity that we see in both of these passages as well as in contemporary rape legislation—the positing of a simultaneous attack on both in the event of criminal sex—produces an important backdrop for early twenty-first century sovereign relations: while the focus on integrity reduces to nothing the possibility of autonomy, the focus on autonomy reduces to nothing the possibility of integrity. The result is a completely passive sexualized body, a body ready (via integrity) and willing (via autonomy) to operate as a setting for the spectacle of the rule of law.[144]

Indeed, this spectacle and the newly articulated role of the body in it have been central to the interrelated development of forensic medicine and embodied rights discourse, especially in the context of rape legislation. As Hyde has noted, the tension between the body as a field of juridical inquiry and the body as an individual interest has produced a number of apparent legal contradictions. In a 1985 case, for example, the United States Supreme Court decided that "a compelled surgical intrusion into an individual's [Rudolph Lee's] body for evidence … implicates expectations of privacy and security of such magnitude that the intrusion may be 'unreasonable' even if likely to produce evidence of a crime."[145] This approach to bodily integrity, as Hyde argues, seems completely contradictory to both the apparent legality of issuing search warrants for women's vaginas in the United States—which I will discuss in more detail below—and also to the apparent legality of, for instance, subjecting a female high school student, Angela Williams, to "a strip search because *one fellow student* told the principal that Angela and a girl named Michelle had a clear glass vial containing a white powder [italics in original]."[146] Hyde addresses these apparent contradictions by stating that in general, there is "a hierarchy of bodily intrusions, under which surgery under general anesthetic is more intrusive, less likely to be ordered, than a urine sample or breath test, which … may be ordered even without individualized suspicion."[147]

143 As discussed in Bergelson *forthcoming*, 66.

144 Engle notes one logical conclusion to this scenario in the case of the former Yugoslavia: "If female victims of rape have long encountered the difficulty of being believed, an odd reversal took place here. It was often women and girls who denied having been raped that were not believed. At some level, all Bosnian Muslim women were imagined to have been raped." Engle 2005, 794.

145 As quoted in Hyde 1997, 156-7.

146 Ibid, 171.

147 Ibid, 159.

What is it, though, about a general anesthetic that immediately prompts concerns of violations of bodily integrity—concerns that strip searches, vaginal examinations, and, as we shall see, post-rape medical examinations apparently do not? One answer has to do with the role played by consent in such situations. The passive, inert body of Cardozo's judgment may be more politically active than its physically active counterparts, but only if this political activity is mobilized in support of the liberty of the sovereign citizen him or herself. Liberal individuals consent to medical anesthesia for their own, *individual*, greater good. If the passive, inert body is nothing more than a political *setting*, however, a field from which to gather evidence for a common good, then there is no liberal political activity to speak of. The rhetoric of consenting citizenship breaks down.

More important than the role of consent in these approaches to general anesthetic, though, is arguably the sexual connotations that have grown up over the past few centuries around medicinal unconsciousness. As Dudley Buxton, writing in 1888 on "The Criminal Use of Chloroform," noted,

> many cases have now been reported in which the prosecutrix has affirmed that a dentist or surgeon has violated her person while she was under the influence of anaesthetic ... [B]ut it is not only designing, bad women who bring such charges. Modest, virtuous, and refined gentlewomen have been prosecutrices in these cases. The cause for this remarkable and deplorable state of things is fortunately not far to seek. Chloroform, ether, nitrous oxide, gas, cocaine, and possibly other carbon compounds, employed in producing anaesthesia possess the property of exciting sexual emotions and in many cases produce erotic hallucinations. It is undoubted that in certain persons sexual orgasm may occur during the induction of anaesthetic.[148]

It is not just the mockery of consent that is at stake in such situations, in other words—it is also involuntary (female) sexual pleasure. It is true that J.P. Payne, commenting on Buxton's assertions 100 years later, argues that such analyses of the effects of chloroform were patently incorrect.[149] But the fact remains that alongside the fear that the physically passive body might slip into political passivity, there is the simultaneous fear that the physically passive body might slip into sexual activity. General anesthetic thus plays up—as a trope if not as a reality—the fundamentally sexual nature of assaults on bodily integrity.

As such, again, it presents the horrifying possibility that sexual behavior or sexual identity might slip outside the bounds of the political, and in the process render legal violations of bodily integrity suddenly illegal. Strip searches, the collection of urine samples, and vaginal examinations are self-consciously modern and humane political and legal processes. All three may *seem* no different from early modern torture—each involving an obvious violation of bodily boundaries performed for the sake of (non-verbal) truth, testimony, and evidence. But they are not *actually* torture in that they do not involve—or are not meant to involve—the undermining of subjectivity, the disordering of the self, or the political and intellectual incoherence that arises from torture (or labor pains) in non-modern contexts. The unconscious

148 Buxton 1888, 149-150, as cited in Payne 1998, 686.

149 Ibid, 686.

orgasm of the anesthetized body, however—whether it happens in reality, or merely hovers as an unrealized possibility (or fantasy) around the passive body—shifts modern, humane violations of bodily integrity into the realm of torture and lawless violence. The basic point of the right to bodily integrity as it was articulated by Cardozo and countless others was that even and especially in an unconscious state, the liberal citizen was a coherent, politically active, self. That a sexual orgasm—*the* manifestation of the shattered, incoherent, loss of subjectivity[150]—might occur in the midst of this unconsciousness completely undermines the very foundation of embodied political rights. In the context of rape legislation, therefore, it becomes particularly frightening, given the very slight difference between the crime of rape—an illegal violation of bodily integrity—and the gathering of forensic evidence following rape—a legal violation of the same bodily integrity.

Indeed, much of the discussion surrounding the gathering of forensic evidence prior to rape trials is implicitly an attempt to ensure that the crime (a form of torture that combines a violation of bodily integrity with an undermining of subjectivity) not be confused with the investigation (a form of not-torture that combines a violation of bodily integrity with a reinforcement of subjectivity). As Jennifer Temkin has noted, for example, rape "victims are not allowed to wash or change their soiled clothing before they are examined and are frequently denied food and drink because the police officer does not feel able to take oral swabs herself … [T]he victim may also be denied medical treatment … [s]o as not to disturb forensic evidence."[151] Temkin suggests, therefore, that at least one solution to this implicitly dehumanizing process of gathering evidence should be a strengthening of the role of consent in the victim/patient-investigator/doctor relationship:

> the normal doctor/patient relationship is very different from that which exists between a victim and the doctor who examines her forensically. One aspect of the difference is that the rules of disclosure ensure that information obtained from the victim as well as evidence obtained from the examination itself are frequently disclosed to the defense and other involved parties. Thus the victim's understandings are misplaced as are her assumptions about the confidentiality of what is to occur … [V]ictims need to be warned about the true situation so that an informed consent may be given to the proceeding and an informed decision made as to how much information to provide.[152]

One basic goal of critiques of the post-rape gathering of forensic evidence, in other words, is to keep rape victims conscious, active, consenting, and—no matter what the discomfort—in full possession of a coherent self. The declarations of consent are repetitive; the extent to which the rape victim is always hyperbolically *aware* of what is going on is extraordinary. And again, the purpose of this insistence is to highlight the legality of these new violations of the victim's bodily integrity, to fortify the rape victim's political rights even as physically they are being undermined. It may

---

150 As has been noted by a number of poets as well as theorists. From among the latter, see Georges Bataille, who argued that "the whole business of eroticism is to destroy the self-contained character of the participants as they are in their normal lives." Bataille 1986, 17.

151 Temkin 1998, 828.

152 Ibid, 830.

be, in other words, that the gathering of evidence involves an intimate regulation of the sexual and the biological, it may be that it involves disturbing and indeed completely erasing bodily borders and boundaries, it may be that all of this occurs in the name of securing truth and testimony. But the process is *not* (like rape) torture. It is the opposite of torture—the violation of bodily integrity happening here is a reinforcement of the rights and the political subjectivity that the rape itself has undermined. At the same time, however, this rhetoric of political subjectivity that surrounds the forensic examination is the only obvious difference between the two processes—physically, they are nearly identical.

Indeed, the post-rape gathering of forensic evidence is not the only process that involves a violation of bodily integrity in the name of political subjectivity—a violation of bodily integrity, in fact, in the name of the very right to bodily integrity. Virginity examinations in Turkey and the issuing of search warrants for women's vaginas in the United States are two similar activities that play on this late twentieth century rhetoric. As for the first, the debate surrounding the use of virginity examinations in schools, hospitals, and prisons became increasingly vocal in Turkey throughout the 1990s. The issue first became a subject of widespread public scrutiny in May of 1992 when, as Gülşan Seral notes,

> the Turkish media explored the unauthorized virginity tests of several high school students as they were ordered by the principal of the schools located in an Anatolian town, Simar-Kütahya, and which unfortunately led one of the girls to commit suicide. At the time of the discussion about virginity tests and suicide, it was found that the Minister of Health at the time, Yıldırım Aktuna, a medical doctor himself, had ordered regular monthly virginity tests for the women patients during his period as Chief Physician at the Istanbul Bakırköy Mental Hospital. His justification for this practice was "to protect women from the sexual abuse of men (both patients and staff).[153]

By 1995, a new statute went into effect in Turkey on "discipline in the high school education institutions," which stated that "'proof of unchastity' [was] a valid reason for expulsion from the formal education system; and in reading this decree, one determining criterion [was] the sex of the student."[154] It eventually became apparent that virginity testing was being used in a vast array of settings, that the police could "send women detainees (especially political detainees), sex workers, or crime suspects to have their virginity tested," and that "juridical authorities" could "require such a test as a means of gathering forensic evidence in relation to cases of alleged rape, encouraging prostitution, or acting as an intermediary, or sexual contact with minors."[155] Finally, in 1999, following a number of protests and discussions by women's groups, an amendment was passed that required a woman's consent for a virginity examination[156] and that limited the use of examinations to evidence gathering for sexual crime.[157]

153 Cındoğlu 2000, 221.

154 Seral 2000, 414.

155 Ibid, 413.

156 Parla 2000, 66.

157 Seral 2000, 415.

Most discussions of virginity examinations in Turkey emphasize the extent to which they are a violation of a woman's right to bodily integrity and thus contradict both constitutional law in Turkey, and international human rights norms.[158] Ayşe Parla, however, has analyzed virginity examinations on a more critical level, providing a much needed corrective to the discourse surrounding them, and challenging especially scholarship that attributes such legislation to some notion of "tradition" in Muslim or Middle Eastern states. In particular, Parla argues that "neither throwbacks to tradition, nor protections thereof, virginity examinations must be viewed as a particularly modern form of institutionalized violence used to secure the sign of the modern and/but chaste woman, fashioned by the modernization project."[159] She concludes that "the state's routinized intrusion into women's bodies comprises a fundamental facet of its sovereign claim over social relations in the name of the nation."[160] As such, Parla's analysis serves as an excellent bridge between the first of my two examples and the second.

The role of "the legal vagina" in United States legal discourse is, as Hyde notes, an increasingly important one. Indeed, Hyde's discussion of this rhetorical space is a compelling one, which he grounds particularly in an analysis of a 1991 Court of Appeals case, *Rodriques v Furtado*. In this case, Hyde notes, Shirley Rodriques sued police officers, a physician, a Massachusetts town, and a hospital after the possibility that she might be smuggling or selling drugs led to the issuing of "search warrants for appellant's apartment and vagina … by an assistant clerk of the Taunton (Massachusetts) District Court."[161] After searching her apartment, police officers "offered the opportunity to remove whatever might be hidden in her vagina voluntarily … [A]ppellant declined this suggestion and was escorted to the Morton Hospital."[162] At the hospital, "Dr. Falkoff conducted a visual and manual inspection of appellant's vaginal cavity," at which point "the search revealed an absence of foreign bodies."[163] Rodriques lost the lawsuit. In analyzing this case, Hyde compares it to the 1985 case that I mentioned above, in which Rudolph Lee's bodily integrity was, unlike Shirley Rodriques's, maintained, and indeed incorporated into protective political and legal structures and ideology. Hyde argues that, given the outcome of both cases,

> it is plain that the legal body of Shirley Rodriques is, somehow, less firm, more porous, more absent, than the body of Rudolph Lee. Like the body of Rudolph Lee, the body of Shirley Rodriques is a juridical artifact that is discursively constructed, then weighed. His is constructed as subject to "intrusion;" the state wrongfully proposed to "take control." Her body, by contrast, is constructed without reference to boundaries at all, a significant omission in a legal discourse often obsessed with the boundaries of the body.[164]

---

158 For example, Seral 2000, 414.

159 Parla 2000, 66.

160 Ibid, 66.

161 *Rodriques v Furtado*, 950 F.2d 805, 807 (1st. Cir. 1991) as cited in Hyde 1997, 165-166.

162 Ibid.

163 Ibid.

164 Ibid, 169.

Hyde likewise comments on the language and vocabulary of the Rodriques case:

> I do not think that the odd phrase "search revealed an absence" is careless or coincidental here, although I realize that in context it means an absence of drugs, not an absence of anything. Still, this is not the ordinary way in English of saying there were no drugs in Shirley Rodriques's vagina; the Court was reifying absence into a thing that can be verified.[165]

Throughout the 1990s, in other words, the "legal vagina" as a searchable space became an intricately defined political reality in both Turkey and the United States. In Turkey, the search was for virginity—something that could be found or not found, something the absence of which, in Hyde's words, could be verified. In the United States, the search was for drugs—again, something that could be found or not found, and something the absence of which could be verified. In Turkey, virginity examinations had far more to do with modern political belonging and sovereign relations than they had to do with sexual purity in and of itself. The repeated examination of political prisoners especially is an obvious indication of the political meaning of the examinations. In the United States as well, vaginal searches have far more to do with modern political belonging and sovereign relations than they have to do with drug possession in and of itself. The focus on searching (for) "foreign bodies,"[166] for instance, the extent to which searches happen most frequently at borders and in airports, and the fact that the vast majority of the searches are "unsuccessful"—and are known to be unsuccessful—are likewise obvious indications of the political meaning of the examined vagina.[167]

Perhaps most important, however, is that in both Turkey and in the United States, it is the very notion of a protected right to bodily integrity—the maintenance of a hyperbolic political subjectivity—that makes these legal violations of bodily integrity possible. In Turkey, especially after 1999, this political subjectivity was maintained via a recourse to consent. Undertaken on the bodies of "consenting citizens" who had, in consenting, waived their rights, the violation of bodily integrity implicit in the virginity examination was simultaneously a fortification of the right to bodily integrity. A waived right is still a right. Consent plays less of a role in the vaginal searches undertaken by United States police officers and customs officials—indeed Rodriques insisted that she had been physically forced onto and held down on the examination table. But a second, equally effective protector of rights was mobilized

165 Ibid, 168.

166 As Hyde points out "'The search revealed an absence of foreign bodies,' only Rodriques's body, which may or may not be foreign. (The body with drugs ingested is often conceptualized as a foreign assault on a pure American national body…)." Ibid, 167.

167 See also, "a recent case awarding damages to a traveler found to have been searched illegally—there was truly no basis for suspecting her of anything, except that she was Nigerian—nevertheless noted how common body cavity concealment has become as a method of drug smuggling … [I]n the year before the search held illegal, five people had been apprehended at the same airport smuggling drugs in body cavities. The court did note, however, that three-quarters of the passengers whose body cavities were searched, at the hospital performing such searches for Logan Airport in Boston, had concealed nothing in them…" Ibid, 169.

instead—that is, the issuance of a search warrant. Like the right to consent, the search warrant exists to protect United States citizens' rights, particularly their right to privacy—a right which by the 1990s had become inextricably entangled with the right to bodily integrity. The issuance of a search warrant, however—like consent—waives this right even as it reinforces it. It is precisely the protected nature of Rodriques privacy and bodily integrity—the existence of her rights—that make possible a legal search of her vagina. Neither the virginity examination nor the vaginal search is thus a rape. Neither is torture. Each is instead nothing more nor less than a reinforcement of a woman's right and duty to protect her bodily borders and to protect her political subjectivity via the violation of each.

What, then, is a rape? I have addressed over the past few pages the line between criminal sexual activity and non-criminal sexual activity both theoretically and anecdotally. We have seen that the coming together of consent and bodily integrity, as well as the conflation of autonomy and integrity, has led—theoretically, at least—to a situation in which all sex is a crime, mitigated merely by the existence of consent. We have likewise seen the complex process by which rape, newly defined as torture, has been differentiated from legal violations of bodily integrity—how the undermining of political subjectivity that accompanies rape and torture is held up against the fragile, coherent political self that is maintained when evidence (of rape, drug smuggling, or virginity) is gathered from a passive, trespassed body. Finally, we have seen the coming together of biological or bodily and political borders in these legal violations—a process nearly the opposite of the separation of the political from the biological or bodily that occurs in criminal violations.

What I would like to do now is look specifically at Turkish, French, and Italian adultery and rape legislation, and how this legislation conforms to these broader processes. After the Second World War, the Turkish government continued the process of almost continual legislative change that it had initiated in 1923. In 1953, the chapter of the criminal code addressing adultery was revised. Adultery remained a crime against public morality and the constitution of the family, but the punishments were made slightly heavier, the partner of the adulterous wife also had to be aware that she was married to be convicted, and although legal separation lightened the punishment for everyone involved, it was still heavier than it had been in the 1926 and 1938 laws.[168] The adulterous wife/concubine keeping husband dichotomy remained in place, with the wife designated "a wife who commits adultery,"[169] and the husband clumsily if significantly designated "a husband who keeps a woman not his wife together with his wife in their domicile, or who lives as man and wife in another place with this woman, such that everyone knows about it."[170]

These provisions remained in place until the 1990s, when various jurists and public figures began to look into abrogating them. Eventually, between 1996 and 1998, adultery ceased to be a crime in Turkey. Adultery did not, however, upon its decriminalization, disappear entirely from Turkish legal discourse. Indeed, by 2004,

168 "Türk ceza kanunu" 1994, Art. 440-444.

169 "*zina eden karı.*"

170 "*karısı ile birlikte ikamet etmekte olduğu evde yahut herkesçe bilinecek surete başka yerde karı koca gibi geçinmek için başkası ile evli olmıyan bir kadını tutmakta olan koca.*"

adultery had become an issue not just of national import, but of international concern, as European Union officials followed Turkish parliamentary debates over whether the abrogated articles of the criminal code ought to be revised and re-introduced.[171] Interestingly, however, both national and international conversations on the subject were couched not in the liberal political language of consent or liberty, but in the biopolitical language of bodily integrity. The issue at stake was whether legislation on adultery would or would not, first, undermine women's bodily borders, and second, assault national or civilizational borders. Whereas the Turkish Prime Minister Recep Tayyıp Erdoğan argued that the adultery legislation would protect women, "critics argue[d] it would be used mostly against women."[172] Guenter Verheugen, the European Union enlargement official, further argued that "the anti-adultery measure would create the impression that Turkey was moving toward Islamic law," and thus away from "Europe"[173]

The argument, in other words, became an argument primarily about the proper means of "protecting" women *and thus* notions of Europeanness as well as Turkishness. Whereas Erdoğan claimed that legislation against adultery would be the most protective of both, various European officials claimed that the absence of legislation would be the most effective. There was, contrarily, no debate whatsoever about 1) the assumption that adultery is an issue having to with women's bodies and 2) the assumption that it is the duty of the modern state to define and protect the borders of these women's bodies. The further fact that adultery became *the* stumbling block in the national and international redefinition of Turkey-as-European—that out of 348 new articles legislated during 2004, concerning everything from political crime to torture to personal status to corruption, it was the text on adultery that drew national and international attention—indicates the extent to which sexual legislation had irrevocably left the realm of the juridical and entered the realm of the biopolitical. Leaving aside the assumption that criminalizing adultery is an "Islamic" or un-"European" move[174]—such that the few reporters aware of the provenance of Turkey's earlier law almost but not quite succumbed to the temptation of turning Mussolini into a Muslim—what we see in both the legislation and the debate surrounding it is the complete overlap between political and sexual borders.[175]

171 Avcı 2005, 3-4.

172 Boland and Dombey 2004.

173 Meixler 2004.

174 I will address the various ways in which sexual and reproductive legislation has defined "Europe" in more detail in the next chapter.

175 There has not been a similar trend in European Union countries presumably because the adultery clauses in most European criminal codes have not been repealed. In Italy, for example, articles 559 and 560 of the Criminal Code remain in place, but have been declared unconstitutional and thus are not enforced. This, obviously, is quite different from actually de-criminalizing the behavior, as occurred in Turkey. On sex legislation in Italy, see Rains and Benedetti 2001, 12, note 76. Another likely reason for the discussion surrounding adultery in Turkey but not in European Union countries is the continuing neo-colonial logic that links deviant sexual behavior (and deviant sexual legislation) to "non-Western" and particularly Muslim populations and states.

Far more so than adultery law, however, rape law has provided a context for the articulation of women's bodies as biopolitical space, even as bodily integrity has become the most prominent right to protect. In Turkey, legislation enacted throughout the late 1980s and 1990s sought to establish gender equity via an overtly biological language.[176] The Turkish Constitution explicitly condemns gender privilege, for example, while nonetheless "respect[ing] women's objective biological and functional differences from men."[177] Turkish criminal law did not always conform to these Constitutional stipulations,[178] but various efforts were made to bring the two into conformity with one another. In 1989/90, for instance, following "a feminist campaign," in which "women went to the famous street of brothels in Istanbul to protest the Penal Code … [with the slogan] 'neither virtuous nor non-virtuous, we're just women,'"[179] the provisions reducing rape and abduction penalties if the woman was a prostitute were repealed. In 2003, the provisions reducing the penalty for the homicide of an adulterous spouse were likewise abrogated.[180] The hierarchy of penalties for abduction, based on the victim's marital status, however, was not.[181]

In 2004, completely new legislation concerning sexual crime was enacted in Turkey. In these new articles, rape is defined as a "crime against sexual inviolability," rather than a crime against morality or family order, and anyone who violates another's "bodily inviolability by sexual conduct," is punished. The penalty is increased if the violation involves "entering an organ or device into the body," spouses can be punished for violating one another, and the penalty is likewise more severe when

176 The 1953 legislation was not hugely different from that which preceded it—focusing a bit more on mental health issues and shifting the penalties to some extent. See, "Türk Ceza Kanunu" 1994, Title 8, Chap. 1, Art. 414-418, 421, 423-425, Chap. 2, 429-431, Chap. 4, Art. 437-439.

177 "In relation to gender equality, the Constitutional Court affirms that the principle of equal rights before law must be interpreted as conferring gender equality while seeking to 'respect women's objective biological and functional differences from men.' This view leads the Constitutional Court to the conclusion that if biological and functional differences create a differentiated behavior or privilege for one party only, such an interpretation is not constitutionally acceptable." Elver 2005, 284.

178 See, for example, "The equality between women and men paid lip service to by the Constitution is contradicted by the Penal Code which posits that attacks on the body constitute a breach of individual rights only when the bodies in question are male. The woman's body under sexual attack, on the other hand, is constructed not as a violation of individual rights, but of family order." Parla 2000, 77.

179 Gözaydın 2006, 64.

180 Avcı 2005, 5.

181 "Article 429 of the Code applies double standards according to the victims' marital status in cases of kidnapping. As such, basic principles of human rights are violated. These provisions have never been challenged by the Constitutional Court, despite endless discussions organized by women's rights groups. Similar discriminatory rules also can be found in the treatment of rape crimes. Article 438 provided reduced penalties for a man convicted of rape and abduction whenever the victim was shown to be a prostitute. This article was challenged in the Constitutional Court, but the Court rejected the claim on the grounds that 'dishonest women, i.e., a prostitute, should not be treated the same as honest women.' After much public debate, the Turkish Parliament in 1989 repealed the provision." Elver 2005, 299.

rape is committed by those in "public authority" or with "authority arising in working relations." If there is a blood relationship, if a gun or multiple people are involved, or if the victim cannot protect him or herself bodily or psychologically, the penalty is also heavier. Loss of health, battery, force resulting in the victim's entry into a vegetative state or in death all likewise increase the penalty.[182]

When we compare these stipulations to similar revisions made to the French and Italian codes throughout the 1990s and into the early twenty-first century, we can see that all three in various ways are conforming to the norms developed in international law. In France, for example, rape had by the late 1990s become a "crime against physical or mental (*psychique*) integrity," situated alongside provisions on torture and "acts of barbarism." Rape itself is defined as "sexual penetration of any sort, by violence, constraint, threat, or surprise." The penalty for rape becomes heavier if the rape results in a permanent illness or infirmity, if the victim is under 15 years of age, if the victim has a particular vulnerability, known or apparent to the perpetrator, due to age, illness, infirmity, physical or mental deficiency, or pregnancy. The penalty is increased if the perpetrator is a legitimate, natural, or adoptive blood relative, an individual with any authority over the victim, or an individual who is abusing an authority conferred by his or her function. The penalty is also heavier if the rape involves multiple perpetrators or multiple victims, if the victim made contact with the perpetrator by using a public telecommunications network, if the rape was undertaken because of the victim's sexual orientation, or if the perpetrator was the victim's partner, concubine, or an individual joined to the victim with a civil contract. Finally, particularly harsh punishments are reserved if the rape results in death, or if it was preceded or followed by torture or "acts of barbarism." The subsection following these provisions covers "sexual aggression" aside from rape, and the final subsection covers torture and "acts of barbarism."[183] The fascist Italian law was reformed in 1996, and is the most conservative of the three. Now designating rape a crime against the individual (and not against bodily integrity *per se*), it nonetheless de-emphasizes penetration and emphasizes a broader notion of "sexual violence." It also narrows the definition of "statutory rape" significantly, such that consensual sex between minors of 13 to 16 years of age is no longer prohibited.[184]

The Turkish code, in other words, speaks the new biological language of international law the most comfortably, emphasizing health, the inviolable body, and even the possibility of entering a vegetative state, while discarding the talk of "sexual penetration," "sexual aggression," and "violence" that remains in the French and Italian texts. The French code associates rape more explicitly with torture or barbarism, however, following the tendency in international law to see sexual crime as both a type of hate crime (against, for instance, a victim defined by his or her sexual orientation) and a "barbaric" act undertaken against humanity. In this way, far more than the Turkish or Italian codes, it re-invokes the late nineteenth and early twentieth century collective "civilization" as the victim of rape. None of the three

182 Gözaydın 2006, 68. See also, "Yeni Türk Ceza Kanunu—Yeni TCK 5237 sayılı kanun, 29.9.2004," 2004.

183 "Code Pénal" 2006, Chap. 2, Paragraph 1, Art. 222-23 to 222-26.

184 Everhart 1998, 692-695.

addresses consent in the way that international human rights norms have, but arguably the conflation of consent and bodily integrity remains in both the French and the Turkish laws—in the continuing references to guardianship or public contracts, for instance, as well as in the sliding scale of "force" that plays a central role now in the punishment of the crime rather than in its definition.

There is, moreover, an unambiguous overlap of autonomy and integrity in each text. The repeated references to the "bodily" and the "psychological" in the Turkish law and the "physical" and the "mental" in the French, for instance, clearly invoke the unbreakable link between a biologically intact body and a politically liberated self. Similarly, the reference to (implicitly non-consenting) victims with physical or mental deficiencies, or victims who cannot protect themselves bodily or psychologically, collapses into a single category: those whose autonomy has been assaulted (i.e., citizens capable of consent) and those whose integrity has been assaulted (i.e., citizens who cannot consent but whose dignity must be preserved).

Finally, and perhaps most importantly, there is the related overlap of political and biological borders in at least the French and the Turkish texts. In the French code, this is most overt, again, in the reference to "barbarism," implicitly held up as a concept "foreign" to civilizational norms in the French nation state. In the Turkish code, the very terminology used to discuss bodily integrity gets at the biopolitical nature of the legislation and at the physically passive, politically active nature of the new Turkish citizen. Literally, "*cinsel dokunulmazlık*," with the word "*cinsel*" a combination of "sexual," "generic," and "bodily," and "*dokunulmaz*" hovering somewhere among "inviolability," "political immunity," and most literally "untouchability," the phrase evokes mixed and overlapping connotations of biology, sexuality, uniformity, political identity, citizenship, and basic physical proximity. An attack on "bodily inviolability" is thus not a crime against "the individual" any more than an attack on "public morality" had been. It is a crime against simultaneously bodily and political boundaries, an assault on the Turkish nation state via a trespassing of the biological barriers surrounding the sexualized citizen's body.

In all of this late twentieth, early twenty-first century legislation, in other words, we can see concrete manifestations of the theoretical situations that I described above. The collapse of integrity into autonomy has produced a situation in which all violations of bodily integrity, including sex, are by definition criminal, mitigated rather than justified by circumstances such as consent. Likewise, the re-positioning of rape as the equivalent of torture especially in the French code creates a spectrum of legal and illegal violations of the body, and in particular plays up the importance of political subjectivity in defining legal trespasses. Finally, there is the fundamental overlap in each of the codes between the biological and the political—an overlap that suggests in the end that the only proper way to protect the right to bodily integrity is a constant legal violation of this right, committed within political structures, and committed upon a citizenry of consenting, physically passive bodies.

Conclusion

I started this chapter with a discussion of Foucault's "gender-neutral" suggestions for reforming late twentieth century French rape law. Unquestionably blind to the realities of patriarchal political, economic, and social structures, Foucault's proposed law has been, I believe correctly, criticized as missing the point completely of rape as a crime. But Foucault's scholarly project had little to do with gender—his interest was in the deployment of sexuality and in the extension of networks regulating both this sexuality and biology writ large. It indeed makes sense that he would not comprehend the full significance of a crime that is arguably as much about gender as it is about sex—and so perhaps he was not the best person to approach on this subject in the first place.

At the same time, Foucault's blindness to gender also seems to have led to a second, more fundamental, oversight in much of his work. In elaborating his theory of biopolitics, he does not seem to have recognized what a perusal of any national or international legal code would have made clear even by the 1970s: it was women's wombs and women's bodies that were playing the part of pre-eminent biopolitical space. Whether or not the French commission had accepted Foucault's proposal, therefore, they would nonetheless have been working within a 200-year-old tradition of situating biopolitical sovereign relations in a place defined at least in part by gender. It is thus, perhaps, an irony that advocates such as MacKinnon have triumphed over scholars such as Foucault in influencing recent legal trends; what they have created, indeed, is precisely the set of structures foretold—or perhaps threatened—by his work.

Chapter 4

Defining Europe

Introduction

Near the end of her discussion of "displaced persons" in *The Origins of Totalitarianism*, Hannah Arendt comments that

> the best criterion by which to decide whether someone has been forced outside the pale of the law is to ask if he would benefit by committing a crime. If a small burglary is likely to improve his legal position, at least temporarily, one may be sure he has been deprived of his human rights … [O]nly as an offender against the law can he gain protection from it.[1]

Arendt contextualizes this apparent failure of human rights doctrine within both the immediate political reality of the refugee camp, and within the broader historical reality of eighteenth and nineteenth century law and liberalism. In a footnote, she provides a concrete example of it, noting that whereas declarations of loyalty would not have preserved what she calls the constitutional rights of interned Japanese Americans during the Second World War, a jail sentence in fact would have.[2] In the section that follows, on "the perplexities of the rights of man," Arendt brings this paradox to its logical conclusion, arguing that "those outside the pale of the law may have more freedom of movement than a lawfully imprisoned criminal," and that in general they may be more physically free than rights-bearing citizens, but this type of liberty cannot change "in the least their fundamental situation of rightlessness."[3]

Although it is to some extent removed from a discussion of sexual and reproductive law, I would like to frame the final chapters of this book within Arendt's analysis of human rights. When she talks about the incarcerated, immobile, incapacitated prisoner as a bearer of rights that the free, mobile displaced person does not possess, Arendt is making a basic, if perhaps unintended, point about the relationship between political activity and physical inactivity. She is anticipating Scarry's analysis of consent, in which the physically incapacitated, anesthetized, dead body is the bearer of rights that the capable, alert, healthy body possesses only in theory. Both Arendt and Scarry are describing a biopolitical reality in which physical passivity is directly proportional to political activity. In Arendt's universe, the politically free "lawfully imprisoned criminal" is set up in opposition to the physically free "displaced person"

1 Arendt 1976, 286.

2 Ibid, 287, note 42.

3 Ibid, 296. She continues, "their freedom of movement, if they have it at all, gives them no right to residence which even the jailed criminal enjoys as a matter of course; and their freedom of opinion is a fool's freedom, for nothing they think matters anyhow."

whose politics do not matter. In Scarry's universe, the politically active, unconscious, consenting citizen is likewise set up in opposition to the physically and biologically active individual whose politics, again, do not matter. Each in a different way is hinting at one result of biopolitical rights-granting: a hyperbolically active political citizenry in a state of complete physical, biological, and sexual passivity.

I have addressed this aspect of rights-granting obliquely in the first two chapters of the book. When abortion, adultery, and rape legislation became central to sovereignty and citizenship formation, when this centrality was articulated in notions like "race suicide" on the one hand and in new rights-based sexual and reproductive readings of the social contract on the other, one of the major consequences was a redefining of both political and biological space. Each was transformed into *biopolitical* space, written across the bodies of a newly articulated biopolitical citizenry. The fact that it was precisely the rights most commonly associated, first, with juridical freedom, and second, with biological dignity—the right to consent and the right to bodily integrity—that were at the heart of sexual and reproductive legislation simply indicates the extent to which this linkage between political activity and sexual or biological passivity was key to even the most basic of sovereign relationships.

And indeed, this interpretation of the sovereign relationship and the central role played by sexual and reproductive legislation in defining it has continued into the twenty-first century. The broadening of the categories of those incapable of consent but also protected by consent theory that we saw in the fascist period, for example, has by no means diminished in contemporary legislation—predicated as it is on Arendt's notion of the rights-bearing criminal, protected by law only because he or she has violated it. The collapse of bodily integrity into bodily autonomy with which we ended the twentieth century has likewise been essential to twenty-first century trends, producing a situation in which sexual behavior is by definition a criminal trespassing of bodily borders—an assault on the citizen described by Scarry, who exists solely as a biologically passive space with boundaries, a physically inert setting with borders, but who is nonetheless politically active by virtue of this same physical passivity.

In fact, as I will argue over the rest of this chapter, contemporary jurisprudence has not been a simple by-product of, but has been aimed precisely at constructing, this biologically/sexually passive, politically active sovereign subject. The citizen, as he or she was articulated in nineteenth and twentieth century abortion, adultery and rape legislation has become the citizen at the heart of twenty-first century sovereign relations. Defined first and foremost as a biological (sexual and reproductive) criminal in need of regulation, this citizen can operate only in (and as) biopolitical space. Indeed, as I will suggest, the point of legislation aimed at those who do not possess full citizenship rights (refugees, for instance) is not to render illegal biological activity on their part legal, but to render irrelevant biological activity on their part "criminal." To the extent that reproductive and sexual legislation has helped to define "Europe" in other words, sketching a civilizational line between the inside and the outside, it has also defined an emphatically biopolitical European citizenry.

Europe

I have already gone into some detail about late nineteenth and early twentieth century fears of race suicide, about the fact that by the late nineteenth century "not only did a woman carry the fate of her kin in her womb, now she also carried the fate of an entire class, ethnicity, race, and nation,"[4] and about the interesting turn of contemporary scholarship that sees the French correct about their depopulation and the Turks mistaken. I do not want to dwell too extensively on these issues again here. I do, however, want to pick up on a few of their implications, and how these implications have affected contemporary legislation. With that in mind, in 1878, a traveler to the Ottoman Empire wrote within a larger discussion of the imperial harem that,

> a few years ago the mother of Sultan Abdul-Aziz, desirous of further reducing the number [of women with the "honorable title of wife"], brought forward an old palace regulation that every woman found *enceinte* should be subjected to the operation of artificial abortion, with the exception of the first four wives.[5]

In 1920, the American birth control advocate Margaret Sanger situated an analysis of population growth within a broader discussion of the "ignorant resignation" of women worldwide and of their lack of knowledge about their "reproductive nature." She made the point that,

> obeying the inner urge of their true natures, *some* women revolted. They went even to the extreme of infanticide and abortion. Usually the revolts were not general enough. They fought as individuals not as a mass. In the mass, they sank back into blind and hopeless subjection. They went on breeding with staggering rapidity, those numberless, undesired children who become the clogs and the destroyers of civilization.[6]

And she continued,

> among the Hindus and Muhammedans, artificial abortion is extremely common … [I]n Persia, every illegitimate pregnancy ends with abortion. In Turkey, both among the rich and the poor, even married women very commonly procure abortion after they have given birth to two children, one of which is a boy.[7]

In 2001, a French senate commission stated that although it was important for women to attain economic and political equality with men and to exercise their juridical rights, this equality would be meaningless without the more basic right to control their reproductive behavior. The commission continued, "it is for this reason that the progress of this right in the West, and especially in France, has attained such importance, and that it was at the vanguard of the historical movement of

4 Stormer 2000, 115-116.
5 Blunt and Lane-Poole 1878, 254.
6 Sanger 1920, 5.
7 Ibid, 14.

societies toward modernity."[8] Indeed, the "birth control movement" is attributed to "feminists in Anglo-Saxon countries at the beginning of the twentieth century," it is seen as a movement based in the principle that women should be granted "sanitary security," and it is historically linked to the fact that even prior to the legalization of birth control, abortions were frequent, even though the "rudimentary nature of the techniques employed" produced unfortunate results, disabilities, or even death.[9] The commission's statement concludes that if the goal is to diminish the number of abortions in general, restricting access to them in fact makes little sense—that even if France adopts legislation regulating abortion, most of its neighbors in the European Union already have more flexible laws.[10]

Obviously each of these analyses of abortion is mobilized for different goals and is grounded in different political (and civilizational) assumptions. The first is a mid-nineteenth century variation on the late eighteenth century discourse adopted by Pouqueville: abortion is an Eastern, Ottoman oddity, the product of a tyrannical household/state, in which the irrational needs and desires of the sovereign (or his mother) result in the subjection of women to artificial attacks on their bodies and their reproductive capacities. Implicitly invoked in the quotation is the decline of the Ottoman state as well as the relationship between political decline and these inappropriate forms of governance or reproductive behavior. In the second quotation, abortion is still an Eastern oddity—indeed so weirdly commonplace that "every illegitimate pregnancy ends with [it]." The rhetorical purpose of invoking this oddity is different, however. Abortion is still linked to civilization, to politically resonant "mass revolts" and individual struggles, but it is described such that "we" should think to ourselves how backward it is that "even in the East," women control their reproductive behavior, whereas we still do not. The final passage is essentially a mirror image of the first two. Here, abortion is not an Eastern oddity, but part of a Western progress narrative. It is one aspect of the "historical movement of societies toward modernity," it is linked intimately to broader economic, political and social rights, and it is the product of a particularly French (and/or "Anglo-Saxon") philosophy of "sanitary security" that traces its origins back to the early twentieth century. Abortion legislation is a way of defining France's relationship to Europe, and Europe's relationship to the rest of the world—a way of defining in a quite elementary way whether or not a nation state is part of the Western project.

The most basic detail that connects these three passages, in other words, is that each invokes abortion as a civilizational identifier. In the first two, there is Europe and then there is the land of the "Hindus and the Muhammedans." The former is a place with no abortions, whereas abortions are everywhere in the latter. This situation is indicative either of the political weakness, tyranny, and decline of the latter, or of the extent to which the former must pay close attention to its eroding civilizational superiority. In the third passage, there is still Europe, it is still placed into the West, and there is still the rest of the world implicitly held up against not-Europe and the East. This time, however, it is the former that is defined by access to abortions,

8 Terrade 2001.
9 Ibid.
10 Ibid.

indeed by the fact that the movement toward reproductive freedom started there. It is now implicitly in the latter—a not-Europe, not at the vanguard of progress and modernity—that reproductive freedom has been stifled, obstructed, and frustrated. Whatever its broader rhetorical purpose, in other words, abortion legislation is also playing a more narrowly defined role in all three of these passages, operating as an indicator and symbol of political and civilizational boundaries. Europe is progressive because abortion does not occur within its borders. Europe is progressive because abortion does occur within its borders. Whatever the case, Europe is both Europe and progressive because, fundamentally, of abortion.

That sexual and reproductive behavior, norms, standards, or laws, however—regardless of their actual meaning or resonance—operate as civilizational identifiers is certainly not something that has gone unnoticed over the past decades.[11] For my purposes, therefore, far more meaningful than the fact that these political and civilizational walls and boundaries were constructed is the *way* in which they were constructed. It is indeed arguably this language of reproduction in particular that has been instrumental in the elaboration of a biologically passive, politically active citizenry within Europe. When we look in more detail at each of the passages, we can see that each is operating as far more than a simple signpost along the border of the East/West divide.

In the first quotation, for example, what the writer finds particularly striking is not simply that abortions occur in the Ottoman Empire, but that they a) occur among women imprisoned in harems, b) occur among women imprisoned in harems who do not possess the *quasi* political title of "honorable wife," and c) occur at the likewise *quasi* political behest of the Sultan's mother. The writer, in other words, is mobilizing well worn themes of the harem as prison and of the harem as state. The women subject to abortions are imprisoned, but they—unlike Arendt's "lawfully imprisoned criminal"—do not have political rights, or even a *quasi*-political designation. What is particularly meaningful in the description of the abortions in the Ottoman Empire, in other words, is not that they happen at all, or even that they happen only in the East, but that they happen among a physically passive *and* politically passive population—a group utterly inactive, deprived of rights, and only *in this way* indicative of a deeper Ottoman political malaise. What is at issue in the description is the physically, politically passive Ottoman subject held up against the physically passive, politically active European citizen.

The "Persia" described by Sanger would seem to operate according to somewhat different standards. Sanger introduces her discussion of reproduction by juxtaposing the politically doomed nature of the individual woman's revolt—a desperate revolt undertaken by a woman without hope of changing her political status and driven to the "extreme" of abortion or infanticide—with the likely success of a mass revolt undertaken by knowledgeable women possessed of a revolutionary consciousness. When Sanger turns to the "Hindus and the Muhammedans," therefore, she has already both described one type of inappropriate reproductive behavior and set it up against the backdrop of another type of appropriate reproductive behavior. Birth control taken or abortions performed by women who do not understand the

11 See Said 1979, *passim*.

political meaning behind them, by women who are simply one part of a group of ignorant individuals, by women who are emphatically not members of the politically defined "mass," cognizant of its role in a political movement, are inappropriate. They suggest physical activity, but not political activity. They produce, in other words, a citizenry biologically active but politically passive—just as irrelevant to functional modern political structures as the biologically passive, politically passive women imprisoned in the Ottoman harem. Although the women of Persia are active reproductively, therefore, their political inactivity disqualifies them from membership in a progressive, rights-based "West."

And indeed, the early twenty-first century French senate commission describes this rights-based West in detail. Intent on defining France, Europe, and Western Civilization in general, explicit about the connections between reproductive behavior and social, political, and economic rights, the commission's statement makes absolutely clear the relationship between political activity and modern citizenship, as well as the relationship between *women's* political activity and France's position in Europe and the West. At the same time, as it maps these boundaries and reinforces these rights, the commission's statement links them to a physical or biological passivity. The passage, for example, emphasizes above all sanitary *security*—not sanitary freedom or sanitary autonomy. The political activity explicitly exercised by women citizens in Europe, therefore, is conceived of as a product *not* of biological (or sanitary) activity—*not* of liberty or autonomy—but of biological passivity, dignity, and security. The politically active woman citizen described in the commission's statement is thus also a physically passive one—emphatically secure but just as emphatically not biologically active. The civilizational barriers, in other words, are just as much predicated on the ideal reproductive citizen, politically active and physically passive, as their eighteenth and nineteenth century counterparts were.

There is a similar trend in scholarly discussions of the West, the not-West, and sexual or reproductive legislation. One analysis of the contemporary adultery discourse and human rights rhetoric, for example, addresses the colonial language in which Islamic law in Nigeria is examined.[12] Focusing in particular on the case of Amina Lawal, sentenced to death by stoning for adultery, and what is termed the Western obsession with "saving" her, the article notes,

> this bias toward issues involving gender and sexuality ignores the breadth of Nigeria's *Sharia* related human rights violations. Despite gender disparities in Islamic substantive and procedural law, men have also been sentenced to death by stoning. People have lost limbs under Nigeria's newly instituted *Sharia* law as punishments for thefts of items worth less than one hundred dollars. Yet in the West, knowledge of *Sharia* in Nigeria

12 "Saving Amina Lawal" 2004, 2367. "The second reason for alarm at the focus on 'saving' women is that it evokes a colonialist rhetoric that positions Nigeria's human rights problems within the framework of a conflict between a Western or 'colonialist' human rights ideology and a religion or culture—in this case, Islam. It is significant, and not surprising, that Ms. Lawal is seen as symbol of the conflicts between an Islamic 'fundamentalist' movement and an international community that espouses a human rights ideology."

for the most part remains limited to Ms Lawal's case and other cases involving women sentenced to *hudud* punishments for unlawful intercourse.[13]

In a 2005 analysis of the rape trial, "M.C. v. Bulgaria," heard in the European Court of Human Rights, a second scholar discusses

> the trend in rape jurisprudence across jurisdictions away from a narrow, rigid, and formalistic definition of rape, in which the key focus was on physical force, toward an understanding of rape in which lack of consent was perceived to be the central element. "The development of law and practices in [this] area" the Court observed "reflects the evolution of societies toward effective equality and respect for each individual's autonomy" … [T]he Court observed [in 1991] that "the abandonment of the unacceptable idea of a husband being immune against prosecution from rape of his wife was in conformity not only with a civilised concept of marriage but also, and above all, with the fundamental objectives of the Convention, the very essence of which is respect for human dignity and human freedom.[14]

Again, the primary point to note about these two passages is that each in a different way mobilizes sexual legislation as a means of drawing boundaries between East and West, Europe and not-Europe. The first quotation begins with a critique of the colonial rhetoric that assumes a monolithic East and a monolithic West, the former defined by its uncivilized treatment of women and its barbaric approach to sex. It then concludes, however, with a reification of this rhetoric in the turn toward "Western knowledge of *Sharia* in Nigeria."

There is, in other words, the West, and then there is Nigeria. Nigeria is a place in which assaults on bodily integrity occur, and the specific issue at stake is what is "known" in the West about these assaults. The divide that is produced is thus a divide between the *knowledge* of Nigeria's sexualized assaults on bodily integrity that "we" see in the West, and the *actuality* of generalized assaults on bodily integrity that occur in Nigeria itself. The civilizational boundaries thus remain unchanged, as does the role of sexual legislation in reinforcing them—they are simply rearticulated in an apparent critique of the colonial implications of such discussions. In the second passage, the rhetorical mapping of Europe is simpler. Like the statement of the French senate commission, the decision of the European Court of Human Rights is here situated within an unquestioned progress narrative. Whereas once there was little respect paid to a woman's right to human dignity, freedom, and sexual autonomy, now societies have "evolved." Indeed, as of 1991, European law has become explicitly "civilized" (as opposed, one assumes, to "barbaric") in its interpretation of the relationship between a woman's sexual identity and her political identity.

My purpose in making these points, however, is again less to demonstrate the ways in which sexual legislation has been mobilized as a means of drawing civilizational boundaries—a project that could continue *ad infinitum*—and more to explore the *type* of citizenship in Europe or in the West that the drawing of these boundaries has produced. In the first passage, for example, there are two basic points

13 Ibid, 2366.

14 Conaghan 2005, 151, 155.

being made: first, in the West and in civilized states, the right to bodily integrity supersedes the right to property or the marital contract. If the punishments in Nigeria are disproportionate and a violation of human rights norms, this is because the loss of property (theft) is less important than the loss of a limb (the punishment), or because a violation of the marital contract (adultery) is less meaningful than a violation of an individual's bodily borders (the punishment). The second point being made is that knowledge in the West about these Nigerian issues is partial and even damaging—focusing inappropriately on the stoning/marital contract question and marginalizing the dismemberment/theft question.

All of this is obvious. At the same time, however, in making these points, the author of the piece is likewise making a statement about the nature of citizenship in Nigeria and, more so, the nature of citizenship in the West. In Nigeria, the state values property and contracts over bodily integrity, it regulates and protects property and contracts far more so than it does bodily integrity, and therefore the political identity of its citizenry is linked more to the former than to the latter. The Nigerian citizen is politically active *and* physically active, in other words—his or her body rendered passive only insofar as a crime against contracts or property has been committed. Indeed the citizen's body is defined as *so* physically active that removing the limb that perpetrated a crime is a legally meaningful act.

In someplace called the West, contrarily, states value bodily integrity over property and contracts. Legal systems in these states protect and regulate the former more rigorously than they do the latter, and the political identity of their citizenry is thus linked more to the former than to the latter. By virtue of his or her human rights, the citizen in the West is indeed subject to a constant interest in his or her bodily integrity—the passivity of his or her body integral to his or her political activity. The bodies of citizens in Western states are defined as *so* physically passive, in fact, so subjugated to political activity broadly defined, that their violation is instantly imagined above all as an assault on humanity as a whole. In addition to reifying the East/West divide, in other words, this approach to sexual legislation likewise makes humanity a "Western" phenomenon.[15]

The passage on the European Court of Human Rights operates according to the same assumptions. In addition to defining "Europe" and especially "European civilization," the Court's decision invokes all of the tropes regarding contemporary citizenship that we have seen so far. Downplaying force and emphasizing consent, it posits the trespassing of biological boundaries as the real crime in rape—assuming

15 My intent here is not to make a culturally relativist remark about how Nigerians naturally behave "that way" and about how critiquing this behavior is an imperial move. Rather, I want to discuss the various ways in which discussions of something called Nigerian behavior, and in particular something called the Nigerian violation of bodily integrity, have served to reinforce the East/West divide. Arguably, such behaviors and such violations of bodily integrity are much the same in the "East" and in the "West." The violation of bodily integrity involved in a court ordered vaginal search in the United States, for example, is not less invasive than many Nigerian punishments. As for the inappropriate or disproportionate imposition of the death penalty (i.e., "stoning"), there is a vast literature on similarly inappropriate and disproportionate impositions of the death penalty—especially to the extent that they have served as a means of racist political control—in the United States in particular.

an inert body and an autonomous individual, a politically active, physically passive citizen operating in biopolitical space. Linking sexual legislation to broader notions of "human dignity" and "human freedom" it indeed renders the political nature of this biological trespass hyperbolic—producing an exact overlap between bodily and political barriers.

Moreover, this overlap between the bodily and the political—this emphasis on the biopolitical nature of citizenship—has created a situation in Europe and on its margins in which any dichotomy between left and right, between liberal and authoritarian, has disappeared in discussions of sexual and reproductive law. In Italy, for example, one scholar has noted that "only on those relatively rare occasions when they unite on a specific issue—such as divorce or abortion—have [coalition partners] been able to prevail."[16] Similarly, it is only in the context of abortion legislation that the Italian neo-fascist party, the MSI, has invoked a liberal rhetoric of "constitutional equality"—in this case the "equality of spouses."[17] In Turkey, one of the most fundamental ways in which the far right (and likewise neo-fascist) party, the MHP, departs from its own and other far right political ideologies is in its approach to abortion and contraception:

> The MHP considers a strong family structure as guaranteeing the preservation of Turkish culture … [A]bortion is strictly rejected on the grounds that it is the result of ineffective family planning schemes. Therefore, diverging from many European extreme right-wing parties, the MHP in Turkey is not against contraception.[18]

Similarly, it has been precisely at moments of authoritarian military rule in Turkey that the movement toward sexual and reproductive liberty has been at its most vigorous:

> The 1982 Constitution forbade political associations of youth, women, and other groups, reducing the relevance of citizen action across Turkey. However, women's organizations benefited from these limitations in the long run as they were touted as "less dangerous" by the military than leftist movements. The emergence of feminist movements in this politically sterilized environment of the 1980s is a good example of the possibilities of such policy in Turkey.[19]

I bring up these points simply to indicate the extent to which sexual and reproductive legislation is now operating in a biopolitical, rather than in a classical-juridical,

16 For the most part, they have "parlayed their small portion of electoral support into cabinet positions, in that way gaining a voice in government and access to some patronage." Spotts and Wieser 1986, 16.

17 "For example, the Neo-Fascist Party (MSI) argued that to include a clause stating that the consent of one parent would be sufficient in the case of a minor seeking an abortion would infringe the equality of the spouses provided for in Article 3 of the Constitution." Caldwell 1981, 52.

18 Arıkan 1999, 130.

19 In a footnote, number 64, that follows this passage: "In this period, women's NGOs attempted to get the military government to legalize abortion, which it did in 1983, and to ratify CEDAW, which it did not do until a few years later." Elver 2005, 301.

framework in modern European nation states. Whereas it is true that each of these examples may seem like a minor discrepancy in specifically Turkish or Italian party politics, I believe that they also point to the unique nature of sexual and reproductive legislation. It is precisely within the context of legislation on marriage, divorce, abortion, contraception, and sexuality-related issues that left/right and liberal/authoritarian ideologies and distinctions cease to be meaningful. The ordinarily fractious Italian party political scene unites *only* over such subjects as "divorce or abortion." It is likewise *only* when faced with changes to reproductive legislation that neo-fascist parties in Italy as well as in Turkey abandon their platforms and begin speaking a language of liberal freedom (if, perhaps, a disingenuous variation on this language). Finally, it has been only by virtue of the post-coup authoritarian regime of the 1980s that feminist movements in Turkey have achieved so many decisively liberal goals in their sexual and reproductive agendas. Indeed, the term "politically sterilized environment" in the final passage above is arguably about more than just the absence of debate in a public sphere. It is also indicative of the clash between the inherently biopolitical nature of reproductive law—a law irrelevant to notions of left and right or liberal and authoritarian—and the inherently classical-juridical nature of party politics. Political sterility, in other words, leads directly to biopolitical productivity.

Even as sexual and reproductive legislation has been instrumental in drawing civilizational boundaries, therefore, in defining what is inside Europe and what is outside, it has also produced biopolitical citizens and been itself the product of biopolitical, rather than classical-juridical, discourses. That "women's issues"—and sexuality and reproduction in particular—have been the canvas on which the West/East, civilized/barbaric divide has been sketched is nothing new. The *way* in which this divide has been articulated, however, deserves further attention. It is not just that uncivilized populations outside of a self-described Europe or the West are assumed to misunderstand "women's issues" in abstract, general ways. It is that these populations and state structures are seen to deviate from a very specific formulation of appropriate political belonging. They are composed of illegitimately imprisoned, politically passive, harem-bound women. Or they are made up of wildly sexual, biologically active perpetrators of infanticide. Never, though, do they comprise the politically active, physically passive, biopolitical ideal—the ideal so central to twenty-first century European, international and humanitarian legislation.

Refugee Sexuality

Despite the fact that these apparently non-European or non-Western notions of citizenry are held up as inadequate, however, the citizens of such states are still seen as citizens. They still operate within a space delimited by some variation on national protection and/or liberty. They are still defined first and foremost as individuals with a political identity. Refugees, contrarily, are not "even" that. And over the next few pages, I want to discuss what happens when sexual and reproductive legislation is enacted on behalf of populations who are precisely "not even that"—on behalf of populations who do not possess even the faulty, partial rights attributed to the non-

European national. In doing so, I will suggest that one consequence of nineteenth, twentieth, and twenty-first century trends in abortion, adultery, and rape law has been the development of a new type of sexuality, a sexuality that is neither deviant nor normal, neither legal nor criminal—a "refugee sexuality" unique to displaced populations.

Arendt, again, paints in broad strokes a number of political characteristics unique to refugees, displaced persons, or stateless people. These characteristics are for the most part defined by their absence—active citizens, for example, have rights and identities; refugees have neither. Refugees may be physically free and unconstrained, but they are absent any actual political traits. A list of the things that the active citizen can do by virtue of his or her political identity that the refugee cannot do thus includes not just participating in elections, say, or making use of national health care systems. It also includes the rights-based behaviors that I have discussed in previous chapters—behaviors such as consenting to political and/or sexual relationships, mapping bodily integrity onto some interpretation of national integrity, or securing the health and integrity of a specific nation within an individual womb. It is only the status of citizen, in other words, that makes consent, bodily integrity, and reproductive freedom meaningful. And indeed, sexual and reproductive legislation has been articulated on behalf of the citizens of nation-states in a distinctly different way than it has been on behalf of their stateless counterparts over the past century.

Within the nation-state, for example, it has been the repeated definition and redefinition of the right to consent and the right to bodily integrity that has gradually rendered sexual behavior criminal and reproductive space subject to political regulation. Writing consent across the body and collapsing bodily integrity into bodily autonomy irrevocably transformed the political meaning of abortion, adultery, and rape. Within the international or stateless context, however, although sex has likewise become criminal and reproductive space has also become an arena subject to regulation, this transformation has resulted from the nature and status of the "refugee," rather than from a redefinition or reinterpretation of rights *per se*. Refugees *as* refugees, as non-citizens and non-bearers of rights, cannot consent, and therefore all sex among them is criminal. The wombs of refugees are displaced onto no national collective, they are related to no rights-based national structure, and stateless reproductive space has thus become the responsibility of every nation. To the extent, in other words, that sexual and reproductive behavior and legislation has become inextricably linked to citizenship rights over the eighteenth, nineteenth, twentieth, and twenty-first centuries, refugees, people without rights and without nations, have been excluded from them.

At the same time, it is important to emphasize that refugees have of course not *actually* been excluded. Neither sexual nor reproductive behavior among stateless people has been treated as theoretically or practically criminal since at least the Second World War. Moreover, since Arendt was writing in the 1950s, there has been a concerted effort to lift the notion of rights out of the framework of the nation state, and to produce a set of international norms that hold regardless of an individual's citizenship or lack thereof.[20] Nonetheless, I want to argue over the remainder of this section that it has been precisely this process of endowing refugees with rights, of moving sexual and reproductive autonomy and dignity out of the realm of the nation-state and into the realm of the international community, that has produced the oddity that is "refugee sex."[21] Indeed, what was suggested in the national legislation—the

20 For example, "to paint with a broad brush, the international community created two regimes to address human rights abuses: one, the human rights regime, to monitor and deter abuse, and the other, the refugee regime, to provide surrogate state protection to some of those who are able to cross borders. Human rights lawyers and scholars have viewed refugee law as too embedded in domestic immigration law and institutions. The great innovation of the international human rights movement of the past half-century was to bring human rights 'out of the confines of domestic legal systems' and into the realm of international law and institutions. Under the Refugee Convention, the responsibility to provide international protection—a surrogate to the ruptured, national protection—is placed on states that are parties to the Convention. Thus, refugee law is implemented by states and, to the extent possible, through domestic legal systems. In many other respects, the refugee regime seems different from the international human rights regime. For example, there is no regularized monitoring of states' compliance with their obligation to provide surrogate protection, although the United Nations High Commissioner for Refugees (UNHCR) serves an important supervisory function. No refugee-specific, international institutions hear interstate complaints or individual communications." Anker 2002, 135. See also, "the final step in the development of international refugee law should then be to identify refugee law completely with the human rights that are internationally recognized. A new refugee definition should incorporate the UDHR as the basis for refugee status. A violation of the standards for individual rights embodied in the UDHR would result in refugee recognition. At the point in the definition of the enumerated categories, the new definition might substitute the following: 'Because of persecution or a well-founded fear of persecution on account of a violation of the principles embodied in the Universal Declaration of Human Rights.' Such a general reference to the UDHR, however, would result in ambiguity and thus would not accomplish the necessary aim of deepening the legal foundations of the refugee definition. Therefore, the new definition should include precise language adapted from the UDHR articles themselves." Parrish 2000, 258-9258–9.

21 It is also worth pointing out that the refugee population is predominantly female and subject particularly to gender-related legislation: "Worldwide, throughout the 1990s, there were between 13.5 and 17.6 million refugees living outside of their countries and in need of protection each year. Women and children comprise approximately 80 percent of the refugee population, despite the fact that in many cases they do not play an active role in the crises that have displaced them from their homes, such as armed conflicts, political and racial violence, and natural disasters. Furthermore, a pattern of denying women their basic rights in a refugee-producing home country tends to replicate itself in the community-in-exile … [I]t is critical that refugee women be documented and registered as such because registration is necessary to obtain international assistance and work authorization in many refugee camps. Procedures for registering refugees must take into account women's particular requirements, such as reluctance to speak openly with male service providers, particularly regarding sexual abuse. Indirect questions about gender-based persecution must be utilized, as women feel stigmatized by such incidents, and more women service providers must be available for refugee women to discuss their persecution." Harris 2000, 30. See also, "the phrasing of this commitment is clearly applicable to those refugee girls who barter sex for food, supplies, and

criminalization of sex and the regulation of reproduction—has become an exaggerated reality in international law and transnational European legislation.[22]

Recall that in national legislation, as I argued in the last chapter, sexual behavior gradually came to be seen as a violation of bodily integrity, thus criminal, and only mitigated by the presence of consent. The only non-criminal trespass of bodily borders became that initiated by the sovereign—in the form, for instance, of the forensic examination—and this particular violation of bodily borders paradoxically reinforced the citizen's right to bodily integrity.[23] Reproduction, likewise, became a political act that turned women's wombs into regulated space. As the various rights surrounding it were articulated and then extended to women citizens, their behavior ceased to have any political meaning, while their existence as settings became of vital importance.

In the international and European law directed at refugees, these interpretations of sexual and reproductive crime have been if anything more pronounced. The purpose of international and transnational European legislation on sexuality, for example, has arguably been not to turn a formerly criminal act[24] into a legal act, but rather to turn a formerly irrelevant act into a criminal act.[25] Similarly, the trend in reproductive legislation has been not to render refugees active and autonomous individuals, but rather to make them meaningful biopolitical spaces. Its purpose, in other words, has been to endow rights-less refugees with the same rights as nationals[26]—to turn them into tolerated sexual criminals and regulated reproductive spaces, just as active national citizens are. Put another way, its purpose has been to help Arendt's physically free, politically non-existent stateless refugee become a physically incarcerated, politically significant "lawfully imprisoned criminal."

---

other favors when it is read in tandem with the instructions of article 22, directing States Parties to 'take appropriate measures to ensure that a child who is … considered a refugee … receives appropriate protection and humanitarian assistance in the enjoyment of applicable rights set forth in the present Convention' … Ratified by nearly all nations of the world, with the notable exception of the United States, this explicit responsibility cannot be denied. The Committee on the Rights of the Child, established under this Convention, must be called upon to effectively monitor its implementation. In addition to the categorical protection of children, international law also provides broad protection to women (including girl children) from discrimination and violence, which directly applies to female refugees. The Convention on the Elimination of All Forms of Discrimination Against Women (CEDAW), adopted by the U.N. General Assembly in 1979, 'condemn[s] discrimination against women in all its forms' and includes any distinction made on the basis of gender which has *the effect or purpose* of impairing women's ability to enjoy their human rights.[italics in original]." Murray 2000, 1009.

22 One scholar inadvertently makes this point in her discussion of the role of consent in ICTY rulings: "presumably, the court found that it was not bound to include a consent paradigm because first, consent was only one theory used by major legal systems of the world, and second, a consent paradigm would transpose poorly to the international arena." Kalosieh 2003, 130.

23 Like Arendt's "offender against the law" who in violating it gains protection from it.

24 The violation of bodily borders without consent.

25 The violation of bodily borders with consent as a mitigating circumstance.

26 See above, Anker and Parrish.

From biologically active, politically passive refugees, displaced people are meant to become biologically passive, politically active citizens—even if they are citizens only of "the world" or at most of "Europe."

Perhaps one of the most obvious places in the late twentieth and early twenty-first century in which this process has played out is in the former Yugoslavia. While it is true that Bosnian women have not always been described as refugees in the technical sense, they were effectively deprived of their political identity and their rights as citizens over the 1990s, and they were subject to treatment *as* refugees by both Serbian soldiers and jurists or scholars of European and international law. As Karen Engle has noted in a discussion of sexuality and reproduction in wartime Bosnia, Bosnian women were portrayed repeatedly and relentlessly as individuals absent any political, sexual, or reproductive agency or identity, non-existent in precisely the way that refugees are: "both women's rights advocacy and the ensuing jurisprudence," she argues, "tended to reify ethnic differences, diminishing women's capacity to engage in sexual activity with the 'enemy' during the war, and to downplay the extent to which any but extraordinary women could be perpetrators in war."[27]

Addressing the extent to which this portrayal of Bosnian women influenced the international tribunal's rulings on sexual crime, and in particular on rape, Engle states,

> when the Tribunal made factual findings that the witnesses had engaged in sexual intercourse with the accused it severely limited the possibility of a consent defense. The consent defense was most restricted in the appeals decision in *Kunarac* … [B]ecause the appeals chamber found that the circumstances in Foča were inherently coercive, it did not require the prosecution to prove lack of consent for each of the rapes, concluding that the notion of consent was meaningless in such circumstances … [B]y presuming coercion, the ICTY's jurisprudence essentially makes consensual relationships legally impossible in some sets of circumstances, which would include those around Foča … [T]his broad reading of "armed conflict" suggests that all sexual relationships between Bosnian Muslim civilians and Serbian soldiers in Bosnia and Herzegovina could be seen as nonconsensual, expanding the reach of *Kunarac* well beyond Foča.[28]

---

27 Engle 2005, 784. A similar paradigm held in discussions of rape in Rwanda, where a point of primary importance was the victims' status as internal refugees: "the Tribunal's treatment of the elements and defenses to the crime of rape has evolved. In the 1992 International Tribunal for Rwanda (ICTR) case *Prosecutor v. Akayesu*, some of the victims/witnesses were displaced civilians who had sought refuge in a municipal building. 'Akayesu served as burgomaster of the Taba commune, which gave him exclusive control over the communal police and responsibility for maintaining public order within the commune.' He regularly subjected the refuge seekers to sexual violence by armed local militia. Many acts were committed by more than one assailant at a time, under threats of death and bodily harm. The victims lived in a constant state of fear and psychological trauma due to the sexual violence and beatings they endured for weeks." Kalosieh 2003, 127

28 Engle 2005, 803-806. Engle also argues that "[The *Kunarac*] decision's discussion of consent, torture, and armed conflict combine, I argue, to reinforce an understanding that Bosnian Muslim women had little, if any, sexual agency during the war." For an example of this argument, see "while the ICTY's definition of consent laudably incorporates the notion of sexual autonomy, and is a liberal standard relative to consent requirements globally, the

With regard to *reproductive* crime in Bosnia, Engle makes a similar point, especially to the extent that rape has become equated with genocide:

> Advocates using this definition of genocide [forced impregnation as a means to prevent births] argued that, when a Muslim woman was forced to carry a child (or fetus) that resulted from a Serbian rape, her womb was "occupied" by the enemy, making her "incapable of conceiving and bearing a child of *her own ethnicity*" … [F]or all the discussion of forced impregnation, a surprisingly small number of pregnancies are estimated to have resulted from the rapes, and few of them resulted in births. Nevertheless, the pregnancies or potential pregnancies constituted an important part of the rape-as-genocide argument, providing insight into the assumptions about ethnic and religious identity that many perpetrators, victims, and advocates helped perpetuate. Note that nothing about the coercive nature of rape leads these advocates to this conclusion. If a Serbian sperm implanted in a Muslim egg creates a Serbian child, lack of consent is not necessary to this outcome. Thus, all children born of such a union, consensual or not, would be *not* Muslim [italics in original].[29]

We are presented, in other words, with two consequences of designating Bosnian women rights-less (i.e., refugees) during the war, and of the transnational European and international legislation that was enacted to rectify this situation and to restore to these women their sexually and reproductively defined national identity. The first of these consequences was the criminalization of any sex, regardless of consent, that resulted from the "inherently coercive" circumstances in Foča. Indeed, as Engle notes, this understanding of consent or the lack thereof could easily be applied to a much larger political and geographical area given the Tribunal's "broad reading of 'armed conflict.'" Bosnian women, according to this argument, occupied an inherently coercive space. They were—by virtue of their rights-less status—explicitly incapable of having legal sex.

Whereas the elaboration and extension of the right to bodily integrity produced a theoretical criminalization of all sex in nation states, that is to say, it produced an actual criminalization of all sex in the international or "stateless" context. In the name of restoring some semblance of political identity or political activity to Bosnian women, these same women have been rendered explicitly passive sexually and biologically. Indeed, as Engle notes later on in the article, "if female victims of rape have long encountered the difficulty of being believed, an odd reversal takes place here. It was often woman and girls who denied having been raped that were not believed. At some level, all Bosnian women were imagined to have been raped."[30]

Approaches to reproductive crime in the former Yugoslavia reinforced even further this sexual and biological passivity and the role that it has played in restoring to refugees their political identity. The theme, for example, of the woman as political space becomes overt in the rhetoric surrounding reproductive crime in Bosnia. Bosnian women's wombs were, again explicitly, occupied by the enemy if they had been invaded by the sperm of Serbian men. Moreover, as Engle notes, this stance

---

consent paradigm is inappropriate in conflict situations where rape is used as a weapon of war … [S]econd, the Tribunal improperly transposed national peacetime rape law norms into the international criminal arena." Kalosieh 2003, 121.

29 Engle 2005, 794.

30 Ibid, 794.

is precisely predicated on the idea that when a Serbian sperm fertilizes a Bosnian Muslim egg, the result is a Serbian child—that this reproductive (as opposed to sexual) act is, indeed, genocidal. Bosnian women, in other words, were subject to illegitimate, genocidal, violence *specifically* because they could not carry the fate of their "own" nation around in their wombs—because, quite basically, they were passive refugees. Genocide in this interpretation involves depriving the woman of her right to do her duty to her nation state—depriving her of her right to open up her womb to appropriate, lawful regulation. To the extent, therefore, that international and European law was about restoring a political identity to Bosnian women—to the extent that it was about redressing genocidal wrongs—it was also clearly about turning these same women into biopolitical space, about triumphantly opening and regulating their wombs in the name of a Bosnian, rather than a Serbian, collective. It was about turning Bosnian women into Bosnian space. Both sexual activity and reproductive activity in this context are thus a direct assault on the possibility of political activity—on the possibility of extending rights and a national identity to the displaced person.

Moreover, this articulation of refugee sex has occurred not just in the former Yugoslavia, but also in countless other "stateless" circumstances. In a discussion of the reproductive freedom of Somali refugees, for example, one analyst has stated that,

> there is an impression that about half of adult Somali refugee women are pregnant or breastfeeding, and many are said to be infected with human immunodeficiency virus (HIV). Whatever the true statistics, pregnancy, sexually transmitted diseases, and HIV are common. In addition to rape, women are often forced to provide sex in exchange for food or shelter for themselves and their children. Sex for security during the civil war in Uganda may have been a factor in the high rate of HIV infection in that country … [U]nfortunately, some western aid agencies equate offering of family planning to refugees with genocide, even though it is intuitively likely that many people will not wish to conceive while in the harsh conditions of a refugee camp.[31]

In a more general discussion of "the needs of refugee women," Chaloka Beyani similarly notes that,

> refugee women are often faced with specific abuses from which they need protection. The most perversive (sic) and wide spread are rape, sexual abuse, sexual extortion, and physical insecurity during flight and in places of refuge … [W]omen seeking refugee status in their own right and not in association with their husbands, fathers, brothers, or uncles are often subject to sexual demands in return for refugee status. Women who breach refugee camp regulations in certain circumstances are offered sex by male camp officials in lieu of punishment.[32]

31 "Reproductive Freedom for Refugees" 1993, 929-30.

32 Beyani 1995, 29.

These are, again, simply two examples of a widespread discourse of the trials of refugee women.[33] For my purposes, therefore, the most relevant questions to ask in response to them are, first, what precisely is seen as problematic about the position of refugee women, second, why this is considered problematic, and third, what the—in this case implicit—solution to these inappropriate sexual and reproductive behaviors ought to be.

In the first passage, the most basic problem is that sexual as well as reproductive conditions in the camps are "harsh"—even dangerous. Both pregnancy and sexual activity are linked to HIV, producing an association between sexuality and reproduction on the one hand and individual or collective illness or death on the other. The critique of the contraception-as-genocide argument at the end of the passage is thus bolstered not just by invoking consent (or what the refugees might "wish" for) but more so by an implicit counter equation: sexuality and reproduction lead to HIV/death which leads in turn to genocide. Sexual or reproductive activity in this scenario is thus associated explicitly with national or political non-existence. The dangerous nature of sexuality and reproduction in the camp is a problem, in other words, because it leads directly, if counter-intuitively, to the non-existence of the displaced national collective.

In the second passage, there is a similar emphasis on the camp and the necessarily abusive nature of sexual behavior that occurs there. In this case, however, the issue at stake is less danger than it is deviance. Indeed, rape and the like are not "pervasive,"

33 Among many others, see for example: "In exchange for sex with refugee girls less than 18 years-old, the U.N. peacekeepers and other agencies would allegedly trade the humanitarian services they were supposed to have been freely providing, such as food staples, medicine, or skills training." Levin 2003, 834-5. See also, "over the last decade, we began to legitimate the plight of refugee women as international tribunals recognized rape as a war crime systematically used to terrorize and degrade a particular community. Other forms of sexual violence against refugees exist, however, that are more closely correlated to the specific and rectifiable participation of state, IGO, and NGO actors in the provision of humanitarian assistance. In particular, sexual exploitation of refugee women and girls—prostitution or bartering sex for food, supplies, shelter, or favors—is a direct result of the distribution of aid and refugees' corresponding economic situation. The perpetuation of this kind of sexual violence, though perhaps more 'subtle' than rape, violates the internationally recognized rights of women and children to be protected from sexual abuse, prostitution, degrading treatment, and to obtain the highest possible standard of health." Murray 2000, 987-8. Finally, see "in addition, until recently, public health experts seemed to assume that refugees did not engage in sexual behavior and that 'sexuality was irrelevant in a conflict situation.' Though precise quantitative figures on the extent to which sexual exploitation contributes to the spread of HIV/AIDS do not exist, many experts have rationally speculated that the implications are quite serious. At a minimum, war and instability, even where coerced sex is not an issue (though it increasingly *is* an issue), have been identified as major factors in the transmission of this disease, where, due to the disruption of family and social life and increased movement of populations, migrants move away from their usual sexual partners and seek new sexual outlets … [T]he primary direct health effects of sexual exploitation on refugee women and girls include suffering the repercussions of HIV infection or other sexually-transmitted diseases (STDs), unsafe abortions, as well as the dangers of premature childbearing." Murray 2000, 1002-3

but "perversive"—indicative of a flouting of legal and ethical standards, and thus calling out for regulation and the extension of protective structures. Sexual activity in this scenario occurs in the absence of national political systems that would presumably protect women and eradicate deviant behavior. Each of these passages, in other words, posits the refugee woman as sexually and reproductively active, but politically passive and unprotected. In the first, sexual and reproductive behavior in the camp leads to collective illness or death. In the second, sexual behavior in the camp is indicative of an unprotected, politically passive individual at the mercy of unregulated deviants.

A more fundamental theme that runs through both analyses concerns consent. In the first quotation, the critique of "sex for security" basically implies sex without consent. Likewise, the critique of the contraception-as-genocide argument, resting as it does upon the "intuitive" notion that women do not want to reproduce in a refugee camp,[34] assumes, if not the absence of consent, certainly not its presence. In the second quotation, refugee status is granted in exchange for implicitly non-consensual sex, and similarly non-consensual sex is demanded by camp officials before they will exempt women from punishment. The question that arises upon reading both analyses, therefore, is why this particular form of non-consensual sex—not physically coercive sex, but "sexual extortion" in return for security, for refugee status, or for pardon—should be so particularly problematic.

One answer is that on a certain level it re-invokes the politically and sexually disloyal guardian or authority figure who played such a prominent role in nineteenth and twentieth century national legislation. Officials responsible for security, refugee status, or pardon are also responsible for establishing an *ad hoc* version of the social contract within the camp. When they abuse their position and sexualize (without politicizing) those over whom they have authority, they are attacking not just individual women, but the future political identity of these women, and the rule of law that is supposed to separate the good refugee camp from the bad concentration camp. The refugee camp is meant to mirror the nation state; in the nation state only the sovereign can regulate sexual and reproductive behavior, and when officials do so without invoking some semblance of law, they are undermining sovereign right.

Perhaps more to the point, however, the sex for security/refugee-status/pardon scenario makes it impossible for women to attain the biologically passive, politically active ideal that would render them honorary citizens. It makes impossible the mobile but un-free displaced person's transformation into Arendt's incarcerated but free lawfully imprisoned criminal. When sex is exchanged for a pardon, it leads to the

34 Compare this "intuitive" approach to reproduction in the refugee camp to its mirror image, the intuitive approach to reproduction in the nation state (in this case, China): "Forcing abortions and involuntary sterilization on people because they want to have more that one child is persecution. Furthermore, since the Chinese government imputes a political opinion to violators of China's population control policy, these individuals are suffering persecution based on their political opinions. Aliens who flee China's coercive population control policy are therefore eligible for asylum under current U.S. law. Thus, once the alien has cleared the 'credibility' hurdle, the United States should grant asylum to those Chinese citizens fleeing China because of a reasonable fear of forced abortion or involuntary sterilization." Brown 1995, 769.

collapse of the rule of law responsible for "lawfully imprisoning" the rights-bearing criminal—even if this rule of law is artificially manifested in "camp regulations." It reinforces the refugee woman's status as sexually active but politically passive, absent rights, incapable of having legal *or* criminal sex because her bodily borders overlap no political borders. It holds her up as the opposite of the biopolitical rights-bearing citizen.

Similarly, sex for security or for "refugee status" itself, limits and obstructs the refugee woman's transformation into a *quasi*-citizen. In the nation-state, a citizen reinforces his or her autonomy and possession of rights by invoking consent. Upon actually consenting, however, this same citizen's rights are waived—producing the paradoxical, but nonetheless effective, delimitation of this citizen as biopolitical space. Here, the situation is reversed. In order to achieve the security and political identity that is "refugee status," the refugee woman must engage in implicitly nonconsensual sex. Whereas citizens consent to sex and thus achieve a political identity, refugees *do not* consent to sex and *thus* achieve a political identity. In the case of refugees, it is the absence of consent, the inability to waive their rights, that grants them political security and status. The problematic aspect of the sex for security situation, therefore, is not so much that it involves coercive sex or even that it involves an abuse of political authority. It is that the refugee woman's rights are waived in an inappropriate manner whereas the citizen's rights are waived appropriately.

And indeed, like the explicit solutions to the refugee "problem" articulated by the ICTY, the implicit solutions to the refugee problem here are essentially about transforming irrelevant, apolitical, displaced persons into criminal, politically defined, *quasi*-citizens—about turning them into politically active, biologically passive sovereign subjects. The ICTY sought to formulate judgments that would re-establish Bosnian women's wombs as national space and that would re-establish the criminal, regulated nature of sexual behavior. The passages here seek to prevent refugee women from reproducing until the harsh conditions of the camp are replaced by protective national or pseudo-national structures—until such time as their wombs can be displaced onto nations. Similarly, these passages seek to turn sex into a criminal act regulated by political systems rather than an act that in and of itself reinforces political identity. All of this discussion, in other words, is attempting to turn refugees into citizens. It is trying to turn politically irrelevant, non-criminal sexual and reproductive behavior—i.e., "refugee sex"—into politically meaningful, criminal behavior that will define both the biopolitical subject and biopolitical space.

That this has been the intent of the sexual and reproductive legislation and activism aimed at refugees is clear in the repetition of two themes that I want to address in concluding this section. The first of these themes is the condemnation of the pornographic use of videotaped rape footage during the war in the former Yugoslavia—an issue that has been discussed by a number of activists and theorists since the early 1990s. As Riki Van Boeschoten has noted,

> one of the most disturbing aspects of war rape in Bosnia is the impact of pre-war pornographic culture on the rapists' behavior and the pornographic use of rape, including

> videotaping and televised transmission of actual rapes on the evening news. As was pointed out by Catharine MacKinnon, this pornography was used as a highly effective tool in the propaganda war by shifting ethnic labels. Croatian and Muslim women raped by Serbian soldiers were presented as Serbian women raped by Croatians and Muslims. On one occasion, the fabrication was revealed when the original soundtrack accidentally came through.[35]

The second theme is perhaps less widespread than the refugee-sex as pornography trope, but it is nonetheless telling. It concerns the debate surrounding the precise way in which rape might be designated a crime against humanity. The aspect of this debate that interests me here is the confusion on the part of jurists—a confusion echoing the fascist conflation of the gang and the authority figure—between wartime rape as horrific because multiple people are involved in it and wartime rape as horrific because its perpetrators are soldiers, jailors, or guardians.[36]

---

35 van Boeschoten 2003, 41-54.

36 See, for example, ""The [United Nations] Convention against Torture and Other Cruel, Inhuman and Degrading Treatment or Punishment does not catalogue specific acts in its definition of torture, focusing rather on the conceptual framework of state-sanctioned violence. [The Tribunal finds this approach] more useful in [the context of] international law. Like torture, rape is used for such purposes as intimidation, degradation, humiliation, discrimination, punishment, control or destruction of a person. Like torture, rape is a violation of personal dignity, and rape in fact constitutes torture when it is inflicted by or at the instigation of or with the consent or acquiescence of a public official or other person acting in an official capacity.'" Kalosieh 2003, 128. Also, in the Guatemalan context, see the following direct overlap of gang rape and rape by officials: "Under the current international legal regime, the offenses committed against Sister Ortiz generally would be understood as torture—except for the gang rape. Rape by government officials typically is viewed as an inferior crime and is categorized as cruel, inhuman, or degrading treatment ('ill-treatment') that does not rise to the level of torture." Aswad 1996, 1914. And in the United States context, where there is pressure to understand rape committed by authority figures, at least, as political rather than individual crimes: "Although the Supreme Court avoided declaring bodily integrity a substantive due process right within the Fourteenth Amendment by denying *certiorari* when the case came before it (again), the issue should not be ignored. In fact, the implications of extending the constitutional right to bodily integrity to encompass rape by officials would reach far beyond the Lanier case. Specifically, a constitutional right to bodily integrity would provide victims of rape and sexual assault by state actors with remedies that might otherwise be unavailable. Here, the civil rights statute implicated by rape and sexual assault requires a deprivation of rights 'secured or protected by the Constitution or laws of the United States.' Therefore, recognizing that rape or sexual assault by a public official violates the substantive due process right to bodily integrity would bring this conduct within the purview of 18 U.S.C. 242. Once courts establish that rape by public officials violates a constitutional right, Section 242 provides alternate remedies, namely, fines and/or imprisonment for persons who are deprived of their bodily integrity by state actors." Weiler 1998, 591-2. And an analysis of the same case: "Moreover, concluding that the right to bodily integrity is protected by the liberty interest of the Fourteenth Amendment leads to the seemingly axiomatic principle that a citizen's right not to be deprived of liberty without due process of law encompasses the right not to be intentionally and sexually assaulted under color of law. A fundamental right that protects a criminal defendant from having his stomach pumped against his will must also protect a law

These two themes—refugee-sex as pornography and the collapse of the gang into the authority figure—might seem at first unrelated. When we consider, again, what is particularly problematic about these two aspects of stateless sex, however, we can see that they too point to a relentless attempt to "restore" to refugees their biopolitical status. In the case of the first, it is immediately clear that the horrific aspect of the situation in Bosnia is not just that rapes occurred, or even that they were videotaped, but that they were broadcast on the evening news and that the ethnic labels of victim and perpetrators were shifted. What is shocking here, in other words, is not the act of rape, but its political implications. The footage was shown on the evening news, and thus served to cement further a Serbian, as opposed to Bosnian or Croatian, imagined community. Sexual activity, in other words, was mobilized to reinforce the "wrong" national collective.

More to the point, the relationship between sexual identity and political identity so central to modern, biopolitical citizenship was destabilized in these narratives. It was not footage of, say, Bosnian men being illegitimately executed that was re-read as Serbian men being illegitimately executed. Nor was it footage of the looting of Bosnian property that was thus reinterpreted. It was footage of rape. Neither the classical-juridical right to life nor the classical-juridical right to property was operating at the heart of this post-modern variation on genocidal activity. Instead it was biopolitical sexuality. The "pornographic" nature of refugee sex is thus pornographic not because it is sexually deviant or obscene,[37] but because it separates the sexual identity of refugee women from their political identity. Indeed, the solution to these crimes against humanity is presumably to restore to Bosnian women their right to have criminal sex—to re-sexualize them and to de-sexualize their Serbian counterparts. It is Bosnian women who cannot consent, say those who decry this particular act of barbarity. It is not Serbian women—and implying the opposite is a humanitarian outrage.

The tension between the gang and the authority figure is likewise an attempt to restore to refugees their biopolitical rights. What the gang and the authority figure have in common is their ability to disrupt sovereign order, to move across and beyond the boundaries of the rule of law. The authority figure is an authority figure precisely because he or she is responsible for keeping political violence within the bounds of the law. The jailor or soldier who rapes his or her charge is thus particularly threatening because in doing so he or she is situating both violence and sexuality—or in this case sexual violence—outside of the rule of law, disordering sovereign relations writ large, and making impossible the essential connection between the victim's sexual and political identities. Rape committed by an authority figure, in other words, is as much a mockery of the modern citizen's biopolitical identity as the shifting of ethnic labels was in the pornographic footage. Rather than sexual behavior reinforcing

abiding citizen from having her jaws forced open and being coerced into engaging in oral sex. If bodily integrity is to have any substantive meaning in our society, it must encompass the notion that the most intimate and private aspects of our bodies are protected from intrusion by the state and its agents." Simons 1997, 1044-5.

37 In this case, after all, it was broadcast on the evening news.

political and legal structures, it undermines them—indeed upsets them—and this in and of itself is a threat to sovereignty as well as to potential citizenship.

The gang is likewise an inherently political unit—unofficially responsible for tracing the boundary between behavior within the rule of law and behavior outside of it. Indeed, the line between criminal gang violence and revolutionary mass violence is a fuzzy to non-existent one, and gang-related crime, including gang rape, can easily be read as a political act.[38] But it is, once more, an inherently *undermining* political act in the same way that rape committed by an authority figure is. It moves sexual behavior beyond the rule of law, and detaches the sexual identity of the rape victim from his or her political identity. It is therefore just as much of a crime against humanity as torture and the like, striking at a victim's political subjectivity as well as his or her bodily integrity.

The invention of refugee sex—as well as the international and transnational European legislation that seeks to transform it into rights-based sex—is, in other words, a basic part of the humanitarian project. Refugee sex and the laws that address it are first and foremost about granting rights to every individual regardless of national affiliation. They are about endowing stateless people with some form of political subjectivity. To the extent, therefore, that abortion, adultery, and rape law produced on behalf of citizens has sought to articulate for these citizens a framework of sexual and reproductive rights, so too has international and transnational European legislation. Similarly, to the extent that these national laws have suggested the criminalization of sexual behavior and the regulation of reproductive space, so too has the international legislation.

If anything, in fact, the logical conclusion to the national legislation has been reached in its international and transnational European counterpart. The self-conscious construction of a biopolitical identity for displaced people—the relentless transformation of mobile, politically irrelevant persons into incarcerated, rights-bearing individuals—has been met with remarkable success. Bosnian women's wombs have been rescued from their Serbian occupiers and redeployed as spaces that serve a Bosnian national collective. Somali women have learned that they must not have sex unless they have first been granted the political right to consent. The refugee in general has been and continues to be incorporated into and incarcerated within—if not a state structure—at least a surprisingly effective simulation of one.

38 See again, the discussion of Schmitt and the politicized "mob" in Chapter 3: "*Der Begriff des Politischen* suggests Schmitt's awareness of political facts used by the elite theorists and crowd psychology, but this theme works its way through the text more as an intrigue than a statement. There is only one reference to that literature (Pareto) and no discussion of the political movements of the day. The underlying urgency of the text, however, conveys a sense of the political as irrational and unpredictable. While the elite theorists saw only the fact of the crowd, Schmitt sees it as something that can be transformed into the Volk of public law while recognizing (as they did) its volatility." Kennedy 1997, 47. For a more concrete example of this thinking in the case of Indonesia: "through brutal gang rapes, women have been used as tools to terrorize the society. Until democracy is instituted in Indonesia, allowing those who oppose the dominating elite to freely express their views without fearing they will become the victims of violence, Indonesia will have rule by law, not rule of law." Primariantari 1999, 276.

Chapter 5

Women and the Political Norm

Introduction

A significant player in the modern, liberal sovereign relationship is the normative neutral citizen. For the most part a legal fantasy, this neutral citizen is rational and politically inviolate, operates faultlessly in the public sphere, and exercises rights or performs duties under the aegis of a classical-juridical social contract. As a matter of course, this neutral citizen is also male.[1] It is in his name that ideological and bureaucratic structures have been constructed over the past 200 years, and in his name that political theories have been advanced, debated, defended, or attacked. Indeed, to the extent that women[2] have acquired political identities, they have been expected to conform to this masculine norm—and a fundamental argument advanced by almost all feminist theory over the past two centuries has been an argument criticizing this interpretation of political belonging which posits men as citizens and women as honorary men.

At the same time, it is important to keep in mind that these interpretations of the political neutral, along with the arguments criticizing it, hold only if we assume that classical-juridical theory has indeed served as a model for sovereign relations over the past 200 years—if we assume that modern nation states have in fact been operating according to a liberal social contract. If, however, we assume that the predominant model of sovereignty has been biopolitical, that the fundamental sovereign right has been the right to make live and let die—if we place sexual and reproductive legislation at the center of citizenship formation, and understand political activity as biological passivity—then we need to re-think this analysis. Rather than understanding men as the norm and women as artificial facsimiles of men, it makes far more sense in a biopolitical framework to understand women as the norm and men as their copies. It is the womb that has become the predominant biopolitical space, it is women's bodily borders that have been displaced onto national ones, and it is women who have taken the concept of consent to its logical conclusion. It is thus the citizen with the womb who has become the political neutral—and rather than grudgingly granting women the artificial phalluses assumed by liberal theory, one can in fact advance an argument that men instead have been granted the artificial wombs assumed by its biopolitical counterpart.

My intent in this chapter is to develop this alternative reading of citizenship in detail. In doing so, I will first give a few anecdotal examples of women playing the political neutral in both international and national structures and in both sexual/

1 See the work of Pateman, Brown, Fraser and others.

2 Or transsexuals—or anyone defined as not-male.

reproductive legislation and broader political theory. Second, I will suggest that one possible reason for this centering of the woman citizen has been the collapse of abortion, adultery, and rape into a single political/legal category over the modern period. Finally, I will address a number of implications of both the woman citizen as the norm and this collapse of sexual and reproductive crime into one.

Women as Citizens and Citizens as Women I

In commenting on the ICTY's February 22, 2001 Kunarac ruling, Bergoffen makes the following point about women, violence, humanity, and changing notions of political belonging:

> before this ruling, the standard against which evidence for or against the charge of a crime against humanity was the normative "neutral" body. Using this body as a measure, torture, understood through the criterion of physical pain, was identified as a crime against humanity … [T]he Court took a different position. It identified an act as rape, a crime against humanity, whether or not there was evidence of violence or physical pain and injury. It decoupled the idea of forced entry from the idea of painful entry … [T]he woman's body [became] not only not property, not only a mark of *her* subjectivity, but the site of humanity, the species, the universal … [I]ts ruling addresses the way in which women's bodies, signified by patriarchy as the uniquely vulnerable body, signify the vulnerability of all human bodies … [D]oes this ruling inaugurate a politics of the body where the particularity of a woman's sexed body replaces the man's "neutral" body as the standard of the human body—humanity? … [I]ts judgment leads us to challenge the myth of the male invulnerable body and to interrogate the ways in which this mythical body has come to represent the human ideal.[3]

Bergoffen is not arguing here that women's bodies have become the neutral. Indeed her point is that it is precisely the patriarchal dichotomy between a masculine neutral and a feminine marked or vulnerable that has rendered women's bodies representative of a human ideal. What her argument does imply, however, is that the invocation of the right to bodily integrity as the fundamental right motivating rape and torture law has centered women in a different way—as emblematic of the political concept, "humanity." Women's bodies, their physical identities, may be particular, in other words, but their political identities have become universal. It is in fact their very biological particularity that *turns* women politically neutral.

Men can be raped as well, it is true—and the self-consciously ungendered vocabulary of contemporary rape legislation emphasizes this trend in national sex laws as well as in human rights law writ large. But like the woman citizen of liberal theory, whose political identity is predicated on her status as an honorary man, the male citizen in this new framework achieves a political identity only to the extent that he conforms to the feminine neutral. Now it is no longer men who can be political actors and women who can be honorary men, but women who can be raped and men who can be honorary women. Political identity in this scenario is thus linked directly to biology and sexuality, to the trespassing and fortifying of bodily borders, and in

3 Bergoffen 2003, 118-120.

turn to the citizen who most effectively embodies these ideals and the threats against them. It is infinitely removed from the rational, inviolate, self-contained individual who consents to the liberal social contract. It is therefore "natural," in the eighteenth century Enlightenment sense of the term, that women citizens should be the norm.

If we look in more detail at the logic of the legislation, in fact, we can see a distinct movement away from understanding the male citizen as the neutral and toward understanding the woman citizen as such. To the extent, for example, that bodily integrity is less significant than physical pain in the pre-Kunarac discussions of torture, the political subject, or at least the subject's body, is understood to be male. When bodily integrity—trespass rather than pain—takes over as the right in need of protection, however, the political subject is immediately assumed to be female. This is not, presumably, because women do not feel pain in the same way that men feel pain, or that men's bodies cannot be invaded just as women's bodies can be. Instead, some other aspect of pain, bodily integrity, and the relationship of each to political subjectivity must be coming into play—producing this dichotomy between the pre-Kunarac neutral male citizen who feels pain, and the post-Kunarac neutral female citizen who undergoes trespass.

Arguably, this other aspect is the linkage between pain and politics on the one hand and between trespass and biopolitics on the other. Whereas pain has to do with political behavior, trespass has to do with biopolitical space. Whereas pain shatters an individual's subjectivity by disordering that individual's behavior, rendering that individual incapable of coherent speech or action, trespass does so by disordering space, wrenching bodily borders away from protective political borders. Pain is violation of political rights—it is about the right to life and liberty, about the individual's freedom to continue living. Trespass is a violation of biopolitical rights—about the right to health and dignity, about the population's capacity to continue reproducing. And it is here that the shift from the male neutral to the female neutral makes sense. It is women's bodies that are and have been mobilized in the delimitation of biopolitical space. It is women who represent the vulnerable, biologically passive political ideal. It is thus women who have taken center stage, playing the neutral citizen, as biopolitics has displaced politics, as bodily integrity has displaced pain, and as the sovereign right to make live has, in all spheres, displaced the sovereign right to make die.

Indeed, given this biopolitical reading of the neutral citizen, the trajectory of reproductive discourse and legislation takes on a new and salient meaning. When in 1922, for instance, the compilers of the annual Red Cross report repeatedly insisted upon "the close relationship of a nation's health to the condition of a nation's womanhood,"[4] their primary point was not *just* that healthy, well educated women make good mothers who in turn bring up good citizens.[5] Nor is this statement simply a

4 Red Cross 1922, 83.

5 There are a number of excellent analyses of this early twentieth century approach to women as citizens. In the Middle Eastern context, for example, see Abu-Lughod 1998, *passim*.

reinterpretation of the trope of "woman" as cultural signifier.[6] This is the Red Cross, after all—explicitly seeking to improve the health of populations—and their point was necessarily a medical and biological one as much as a social and civilizational one. "Womanhood" and national health are linked here, the nation is politically displaced onto women, but this is not a result of women's place in something called "traditional" interpretations of honor or civilization. Nor is it a result of their role in preparing children for a liberal education. It is instead that women are biologically and medically linked to the nation, and that in this emergent *biopolitical* framework, women are the political actors.

Similarly, when Pederson elaborates on early twentieth century French pro-natalism, she argues that "the exhaustive list of prohibited substances included all female methods of contraception but did not include condoms. This indicates that the French legislators' expanded political and medical authority to intervene into family life was extended through the bodies of women."[7] Pederson's argument is without question a convincing one. At the same time, however, it is important to keep in mind that this legislation, again, was enacted specifically within the broader discourse of race suicide. Women were linked *biologically* to the health of the political collective and it was only as a result of *this* linkage that political and medical authority was extended through their bodies. The resulting situation was no doubt oppressive and—obviously—gendered. But this oppressive and gendered situation did not come about because men played the role of the neutral citizen while women were forced to conform to this neutral or lose their political subjectivity. On the contrary, the neutral citizen was emphatically female in this formulation. She was also, however, defined biopolitically rather than politically, her political activity predicated on a biological passivity, and her bodily and biological identity therefore subject to intimate regulation.

In a purely medical context, in fact, the concept of the woman as the sexual and reproductive neutral has been a long standing one. As van Kammen has noted with regard to research on contraception and fertility, "instances in which the sex of future users was made explicit in researchers' texts were occasions when users other than women were at stake. In contrast to most walks of life, in reproductive sciences women are the unlabeled sex."[8] This is not a minor or an apolitical point—and arguably there is not the strict dichotomy between reproductive sciences on the one hand and "most walks of life" on the other that van Kammen implies. The basic purpose of the modern, biopolitical state is after all to produce and reproduce populations. The sexual and reproductive normativity that she mentions is therefore crucial—leading directly to a political and a biopolitical normativity in turn.

---

6 Critiqued, for example, in the article "Saving Amina Lawal,": "challenging this symbolism means seriously examining current human rights comparisons and moving away from the centuries old method that confuses women's issues with cultural issues." "Saving Amina Lawal" 2004, 2384.

7 Pedersen 1996, 676-7.

8 van Kammen 1999, 322.

Collapsing Categories I

Indeed, I want to suggest that this construction of a feminine norm—a norm sexual, reproductive, political, *and* biopolitical—has been the result of two ongoing post-Enlightenment processes, each related to the broader shift from politics to biopolitics. The first of these processes is the collapse of sexual and reproductive crime into a single category. The second is the more widely noted collapse of law, politics, and war into a single category. What I would like to do over the next few pages therefore is to address, first, the gradual erasure of the lines dividing rape from adultery from abortion, and second, the parallelism between this process and the coming together of war, politics, and law. I will conclude by discussing the various ways in which these two trends have led to the construction of this biopolitical feminine norm.

Again, the distinction among rape, adultery, and abortion has always been a fuzzy one in European and Middle Eastern criminal law. This was particularly true in medieval and early modern interpretations of sexual crime (rape/adultery/fornication)—Catholic canon law of the period as well as its Islamic counterpart understanding sex outside of a sanctioning contract, no matter what the circumstances, to be an act against God.[9] The temporal legislation enacted by states at the time adhered for the most part to these religious prohibitions, downplaying, perhaps, the divine character of sex law but nonetheless emphasizing its monolithic nature.

The overlap of adultery/rape as a crime with abortion as a crime was equally apparent in medieval and early modern legislation. Abortion, for example, was understood by both religious and temporal authorities primarily as a crime accessory to the original sin of sex outside of the sanctioning contract, and interpreted or punished as such. In the medieval Islamic context, the jurist Ibn al-Jawzi assumed that the divine punishment for an adulteress and for a woman who has committed infanticide and/or undergone an abortion was the same. As Avner Giladi states, "an adulterous woman is described [by Ibn al-Jawzi] as being devoured by serpents; this was the divine punishment for murdering three infants born as a result of her sins."[10] Even into the nineteenth century, abortion was linked in this way to adultery—in the United States, for example, it was "criminal when it concealed illegal activity [i.e. seduction, fornication, or adultery]."[11] As Susan E. Klepp has noted, the memoirist Ann Carson denounced in 1822 "an unnamed local doctor who had seduced and would abort his wife's cousin, Susan Elliot … [C]arson condemned the doctor because he intended to remove the evidence of his adultery and of his seduction of Elliot."[12]

9 There are obviously a number of exceptions to this blanket prohibition—and I will discuss some of them momentarily.

10 Giladi 1990, 192.

11 Klepp 1998, 937.

12 As Klepp argues, however, by 1822, changing approaches to sexual and reproductive issues were already apparent: "This transformation can also be seen in the 1822 autobiography of Ann Carson. She denounced an unnamed local doctor who had seduced and would abort his wife's cousin, Susan Elliot … [A]bortion had traditionally been criminal when it concealed illegal activity, so Carson condemned the doctor because he intended to remove the evidence of his adultery and of his seduction of Elliot. Elliot, however … did not see herself as the

At the same time, by the mid to late nineteenth century, and certainly by the early twentieth century, this blurring of the lines between sexual and reproductive crime had taken on a new meaning. The medieval and early modern legislation undoubtedly set a foundation and provided a vocabulary for its modern and eventually post-modern counterpart. But the political context had changed by the end of the nineteenth century, and what had once been a means of defining a religious community had now become a means of defining a citizenry and a population. Just as the *zina* of medieval Islamic law bears very little resemblance to the radically modern *zina* punished by late twentieth and early twenty-first century nation states like Afghanistan and Nigeria,[13] in other words, the rape/adultery/abortion of modern European law is only a distant relative of the *raptus*/fornication/"infanticide" of the fifteenth and sixteenth centuries.

In order to provide something of a bridge between these two periods, therefore, I want to turn to an 1898 analysis of "sex in crime" from the *International Journal of Ethics*. In this analysis, the author, Frances Alice Kellor, begins by setting forth the intersecting race and gender categories that will serve as a foundation for her argument—noting for instance that "negroes furnish an abnormally large percentage of criminals in proportion to their population, their crimes generally those of a sexual passion which woman is incapable of committing."[14] Kellor then elaborates on her argument, providing a number of other illustrations of racial types, the crimes that they commit, and the extent to which gender intersects or does not intersect with these racially specific behaviors. In Italy, for example, "where the percentage of crime against the person is so large, women contribute only nine percent of the total, while in England, where crimes are largely against property, their proportion rises to eighteen percent."[15] Kellor then concludes by addressing gender on its own, arguing that,

> while excess of passion in man, not directed into proper channels, leads to assaults and sexual perversion, in woman its existence more frequently culminates in mental degeneracy or physical disease … [T]he criminal age in women is less than in man, depending upon functions peculiar to women. This operates particularly in such crimes as abortion, infanticide, etc., and is more related to crimes of passion and prostitution, women becoming sexually indifferent at an earlier age than men … [T]he crimes of women are more insidious. Prostitution, abortion and allied crimes exist to an alarming degree among women, and, from the view of public policy alone, are among the gravest, as they strike at the very root of society by decreasing population. The seriousness of the crime of abortion is twofold—it lowers the moral standard of the women of a nation, and it destroys the physical health of the mother, who, when a child is born, transmits her own deficient

innocent victim of a seducer but interpreted the plan to abort the pregnancy as the destruction of the innocent. This moment of miscommunication captured the sea change in attitudes on pregnancy, fertility, and legitimacy. Pregnancy either represented a woman's choice, when choice was essential to her identity as wife and citizen, or it represented the fetus, which emerged as a being with some characteristics of a separate person." Klepp 1998, 937.

13 Regardless of the fact that it is so often designated as "traditional" by its critics and its supporters alike.

14 Kellor 1898, 75-6.

15 Ibid, 79.

> physical condition. The fact that abortion is so prevalent among married women is of the gravest importance [footnote: "this is based upon facts gleaned by original investigation among reputable and trustworthy physicians and alienists"] as it shows a decrease in the maternal sentiment which has preserved women from much crime and degradation, and which is distinctly recognized as the crowning honor of womanhood.[16]

This analysis of race, gender, and crime is not particularly unique for its period,[17] nor is the construction of a relationship among sexuality, national identity, and civilization. Nonetheless, I would like to highlight five aspects of Kellor's argument that will serve as useful transitional points between my discussion of the medieval and early modern collapse of sexual into reproductive crime and the modern variation on this process. First of all, Kellor argues that crimes against the person or crimes of sexual passion are committed primarily by non-White populations, and never by women. Second, to the extent that women do possess an excess of sexual passion, they become mentally or physically ill rather than violently criminal. Third, abortion, infanticide, and prostitution are all "allied crimes," implicitly the result of this mental and physical deficiency. Fourth, these related sexual and reproductive crimes are committed more often by married women than by single women—meaning that the marital contract has become largely irrelevant. And finally, this simultaneously sexual and reproductive crime, the result of mental illness, is far more serious than other crimes, leading as it does to a decrease in, or weakening of, the nation's population (i.e., leading as it does to race suicide).

Whereas there is unquestionably an overlap between abortion and fornication[18] in this analysis, in other words, the overlap is quite different from earlier versions of the same. No longer is abortion a crime accessory to adultery or fornication, the purpose of which is to cover evidence of these more serious sexual crimes. No longer is sexual crime, regardless of the circumstances, criminal in that it undermines the marital contract. Instead, "allied" reproductive and sexual crimes are attacks on a racially defined nation state. They are the same thing not because they attack a contract, not because each covers evidence of the other, but because each, undifferentiated, is an assault on a population.

The mentally ill women who commit these crimes, for example, are both part of the collective (i.e., "not negroes") and also not part of it (i.e., degraded and threatening to public policy). The only crimes that they can commit are sexual and reproductive, but it is precisely sexual together with reproductive crime that is the most dangerous politically. Whereas Rousseau, working in a classical juridical context, saw adultery as treason,[19] therefore, here adultery has become the same as prostitution which is likewise the same as abortion—and all three, undifferentiated, are treason. The collapsing categories in this narrative are thus not about a traditional or even a liberal understanding of sexuality and reproduction. They are the product of an exaggeratedly biopolitical interpretation of violence and national belonging.

16 Ibid, 80-1.

17 Coinciding in particular as it does with the work of positivist criminologists such as Enrico Ferri and Cesare Lombroso.

18 Or, given that married women are more likely to commit it, adultery.

19 See above, Hanley 1997, 46.

I am emphasizing this point not because it has been absent from earlier sections of this book or because it has been missing in the work of others. Rather I want to make clear that Kellor's racist and gendered fusing of sexual and reproductive crime above is operating within the same rhetorical framework as the humanitarian fusing of sexual and reproductive crime that we see in national and international law today. Each presupposes a close, intimate relationship between sexual, reproductive, or biological identity and political identity. Each assumes that major threats to political structures and political collectives are likewise sexual, reproductive, and biological. Far removed from the medieval and early modern collapse of rape into adultery into abortion, or the liberal rhetoric that solved the problem of sexual violence by drawing apparently ineradicable lines between "public" and "private," this biopolitical interpretation of sexual/reproductive crime explicitly renders biological identity political identity. And it is this interpretation above all that has set the foundation for the late twentieth and early twenty-first century reforms that have been made to sexual/reproductive law by both national and international legislative bodies.

War, Politics, and Law

Indeed, I want to emphasize that this interpretation of sexual/reproductive crime is a peculiarly contemporary one. It is an interpretation that has developed alongside of one of the most distinctive trends of the modern period—namely, the collapse of war, politics, and law into a single category. While it is true that the emphatically separate nature of these three concepts—and in particular the emphatically separate nature of law and politics—has been a cornerstone of classical liberal theory, the fact nonetheless remains that a vast quantity of scholarship over the past hundred years has demonstrated the fragile, or even imaginary, state of this cornerstone. Two of the more influential theorists who have made this point are Carl Schmitt[20] and more recently Agamben. What I would like to do now, therefore, is to summarize their positions and then to return to sexuality and reproduction *per se*.

In his 2005 book, *State of Exception*, Agamben develops a theory of exceptional politics, which he argues now operate as the contemporary norm. Drawing on a number of other theorists—most notably Carl Schmitt[21]—he begins his investigation by noting that "one of the essential characteristics of the state of exception—the provisional abolition of the distinction among legislative, executive, and juridical powers—here shows its tendency to become a lasting practice of government."[22] It is, in other words, precisely the collapse of law into politics that both defines the transitory nature of the state of exception and has become its most enduring

20 There was much discussion in the early and mid-1990s about whether citing Schmitt was appropriate, given his complicity with the Nazi regime. At this point, however, the question appears to have been settled, and I am thus engaging with him here as a theorist in the same way that I would engage with Locke, Weber, Arendt, Agamben, or any other political philosopher.

21 Although Agamben also makes an effort to critique Schmitt, arguing especially that in his (hypothetical?) "debate" with Walter Benjamin, Schmitt was the less persuasive. Agamben 2005, 58.

22 Ibid, 7.

legacy. This erasure of lines between the political and the juridical is, therefore, simultaneously temporary and permanent, a by product as well as a fundamental characteristic of the new political norm.

With regard to the role of the sovereign in this situation, Agamben, invoking Schmitt, continues that,

> the sovereign, who can decide on the state of exception, guarantees its anchorage to the juridical order. But precisely because the decision here concerns the very annulment of the norm, that is, because the state of exception represents the inclusion and capture of a space that is neither outside nor inside (the space that corresponds to the annulled and suspended norm,) "the sovereign stands outside of the normally valid juridical order, and yet belongs to it for it is he who is responsible for deciding whether the constitution can be suspended in *toto*."[23]

Finally, Agamben links his discussion of exceptional politics even more securely to Schmitt's political philosophy—if simultaneously criticizing it—arguing,

> the state of exception is not a dictatorship (whether constitutional or unconstitutional, commissarial or sovereign), but a space devoid of law, a zone of anomie, in which all legal determinations—and above all the very distinction between public and private—are deactivated ... [T]his does not mean that it is impossible or useless to analyze the function they perform in the law's long battle over anomie. Indeed, it is possible that what is at issue in these categories is nothing less than the definition of what Schmitt calls "the political."[24]

The state of exception, in other words, has a number of defining characteristics. First, and most importantly, it is the contemporary norm—and has been for at least the past hundred years. Second, this norm is predicated upon a collapse of the legislative into the executive into the juridical—a collapse of law into politics—that is simultaneously temporary and permanent. Third, even as it is articulated in a vocabulary of law and/or constitutionalism, the state of exception defines a "space devoid of law." Fourth, it defines a space in which exception overlaps with norm and in which law and not-law interact with one another—a space occupied first and foremost by the sovereign. Finally, it is a space in which all legal resolutions, "above all the very distinction between public and private," are deactivated—but in which these legal resolutions nonetheless define Schmitt's "political." The contemporary political norm, therefore, is a temporary/permanent, lawful/lawless, public/private space in which law collapses into politics and, as a result, every behavior can be interpreted as either exceptional and extraordinary or normal in every sense of the word.

Schmitt himself goes into more detail about the repercussions of this collapse of law into politics, as well as the collapse of war into both. I would therefore like to turn to his work now, in particular his *Political Theology*, *Legalism and Legitimacy*, and *Concept of the Political*, to flesh out these ideas. In *Political Theology*, Schmitt outlines a number of corollaries that follow from assuming an overlap between

---

23 Ibid, 35.

24 Ibid, 50-51.

politics and law—from assuming that juridical systems are less about objective, rational, abstract norms than they are about sovereignty and sovereign decision. One of the most basic of these corollaries is that, as he argues, "the exception in jurisprudence [becomes] analogous to the miracle in theology."[25] The exception, in other words—the sovereign violation of the sovereign's law—performs the same non-legal but nonetheless legitimizing role in jurisprudence that the miracle, the divine violation of the (divine) laws of nature, does in theology. Each shatters a system of objective norms, but each in doing so demonstrates the higher existence and sovereignty of law/politics or law/divinity.

As Giacomo Marramao has suggested in analyzing this statement, Schmitt is making a comment here not just about the nature of juridical exceptionalism, but, perhaps more importantly, about the nature of liberal politics. If eighteenth and nineteenth century liberal rationalism rendered the miracle, the divine violation of the laws of nature, impossible—thereby simultaneously legalizing and delegitimizing divinity writ large—this same liberal rationalism rendered the exception, the violation of sovereign law, impossible, thus both legalizing and delegitimizing sovereignty writ large.[26] It is, in other words, not just that the exception, the construction of a lawfully lawless space, lends meaning to contemporary sovereign relations. It is that it lends a particularly *miraculous* meaning to contemporary sovereign relations, predicated explicitly upon an irrational, non-objective, non-verbal acceptance of political power. Sovereign legitimacy rests upon a miraculous absence of legality.[27]

This interpretation of law-as-politics, and of the meaning and purpose of the exception, leads Schmitt to a second important point in *Political Theology*. Namely, he argues that "the political is the total, and as a result we know that any decision about whether something is *unpolitical* is always a *political* decision, irrespective of who decides and what reasons are advanced."[28] This may seem like an obvious point, especially if we accept the political nature of law and jurisprudence. But it also implies a more subtle second critique of liberalism as well as a broader commentary on the nature of contemporary sovereignty. With regard to the critique of liberalism, Schmitt's analysis makes clear not just the undesirability, but the impossibility, of an apolitical juridical system, or for that matter any apolitical sphere within the state

---

25 Schmitt 1985, 36.

26 "Here, Schmitt neatly outlined his opposition—which will remain, from this point on, a constant in Schmitt's thought—to the "deistic" theological-metaphysical presupposition of the "modern State of law," which "eliminates the violation of the laws of nature contained in the concept of miracles, [and] produces, by means of direct intervention, an exception, in the same way it excludes the direct intervention of the sovereign in the current legal system." The case of an exception, repudiated by "illuministic rationalism" in any form whatsoever, "has a significance for jurisprudence that is analogous to that of the miracle for theology." Marramao 2000, 1571-2.

27 Schmitt expands on this tension between legality and legitimacy in his book by the same name.

28 Schmitt 1985, 2. See also, "'In the language of the nineteenth century, "society" faces the "state" independently.' The logical deduction from that dualism is that everything 'social' is 'unpolitical'—either a naive mistake, Schmitt remarks, or a very useful tactic in domestic politics." Kennedy 1997, 39.

structure. As he argues later on in *Legality and Legitimacy*, a liberal, pluralist state "becomes 'total' out of weakness, not out of strength and power. The state intervenes in every area of life because it must fulfill the claims of all interested parties."[29] He continues, therefore, that "what is required is a clearer consciousness of the fundamental constructive connections that distinguish a constitution from some product of the partisan legislative machine."

As John P. McCormick has noted, in Schmitt's view it is thus precisely the liberal obsession with legality or with legal formalism, with an apparently objective, rational rule of law that has allowed "more state intervention than was ever dreamed of by absolute monarchs." Indeed, the only major difference in this regard between the liberal state and the state as it is envisioned by Schmitt is that the totality of the liberal state is "undetected" and dysfunctional, whereas its totality in Schmitt's universe is self-conscious and functional.[30] In addition to positing the simultaneously normative and miraculous nature of the state of exception, in other words, Schmitt also suggests that the collapse of law into politics produces a total state where the primary difference between political structures is a metaphysical one—the choice is between an unexamined political life and a self-conscious one, not between the apolitical and the political.[31]

In his *Concept of the Political*, Schmitt addresses the ways in which war has likewise collapsed into this simultaneously political and legal arena. War, he argues, "is neither the aim nor the purpose nor even the very content of politics. But as an ever present possibility, it is the leading presupposition which determines in a

---

29 Schmitt 2004, 92-3.

30 "According to Schmitt, in their revulsion at arbitrary discretion, liberals sought to eliminate the state institutionally from jurisprudential concerns, just as they wished to eliminate, hermeneutically, the personal, subjective, decision from such matters. But they were equally unsuccessful in each endeavor. Specifically, the adherence to legal formalism under conditions of an emerging welfare-state allows more state intervention than was ever dreamed of by absolute monarchs. To Schmitt's mind, in the early twentieth century, the formalism of liberalism serves as an ideology that belies the so-called materialization of law that is brought about by state activity in the new era of welfare-state or Sozialstaat interventionism. Schmitt observes presciently that, as state activity addresses complex and variegated social and economic situations, law is formulated in a more open-ended, and less discernible, manner. In the service of widespread state intervention into particular spheres of society, more discretion becomes exercised by bureaucratic administrators, including judicial officers, in implementing broadly defined social policy. Rather than a formal guideline for members of society, law becomes a material part of social reality. By repressing the state, the legal formalists not only do not prevent arbitrary state functioning, but they allow its activity to proliferate more extensively, and undetected to an even greater degree." McCormick 2000, 1697-8.

31 At the same time, however, as Marramao notes, Schmitt's universe is an uncertain one: "it lies in defining sovereignty legally, not as a monopoly of 'sanctions' or of mere 'power,' but as 'a monopoly of the final decision.' The decision is thus rendered 'free from any normative constraint and becomes absolute in the true sense.' Therefore, Schmitt's wager rests on the chance that the case of exception, too, will remain 'accessible to legal knowledge, since both elements, the norm and the decision, remain within the realm of the legal given.'" Marramao 2000, 1574.

characteristic way human action and thinking and thereby creates a specifically political behavior."[32] He further argues that the basic function of a political order is to decide upon who will play the role of public friend, and who will play the role of public enemy.[33] Far more important to law and politics than the question of individual life or death, in other words, is the question of collective, political existence or non-existence—friend or enemy in a particularly public sense.[34] Politics-as-law is thus likewise politics-as-war—even if *waging* war is neither the aim nor the purpose of political structures. Indeed, even when universal concepts such as humanity are invoked, they are invoked, Schmitt argues, as a means of maintaining the inherently *political* dichotomy between public friend and public enemy—humanitarianism itself a political concept, with obvious implications for (international) humanitarian law: "the concept of humanity excludes the concept of the enemy because the enemy does not cease to be a human being … [w]hen a state fights its political enemy in the name of humanity, it is not a war for the sake of humanity, but a war wherein a particular state seeks to usurp a universal concept against its military opponent."[35]

As Marramao notes, this construction of the friend-enemy distinction, and the increasing overlap among law, politics, and war suggests a number of further corollaries. Schmitt, he argues,

> activates the methodical criterion of the "extreme" as truth for normal cases: the closer a grouping comes to the extremity and purity of the friend-enemy antithesis, the more political it is. This produces the definitive detachment of political acting from any topological referent, which has led some to see in Schmitt a definition of politics that mirrors, and is the opposite of, the relational, functionalist, or systematic models of power-influence … [S]ince "purity" and "autonomy" are part of the criterion, not the realm in which it is made explicit, it follows that any aggregation of intensity close to the friend-enemy antithesis itself acquires an exquisitely political character, excluding the fact that it is manifested in religious (confessional civil wars), national (interethnic conflicts), or economic (class conflict) areas.[36]

Ellen Kennedy likewise elaborates a number of corollaries of Schmitt's position in *The Concept of the Political*. By defining the political as "the field on which issues

---

32 Schmitt 1996, 34.

33 As Marramao, summarizing Schmitt, argues, "In the first place, the concepts of friend and enemy must be assumed, not as metaphors or symbols, but in their concrete, 'existential' meaning. In the second place, not only must they not be confused with other criteria (according to which, for example, the enemy would be morally bad, or aesthetically ugly, or economically disadvantageous), but neither must they be 'understood in an individualistic-private sense, as a psychological expression of private feelings and tendencies.' Friendship and enmity, therefore, must be conceived exclusively in a public sense: 'The enemy is only the public enemy … it is the hostis, not the inimicus in a broad sense.'" Marramao 2000, 1578.

34 "The authority to decide, in the form of a verdict on life and death, the *jus vitae ac necis*, can also belong to another nonpolitical order within the political entity, for instance, to the family or the head of the household, but not the right of a *hostis* declaration as long as the political entity is an actuality and possesses the *jus belli*." Schmitt 1996, 47.

35 Schmitt 1996, 54.

36 Marramao 2000, 1579.

of life and death are met for the public," she argues, Schmitt is privileging above all the idea of "security within and security outside … [as] the chief purpose of the state."[37] Finally, McCormick suggests one further implication of Schmitt's erasure of the lines between law and politics, and politics and war, especially to the extent that modern sovereignty has become increasingly associated with democracy:

> According to Schmitt, this process is radicalized as sovereignty becomes increasingly defined as *popular* sovereignty—as authority derives not from a specific and definite individual person like an absolute monarch but rather from an amorphous and differentiated populace. As a result, emergency action becomes more extreme as it is soon carried out by an elite whose actions are supposedly sanctioned by such "popular" sovereignty. Concomitantly there is a historical justification for the violent destruction of an old order and the creation of a new one out of nothing. Sovereign dictatorship becomes the power to perpetually suspend and change political order in the name of an inaccessible "people" and an eschatological notion of history.[38]

---

37 "Rejecting attempts to derive a conception of the political from a theory of the state, Schmitt reverses the equation, making the political primary and the state dependent upon it: 'the concept of the state assumes a concept of the political.' The discussion transforms the state as a public law concept into a question about the essence (*Wesen*) of 'the political' which emphasizes its precedence over the legal or formal. The grounds for its preeminent position are existential: the political is the field on which issues of life and death are met for the public; security within and security outside its territory are the chief purpose of the state." Kennedy 1997, 43.

38 The full passage from McCormick follows: "Subsequently, as the practical task of early modern state-builders becomes the expansion of political power through the prosecution of boundary-defining external war and the suppression of internal religious civil war, the normatively-unencumbered and technically-disposed executive becomes the model of political practice. Civil war and foreign war, traditionally considered exceptional circumstances that might occasionally call for a dictator, become something else in the writings of state-theorists such as Thomas Hobbes and Jean Bodin. In line with these historical transformations, Hobbes, who will later become Schmitt's intellectual hero, further inverts the relationship of a normal political situation and an exceptional one with his concept of the 'natural condition' or the 'state of nature.' Civil war becomes the ever-imminent normal state of affairs to which the sovereign state is the exceptional solution. Hobbes's 'sovereign state' is hence a kind of dictatorship that has as its sole task guarding the ever-present exception. And because there is no sustained concept of stable political normalcy its authority cannot be a commissarial dictatorship. It is rather, appropriate to its name, a sovereign one. According to Schmitt, this process is radicalized as sovereignty becomes increasingly defined as *popular* sovereignty—as authority derives not from a specific and definite individual person like an absolute monarch but rather from an amorphous and differentiated populace. As a result, emergency action becomes more extreme as it is soon carried out by an elite whose actions are supposedly sanctioned by such 'popular' sovereignty. Concomitantly there is a historical justification for the violent destruction of an old order and the creation of a new one out of nothing. Sovereign dictatorship becomes the power to perpetually suspend and change political order in the name of an inaccessible 'people' and an eschatological notion of history. Schmitt's chief examples of this development are the writings of the French revolutionary theorists, such as Mably and especially Sieyes, and more immediately the Bolsheviks. Yet from the famous first sentence of *Political Theology* written only a year later it is clear that Schmitt has come to endorse something much closer to this latter kind of dictatorship: 'Sovereign is the one who decides

As politics and war come together, in other words, the political is, first, increasingly defined as that which decides on the distinction between public friend and public enemy. The political in its "normal" form is distilled into something pure and extreme, all other relationships—economic, social, and religious[39]—moving, or being moved, constantly toward the purity and extremity of the friend/enemy distinction. As a result, the primary purpose of the state is security, both internal and external. Finally, to the extent that modern sovereignty is democratic—and legitimate precisely because it is democratic—the extreme nature of the normal state becomes increasingly violent and unstable.

Taken together, therefore, Agamben's and Schmitt's analyses provide a number of insights into the type of sovereignty produced by the collapse of law into politics into war, and by the state of exception more generally. First of all, this collapse produces a sovereignty and a political space simultaneously temporary and permanent, exceptional and normal. Moreover, as Schmitt suggests with his miracle analogy, it is not just that these circumstances exist alongside one another, they also imply one another. The "miraculous" legitimizing function of the temporary and exceptional explicitly reinforces the "rational" legality of the permanent and the normal, even as it violates or suspends it. Indeed, it is upon precisely the non-rational, non-verbal, non-objective, miraculous violation of the norm that sovereign power rests. Secondly, the collapse produces a politically total version of sovereignty. There is no public and private, no political and apolitical. Decisions about what should operate outside the realm of the political are indeed emphatically political themselves—and the only real choice that exists in this space is between denying the reality of politics and accepting it. Finally, the collapse produces a very specific type of total state—derived from a politics whose basic, and indeed only, function is to decide on the public friend and the public enemy. As a result, *all* relationships—economic, social, religious and, I will also suggest, sexual, reproductive, and biological—political as they necessarily are, tend toward reinforcing the public friend/public enemy distinction. There is no relationship in the exceptional state that is not in some way aimed at describing the friend/enemy opposition.

---

on the exception.' He seems to celebrate the very merging of the normal and exceptional moments that in *Die Diktatur* he analyzed as politically pathological. He even encourages it with the ambiguous use of the preposition 'on' [*uber*], which belies the distinction that he himself acknowledges in the earlier book between, on the one hand, the body that *decides* that an exceptional situation exists—in the Roman case, the Senate through the consuls—and, on the other, the person that is appointed by them to *decide* what to do in the concrete particulars of the emergency—the dictator himself. The two separate decisions, one taking place in the moment of normalcy, the other in the moment of exception, are lumped together and yet hidden behind the ostensible directness of Schmitt's opening statement in *Political Theology*. Indeed, further on in the work Schmitt explicitly and deliberately conflates the two decisions: the sovereign 'decides whether there is an extreme emergency *as well as* what must be done to eliminate it' (emphasis added)." McCormick 1997, 168-169.

39 And, as we shall see, biological.

Collapsing Categories II

Indeed, what I would like to propose now is that the collapse of sexual and reproductive crime into one another that I mentioned above and that I will develop in more detail below has resulted directly from this broader collapse of law into politics into war. Abortion, adultery, and rape have become a single crime, undifferentiated, because law, war, and politics have likewise become a single entity. More briefly, the former has come to be understood as an assault on the sovereignty defined by the latter. If political space is temporary and permanent, exceptional and normal, legitimized by the very suspension of the legal, in other words, then the crime of abortion/adultery/rape is an attack on this space. Abortion alone, adultery alone, and rape alone do not pose the same threat—quantitatively *or* qualitatively—that the three operating as one do. If political space is likewise total—erasing the lines between public and private and turning "apolitical" into a meaningless concept—then sexual and reproductive crime together also undermine this space. Finally, if politics is about producing a friend/enemy distinction, and if all relationships are to a greater or lesser degree complicit in producing this distinction, sexual and reproductive crime together—not one alone nor the other alone—destabilize this distinction, support public enemies, assault public friends, and only *therefore* must be eradicated.

If we look, for example, at the collapse of sexual into reproductive crime in actual instances of warfare over the twentieth century, we can see that this collapse is predicated upon precisely the notion of exceptional sovereignty that Schmitt and Agamben sketch above. As Reggiani has observed, it was during the First and Second World Wars that pronatalists and population experts began to influence French policy most effectively,[40] producing "propaganda that focused on the military consequences of a continued decline of fertility, [and] making national security completely dependent on a high birthrate."[41] By the end of the war, especially in defeated countries such as Germany, the relationship between reproduction, sexuality, and criminal versions of each on the one hand and sovereignty or public policy on the other had become overt. Atina Grossmann, for instance, has noted that,

> throughout most of the first year after May 1945, a medical commission comprised of three or four physicians attached to district health offices approved medical abortions—almost up until the last month of pregnancy—on any woman who certified that she had been raped by a foreigner, usually but not always a member of the Red Army … [R]apes were immediately medicalized and their consequences eliminated.[42]

This policy, she continues, was for all intents and purposes an extension of practice already in place under the Nazis, the pronatalist regulations prohibiting abortion and contraception balanced by "secret directives permitting—or coercing—abortions on female foreign workers and women defined as prostitutes and non-'Aryans,' as well

40 Reggiani 1996, 729.

41 Ibid, 733.

42 Grossmann 1995, 56.

as on the growing number of German women who became pregnant via consensual sex or rape, by foreign workers or prisoners of war."[43]

In both France and Germany, in other words—implicitly in the former and explicitly in the latter—criminal reproductive behavior was increasingly linked to, and interchangeable with, criminal sexual behavior. The situation was simply one in which criminal sex (i.e., rape), like criminal reproduction, had little or nothing to do with individual choice, behavior, or coercion, and everything to do with the common good. Sex was rape if it undermined collective health and security. Sex was not rape if it did not undermine collective health and security. Likewise, having an abortion was criminal if it attacked the population. *Not* having an abortion was tantamount to being criminal if it attacked the population. In Germany, evidence of rape, both during and after the war, was evidence of a fetus of "foreign" extraction. Abortion was illegal if the fetus was "Aryan," while not having an abortion was illegal if the fetus was "foreign." In France, reproduction was linked to national security, but this reproduction was predicated upon a previously defined *French* population. Abortion was only illegal because it undermined the French collective. If the fetus was, say, German, the laws did not come into play.

What this means in a basic way is that sexual crime and reproductive crime had become by the end of the Second World War exactly the same thing. If each was defined as criminal because it was a broader attack on a common political good, then neither criminal sex nor criminal reproduction could have any meaning in the absence of the other. The crime of rape assumed the possibility of a "foreign" fetus or at least a "foreign" occupation of the womb as political space. Sex without the possibility of reproduction in this scenario could not, therefore, be criminal. Likewise, both criminal abortion and criminal non-abortion assumed a prior criminal sexual act—a sexual act, however, that was fundamentally a political one, in which the violation of the woman's bodily integrity by the foreigner could be read as a violation of the collective national good. Reproductive behavior without prior evidence of criminal sexual behavior simply could not be criminal. If nothing else, it would be impossible to know whether the reproductive crime to punish was having an abortion or refusing to have one.

Moreover, this collapse of sexual into reproductive crime assumed a sovereignty unabashedly exceptional, a collective in which law, politics, and war all had the same meaning. Again, sexual/reproductive law in this case meant *nothing* without politics—having sex or not having sex, reproducing or not reproducing took on legal meaning only upon the acceptance of an irrational, but political, friend/enemy distinction. If sex/reproduction involved assisting the enemy, then it was criminal. If it involved assisting the friend, then it was required. Sexual/reproductive behavior as behavior was irrelevant. Likewise, just as sovereign space was created and legitimized via a violation of legal norms, via a coming together of the exceptional and the normal, here too, sexual/reproductive space was created and legitimized via a violation of sexual/reproductive norms, via a coming together of the exceptional and the normal.

43 Ibid, 52. Moreover, these abortions both during and after the war were "performed in public hospitals and public cost." Ibid, 56.

Sexual/reproductive space had meaning, for example, only to the extent that the normative legal understanding of "rape" (say, "forced sex") and abortion (say, "expelling a fetus") was suspended and replaced by an exceptional political understanding—"sex with the enemy" or "reproducing enemies." In this way, any sexual/reproductive activity could be simultaneously exceptional and normal—having an abortion could violate norms or refusing to have an abortion could violate them, depending upon a previous sovereign decision. As a result, sexual/reproductive relationships—like social, economic, or religious relationships—could be nothing *but* political, part of a total politics, legally meaningful only to the extent that they conformed to the purity of the friend/enemy distinction. The collapse of sexual and reproductive crime, in other words, was a direct result of the collapse of law into politics into war.

But we are, of course, talking about the Second World War and the immediate post-war years. The totalitarian nature of politics over these years—and the likewise totalitarian nature of sexual and reproductive regulation at this time—has become a given, as has the assumption that national and international law in the latter half of the twentieth century and at the beginning of the twenty-first century has been a self-conscious attempt to move away from this model. Nonetheless, what I want to suggest now is that in fact recent and contemporary national and international sexual/reproductive law has been built upon precisely the foundation set in this historical moment. Indeed, if anything, sexual crime and reproductive crime have become even less distinguishable, and law, politics, and war have become less possible to tell apart since the Second World War—this time, however, in the name of humanitarianism.

Writing in 1996 on the "laws of war," "women's human rights," and the ICTY, for example, one scholar has argued that,

> the suggestion that women's human rights and gender justice might be realized by this tribunal [the ICTY] depends on two assumptions: that including women in the laws of war is equivalent to gender-specificity and perhaps more importantly, that the laws of war are continuous with human rights law ... [S]tarting with gender, this analysis raises doubts about the new world order return to legalism as a peacemaking measure and the efficacy of the laws of war in protecting civilians from wartime violence and abuse.[44]

A second scholar, writing more specifically about the ICTY's February 22, 2001 conclusion that "rape and sexual enslavement were violations of sufficient gravity to be considered as 'crimes against humanity,'" is less critical of recent trends in international law. She nonetheless immediately juxtaposes the "mass rape and forced incarceration of women in so-called rape camps" with the fact that "truckloads of eastern Bosnia's Muslim women arrived in the central cities of Travnik, Zenica, and Visoko, and from there were taken [by Serbian soldiers] in busloads to the nearest

44 Philipose 1996, 47-48. She continues that, "the present application of the laws of war and the inclusion of rape as a crime against humanity is a condemnation of rape as it is used to pursue policies of ethnic cleansing, but not a condemnation of rape as a violation of women's human rights. Rape is not prohibited in this instance as intrinsically illegitimate or illegal." Philipose 1996, 56.

hospitals for abortions."[45] Finally, in 2005, a third scholar, critical once more of trends in international law, invokes the same decision to argue that,

> the sexually violent crimes perpetrated against Muslim and Croat women and female children in the former Yugoslavia are distinct; they were part of a campaign that targeted victims because of both sex and ethnicity and that colonized victims' bodies in order to perpetrate genocide. Current international law fails to address the nuances of such genocidal sexual terrorism because it proscribes either the sexual crimes or the ethnicity-based persecutions while completely marginalizing sex-based persecutions. The current framework therefore fails to grasp the concept of sexual violence being targeted at women of a specific ethnicity in order to perpetrate genocide. It overlooks the fact that genocidal sexual terrorism reduces female bodies to a mere means to a genocidal end. Not only does it overlook reality, it assumes charging the perpetrators with token crimes will address the problem and redress the victims.[46]

As early as 1996, in other words, it was first and foremost the ICTY's "legalism" that was criticized by advocates of an international juridical system more cognizant of gender and gendered crime. International legal norms were not enough, these scholars argued, did not sufficiently address rape as a violation of women's human rights. Instead something more was needed. And this something more was a suspension of norms—a suspension that would explicitly reinforce the ethical and above all *political* (rather than legal) status of women as human beings with rights.

What was necessary, in other words, was an exception, a miraculous violation of formal law that would legitimize women's sovereign status and—paradoxically—*therefore* their relationship to law. Indeed, by 2005, this assumption that international sexual and reproductive law could progress only given a collapse of law into politics into war had become explicit. What, after all, is "genocidal sexual terrorism"—occurring as it does in both times of war and times of peace[47]—if not an act that assumes a state of exception? Objective, formal legal norms will never be developed to define in the abstract a "genocidal sexually terrorist behavior" that might then be applied to some individual or another who has been accused of transgressing these norms. No, genocidal sexual terrorism is a decisionist concept that exists in exceptional space and assumes the suspension of law along with the hyperbolic legitimization of politics. Genocidal sexual terrorism has meaning *only* given the prior existence of a pure, distilled public friend/public enemy distinction. Rape is only rape if we know who can legitimately inhabit, and thus who necessarily illegitimately "colonizes" the political space that is a woman's body. Sexual crime is only sexual crime, in other words, if there has first been a sovereign decision made on who is the enemy, on who represents the *hostis*.

Moreover, sexual crime means nothing in this analysis without reproductive crime. This is implicit in the critique of the ICTY's legalism as well as in the development of the notion of genocidal sexual terrorism. It is explicit in the second passage's

---

45 Boose 2002, 71-72.

46 Abreu 2005, 18.

47 See also MacKinnon below on this issue of wartime rape as something that happens especially in times of peace.

acceptance of the ICTY's decisions. Indeed, "mass rape" is conflated here with "forced abortion"—producing a situation in which, again, sexual and reproductive *behavior* ("forced sex," "expelling a fetus") is irrelevant. If something understood to be a Bosnian fetus is "occupying" the womb, then abortions are illegal—just as the eugenic abortions performed by the Nazis were illegal. If something understood to be a Serbian fetus is "occupying" the womb, however, then refusing to allow abortions is illegal—just as the post-Second World War hospitals performed abortions on German women carrying "foreign" fetuses throughout 1945. The question is not about individual life or individual death. It is not about liberal or post-liberal rights (the contract, consent, or bodily integrity). The sole question at stake, again, is who is the friend and who is the enemy. The purpose of the new juridical system, that is, is to preserve the purity of a racially defined political collective. As a result, sexual crime and reproductive crime become necessarily one precisely as the sovereign exception becomes the norm.

This transformation, moreover, is by no means the product solely of law or advocacy on the international stage—advocates of legal change in various national contexts make identical arguments, or sometimes exaggerated variations on them. As early as 1989, for example, MacKinnon was criticizing the separation of sexual and reproductive legislation in the United States. The two, she argued, were unavoidably one, had been separated for patriarchal political or economic reasons, and should be reconnected to one another rhetorically as well as legally. She suggests that the late twentieth century United States abortion debate is entirely inappropriate, for example, because it

> has centered on separating control over sexuality from control over reproduction, and on separating both from gender. Liberals[48] have supported the availability of the abortion choice as if the woman just happened on the fetus, usually on the implicit view that reproductive control is essential to sexual freedom and economic independence. The political right imagines that the intercourse that precedes conception is usually voluntary, only to urge abstinence, as if sex were up to women. At the same time, the right defends male authority, specifically including a wife's duty to submit to sex. Continuing this logic, many opponents of state funding of abortions would permit funding of abortions when pregnancy results from rape or incest. They make exceptions for those special occasions on which they presume women did not control sex. Abortion's proponents and opponents share a tacit assumption that women significantly control sex.[49]

In 1997, Amy E. Ray linked this criticism of separate sexual and reproductive legislation at the national level to her own analysis of the shortcomings of international sexual and reproductive law. More to the point, however, she also couches her call for a simultaneously national and international, sexual and reproductive juridical system within a redefinition of "war" that essentially renders the latter synonymous

---

48 MacKinnon does not distinguish between "Liberal" (that is, on the center left of the United States political spectrum) and "liberal" (that is, the advocate of an Enlightenment era philosophy of rationality and individual rights) in much of her work. Here I believe she is understanding "Liberal" as it is defined against United States party politics rather than "liberal" as it is defined within the field of political philosophy.

49 MacKinnon 1989, 184.

with politics. Starting with the Balkans, and then making a more wide ranging argument, Ray asserts that,

> given the emphasis on invasion of physical territory as the impetus of war between nations or groups of people within one nation, we may be able to reconceive the notion of "war" in order to make human rights laws applicable to women "in the by-ways of daily life." We could eradicate the traditional public/private dichotomy and define oppression of women in terms traditionally recognized by human rights laws by arguing that women's bodies are the physical territory at issue in a war perpetrated by men against women. Under this broader definition of "war," any time one group of people systematically uses physical coercion and violence to subordinate another group, that group would be perpetrating a war and could be prosecuted for human rights violations under war crimes statutes. Such an understanding would enable women to seek the prosecution of any male perpetrator of violence against women, regardless of whether that violence occurred inside a bedroom, on the streets of the city, or in a concentration camp in a foreign country … [I]n order to address the sexual terrorism that occurs every day in the lives of women in the Balkans and in the lives of women all over the world, human rights and what constitutes war and peace must be reconceptualized. Only by acknowledging that women are sexually terrorized daily in every country in the world and by holding the individual perpetrators, as well as the states, responsible, will the term "human rights" include women's experiences.[50]

Throughout 2005 and 2006, MacKinnon popularized and simplified this view, advocating the collapse of sexual into reproductive legislation and the collapse of politics into war in the name of both national and international women's rights. After presenting talks to a number of United States law faculties throughout 2004 and 2005, she published an article[51] in the *Harvard International Law Journal*, for instance, in which she argued that,

> while daily life goes on almost as if violence against women is legal, daily life lacks the legal benefits to noncombatants that a recognized state of war confers. If women in everyday life are not formally considered combatants, with combatants' rights, neither do they effectively receive the benefits the law of war confers on civilians during combat … [I]f violence against women were considered a war inside one country, an armed conflict

---

50 Ray 1997, 838-40.

51 It is beyond the scope of my analysis to discuss MacKinnon's apparent decision in this piece to ignore the past 30 years of scholarship in international gender studies or post-colonial studies. To furnish one example, however: after first asking parenthetically where the post-modernists with their scare quotes have gone now that the "seriousness" of 11 September 2001 has demonstrated the weakness of their position, MacKinnon states that "women are incinerated in dowry killings in India or living in fear that they could be any day. They are stoned to death for sex outside marriage in some parts of South Asia and Africa. They are dead of botched abortions in some parts of Latin America and of genital mutilations in many parts of the world. Girls killed at birth or starved at an early age, or aborted as fetuses because they are female, are documented to number in the millions across Asia. If foreign men did all this inside one country, would that create a state of war? (Come to think of it, what does that make sex tourism in Thailand?)" MacKinnon 2006, 20-21. What, in other words, would these women in Asia, Africa, and Latin America do without "us" middle class white American women speaking for them and demanding their rescue?

> "not of an international character," much of what happens to women every day all over the world would be crisply prohibited by the clear language of Common Article 3 of the Geneva Conventions ... [T]he absence, for women around the world outside what are termed zones of conflict, of such guarantees for noncombatants in war puts women in the practical position of being combatants in daily hostilities, while at the same time generally being unarmed and considered criminals if they fight back ... [I]nternational law still fails to grasp the reality that members of one half of society are dominating members of the other half in often violent ways all of the time, in a constant civil war within each civil society on a global scale—a real world war going on for millennia. It little imagines a war, or crimes of war, or crimes against the peace taking place in which states as such are neither the source nor the name of the power being violently exercised, nor the object sought, nor the violated party. It does not envision conflicts in which it is not the boundaries of nations or the sovereignty of states that are attacked or defended, but the boundaries of the person as a member of a group that are transgressed, and the sovereignty of members of a group of people to live life every single day that is infringed—all the while being regarded as life as normal.[52]

In other words, both of these passages replicate Carl Schmitt's analysis—war "may not be the aim, the purpose, nor even the very content of politics. But it is an ever present possibility,"[53] and our political behavior must be specifically geared toward the reality of politics *as* war. Moreover, if national or international juridical systems are going to address this reality—are going to address the fact that women are not being legally (or politically or militarily) protected—these systems need to do so not by legislating formal law, but instead by placing women into legally defined lawless spaces. Women need, according to these scholars, to be defined as always inhabiting "zones of conflict." If a woman exists, around her must extend lawless, wartime space. Once this new politics has been established, indeed, women might then be protected by the Geneva Conventions, and this is a good thing.

Again, I want to emphasize this point: it is not by legislation that sexual and reproductive crime will be addressed. It is by placing women, the victims of sexual and reproductive crime, into the miraculous space defined by the state of exception. Doing so will restore something called "sovereignty" to women. Just as Schmitt, in other words, invoking Hobbes, saw civil war as "the ever-imminent normal state of affairs to which the sovereign state is the exceptional solution," and suggested "a kind of dictatorship that has as its sole task guarding the ever-present exception,"[54] Ray implicitly and MacKinnon explicitly see here a likewise constant "civil war" as the normal state of affairs that must also be addressed by redefining sovereign space as exceptional space. Moving beyond Schmitt, however, they then imagine this exceptional sovereign space as a space enclosed by the "boundaries" of a *woman's body* rather than by the boundaries of a *nation state*—boundaries, however, that become *more* political than those of the nation state, impervious to transgression, be it legal, political, military, sexual, or biological.

Moreover, the space enclosed by these borders is one in which the only function of the political is to decide upon the friend/enemy distinction. All relationships—

52 MacKinnon 2006, 7-9, 15-16.

53 Schmitt 1996, 34.

54 McCormack 1997, 168.

including the sexual, the reproductive, and the biological—are distilled into a means of defining the public friend and the public enemy. The discourse surrounding rape/abortion in the former Yugoslavia is, again, a hyperbolic variation on this theme. As Engle has already noted, the countless proponents of the rape/abortion/forced pregnancy-as-genocide position are relentlessly reinforcing essentialist notions of "ethnic identity"—and in particular an early twentieth century European racial/biological "ethnic identity"—as they make their cases. It is worth noting as well, however, that the production of this racialized identity is the direct result of this new discourse surrounding *law* and law-as-politics-as-war.

In a 2003 article, for example, one writer states first and foremost that "in Yugoslavia, the desire of the perpetrators of forced pregnancy was to "dilute" the Muslim population."[55] She then immediately turns to the racially problematic assumptions behind this policy, observing that

> according to critics of the effectiveness of forced pregnancy in ethnic cleansing, the method is only conceivable if one denies both science and culture. Biologically, the fetus shares an equal amount of genetic material between the non-Serb mother and the Serbian father. Culturally, unless that child is raised by the father within a Serbian community, he or she will assimilate the cultural, ethnic, religious, and national identity of the mother.[56]

Upon making this point, however, she effectively undermines it, returning to the trope of essential ethnic difference (that goes beyond, even, the half-and-half "genetic material" mentioned above): "However, "under Islamic and Muslim law, a child's ethnicity is determined by that of the father, so children born of these sexual assaults, committed by the Serb men, would not be considered Muslim or of their mother's ethnicity.'"[57] Her conclusion is that one must therefore take into consideration "the important question of whether to evaluate forced pregnancy the same in matrilineal and patrilineal societies."[58]

This is an argument packed with political, sexual, and reproductive assumptions. The biological and cultural problems inherent in understanding sexual/reproductive crime as genocide—while nonetheless accepting some sort of "biological" difference between Serbs and Bosnians, given their separate "genetic material"—are acknowledged. But these problems are then resolved with recourse to "Islamic law." Biological and cultural realities may make it difficult to read sexual/reproductive crime as the political/legal act, "genocide." But if we replace biology and culture with an equally essential and monolithic thing called "Islamic law," then sexual/reproductive crime can indeed be genocidal. All that is required is a move from the classical orientalist position that Islamic law is a *civilizational* identifier, to a contemporary position that Islamic law is a *biological* and *political* identifier. It is thus *only* by understanding law—in this case Islamic law—as politics and law as biology that the rape/abortion/pregnancy-as-genocide argument holds.

---

55 "Sexual Violence as Genocide: The Developing Law of the International Criminal Tribunals and the International Criminal Court" 2003, 512.

56 Ibid, 512.

57 Ibid, 512.

58 Ibid, 513.

Indeed, the fact that no region of the former Yugoslavia, including Bosnia, was operating under an Islamic law system, and the fact that the vast majority of contemporary jurists of Islamic law, all over the world, commented upon the wartime rape of Bosnian as well as Kuwaiti women by stating that the children born of these unions were innocent Muslim Bosnians or Kuwaitis,[59] merely highlight the extent to which "law" in these narratives operates not as a system of norms and regulations, but in a manner identical to "politics" and "biology." "Islamic law" is what makes it possible, first, to differentiate Bosnians from Serbs biologically and, second, to understand this differentiation as a friend/enemy dichotomy—as a battle between essential groups of people seeking to eliminate one another. At the same time, it is clearly not just "Islamic law" here that has collapsed into politics and thus made possible the creation of simultaneously sexual and reproductive genocidal crime. As the article concludes, the question of forced pregnancy as genocidal, or even criminal, rests upon who the victim is politically and biologically—upon, once again, the friend/enemy distinction and how it might be activated.

Like rape and abortion, therefore, forced pregnancy has nothing to do with an individual and her right to bodily integrity. Indeed, forced pregnancy is barely criminal if the victim's collective is a "matrilineal" one. Instead, it has everything to do with a biologically, sexually, and reproductively defined politics—a politics the sole purpose of which is to determine who is the public friend and who is the public enemy. Far more than simply reinforcing racial and ethnic categories, or playing upon the fantasy of a timeless "Islamic law," in other words, these trends in international and national sexual and reproductive law are producing and productive of a quite explicit state of exception, an exceptional space conforming in detail to its definition in political theory. Current thinking about overlapping sexual and reproductive crime, about sex, pregnancy, abortion, and genocide, can indeed be traced directly back to early twentieth century thinking about how these same issues affected race suicide. The only difference is that it is now the job of the international community, working with national governments, to prevent the death of races by

---

59 They did so primarily within the context of discussions on post-rape abortion. Whereas scholars such as the above understood "Islamic law" as, presumably, some monolithic eleventh century phenomenon that could not and had not changed over the past millennium, actual Muslim jurists were reinterpreting both reproductive and sexual relationships according to changing political, social, and moral standards. What this means is that they were moving away both from the relatively unrestricted right to abortion of the medieval period as well as the relatively restrictive understanding of lineage and legitimacy: "in recent years the muftis were urged by Muslim women to legitimize abortion for fetuses resulting from rape. This came following the atrocious raping of Kuwaiti women by Iraqi soldiers during the Gulf War of 1991, and after Muslim women were raped in Bosnia in the 1990s. Most of the muftis who addressed the issue were unanimous that the child of rape, like *walad zina*, is not to blame for the mother's sin, and he or she does not fulfill any of the terms which justify an abortion. The child of rape is a legitimate *shar'î* child, they claim … [A] significant exception can be found in a fatwa by 'Ikrima Sabri, the Chief Mufti of the Palestinian Authority. In 1999 he permitted Muslim women who were raped in Kosovo to take an abortifacient medicine in order to prevent pregnancy from taking place. He justified the permission by arguing that Muslim women should not bear children of the Serbs, since later on these children might be enlisted by the Serbs to fight against the Muslims." Rispler-Chaim 2003, 87-88.

regulating sex and reproduction. Although the contemporary collapse of sexual into reproductive crime is very much a product of the likewise contemporary collapse of law into politics into war, therefore, it is also the inheritor of a 200 year legacy of placing sex and reproduction at the center of biopolitical states.

Women as Citizens and Citizens as Women II

To return to my original question, though, how has this collapse of abortion into rape into adultery led to the creation of the woman citizen as the neutral citizen? And what sort of neutral citizen does it imply? I have already given a few anecdotal examples of women playing the political norm in modern and contemporary structures. I have also sketched an outline of the collapse of law into politics into war as it is described by Agamben and Schmitt. Finally, I have demonstrated that the modern and contemporary collapse of sexual into reproductive crime has been the result of this simultaneous process. What I would like to do now is suggest that this centering of the woman citizen is in turn a result of the collapse of sexual into reproductive crime. And in order to get at this issue, I want to return to Bergoffen, women, and humanity.

The increasing rhetoric of women as representative of humanity that we see in international law and in discussions of this law[60] is neither a gender-aware reinterpretation of classical juridical theory nor an invocation of the notion of woman-as-cultural-signifier. Instead, it has a specific, biopolitical meaning and produces an explicit linkage between the political "humanity" and the biological "sexual integrity."[61] As Bergoffen argues with reference to this new international humanitarian approach to rape, for example,

> as distinct from slavery, heterosexual rape engages the unique vulnerability of a woman's body. As related to slavery, it shows the way in which a woman's unique vulnerability speaks of a bodied vulnerability that is not unique to women. Not only is it not the case that only women can be raped, it is also not the case that only women can be enslaved.[62]

The assault on liberal or classical juridical categories that is "slavery," in other words, has been completely re-imagined in this interpretation such that women are the citizens whose freedom might be assaulted. It is not a neutral male citizen, possessed of inalienable political rights, who must be protected from enslavement—and a female citizen who, to the extent she can conform to the neutral male, must as an afterthought also not be enslaved. It is now a neutral female citizen, possessed of an inalienable biopolitical identity, who must be protected from rape *and* enslavement

---

60 See, for instance, Bergoffen 2003, 121-122.

61 For example, "In focusing on the matter of consent and in using criteria of consent, rather than criteria of violence or pain, for determining whether or not a crime against humanity occurred, the court took note of the relationship between a woman's humanity and her sexual integrity." Bergoffen 2003, 119.

62 Ibid, 121.

(or, more accurately, rape *as* enslavement). And it is now, moreover, the male citizen who is, indeed, the afterthought.

Conclusion

At the beginning of this book, I suggested that the womb, rather than Agamben's camp, is the most effective example of Foucault's biopolitical space. I then tried to demonstrate that, like the camp, the womb is emblematic of the sovereign exception, a space both included within and excluded from the rule of law, and that the easy political dichotomies of classical juridical systems—law/not-law, citizen/not-citizen, rights/lack of rights—break down precisely within the biopolitical arena represented by the womb. Over the course of the past two chapters, I have taken this argument one step further. I have tried to argue that whereas the camp represents *political* space turned into biopolitical space, the womb represents *biological* space turned into biopolitical space.

On one level, this difference does not seem like a particularly important one. Both, after all, end up as biopolitical arenas. But what the transformation of the biological into the biopolitical has brought about, that the transformation of the political into the biopolitical could not, is a much more fundamental collapse of political and biological categories than we have seen before. It is not just juridical lines that have been erased as the womb has been politicized—not just the elimination of any difference between law and not-law or citizen and not-citizen—but basic biological lines that have been erased—the lines between sterile and fertile, impure and pure, dead and alive. It is not, in other words, that law leads inexorably to lawless space, as it does, say, in the Nazi camp. It is that birth leads inexorably to death, as it does in the Bosnian, Somali, or Rwandan womb. And it is thus above all in the womb that the potential of modern and post-modern politics has been reached.

Chapter 6

Conclusion

A number of themes have appeared and reappeared in this book. The most fundamental of these concerns the relationship between rights and sovereign power. The granting of rights is a modern sovereign prerogative, and I have tried to demonstrate that it has been as much a function of unabashedly authoritarian states such as *fin-de-siècle* France and late Ottoman Turkey or self-consciously fascist states such as Mussolini's Italy, as it has been of liberal and neo-liberal governments. It has not led simply and directly to something called individual liberty, and it has not produced a state full of citizens "reasonably" free from coercion. Indeed, Agamben's point that it has been above all rights-granting that has inscribed "bare life" into modern political structures takes on a new salience in the context of abortion, adultery, and rape legislation.

Irrevocably politicizing the sexual and the reproductive, rights granting in this arena has inscribed not just bare life but potential life into political systems—in the process opening up women's bodies to constant regulation. It was, for example, precisely the fascist obsession with "sexual liberty" and a woman's right to consent that expanded the categories of statutory rape and injurious sex to the point that all sexual behavior became effectively criminal and subject to surveillance. It was likewise the intermingling of sexual and reproductive rights with political rights such as *habeas corpus* in the late twentieth and early twenty-first centuries that turned gang rape and rape by authority figures into attacks on humanity writ large—thus displacing the boundaries of women's bodies onto the boundaries of national and international structures.

Moreover, it was precisely the two rights most closely associated with sexuality and reproduction—the right to consent and the right to bodily integrity—that were also the most instrumental in turning modern and post-modern citizens into inert, passive spaces. As Scarry notes, the right to consent is a right above all written across the body. The ability to consent and the right to bodily integrity come together, therefore, as fundamental indicators of the active citizen precisely as this citizen is redefined in spatial terms—at the moment that the trespassing of boundaries replaces violent attack as the defining characteristic of sexual, reproductive, and political crime. Indeed, when Scarry argues that the individual's political power to invoke consent and bodily integrity is directly proportional to this same individual's physical weakness, passivity, and vulnerability—to this individual's existence as nothing more than an area with borders to be protected—there is an unspoken message in her analysis about the relationship between sexual and reproductive law on the one hand and the modern rights bearing citizen on the other.

We can see this relationship playing out in the twentieth and twenty-first century emphasis on sexual and reproductive *space*, and in the relegation of sexual and reproductive *behavior* to the realm of "tradition." We can see it in the disappearance of the penis and in the focus on the uterus in rape, adultery, *and* abortion law. We can see it in the shifts in national rape law that eventually turned integrity/humanity into the victim of sexual attack—an interpretation that necessarily understood the victim's body above all as a political space. And we can see it in the logical conclusion to the early twenty-first century international rape law that mobilized bodily integrity in much the same way that early twentieth century fascist law mobilized consent—producing a situation in which all sexual activity was a violation of bodily borders, was criminal, was only mitigated by the possibility of consent, and was thus subject to constant surveillance. In each of these scenarios, the politically active citizen was necessarily physically and biologically passive. The citizen's body was a political space, and the nature of this space was articulated above all in legislation having to do with sexuality and reproduction.

The fact, indeed, that explicitly fascist norms should appear with such unexpected regularity in late twentieth and early twenty-first century international and humanitarian sexual and reproductive law is an indication that rights-granting is playing a far more complex role than liberal or neo-liberal theorists might recognize. It is clear from the trajectory of abortion, adultery, and rape legislation in various contexts that what we are looking at is not a progress narrative—we do not move from something called the traditional to the liberal to the post or neo-liberal with unfortunate or aberrant detours into the authoritarian and fascist along the way. Instead, we have seen a collapse of the traditional into the liberal into the authoritarian into the fascist—and this collapse has led us to our contemporary "spectacular post-democratic" situation.

The purpose of the various laws has been to define a collective, to delimit civilizational boundaries, and to posit basic friend/enemy distinctions—whether these distinctions are based on an East/West divide, a Europe/not-Europe divide, or smaller national units. Political ideology *per se* is largely irrelevant. What is important instead is the biopolitical nature of collective belonging, the populations that are formed, purified, protected, and maintained—the refugees or stateless people who are incorporated into these populations, rendered physically immobile and politically active. It is indeed worth reiterating that the actual effect or meaning of the past 200 years of legislation has been in many ways irrelevant in both theory *and* in practice. The criminalization of abortion, for example, indicates the civilizational (and biological) superiority of Europe in the late nineteenth century, whereas its legalization indicates precisely the same European superiority in the late twentieth century. When the womb is occupied by a Bosnian fetus, having an abortion is unethical. When it is occupied by a Serbian fetus, not having an abortion is unethical. It is not what the laws say, it is simply their existence that is important. Political and civilizational legitimacy has nothing to do with legality, that is, and everything to do with the rhetoric of law.

Which brings me to my final point. The usual practice in books of this sort is to end with proposals or suggestions about how to fix the situation. Sexual and reproductive law at both the national and international level has, according to my argument, in no way secured the individual freedom or liberty of women citizens. If anything, the repeated promulgation of norms and codes has gradually tied women more effectively into patriarchal political structures—has left women's bodies more exposed to increasingly invasive and intrusive regulation. It has led to the normalizing of the vaginal search warrant and to the ritual of the post-rape forensic examination. Clearly a solution must be found.

It is not my purpose, however, to recommend a solution. Again, one of the most fundamental themes of this book has been the futility of invoking the liberal progress narrative as a means of understanding abortion, adultery, and rape law. If sexual and reproductive legislation had anything to do with progress, if the goal of granting sexual and reproductive rights had ever been to create rational, inviolate, juridically defined women citizens, then perhaps discussing solutions might be meaningful. As it is, however, sexual and reproductive legislation and rights have served as nothing more nor less than a vocabulary for the expression of biopolitical sovereignty. And given that one of the defining characteristics of biopolitical sovereignty is that one does not stand outside of it and call for reform or revolution—that rights rhetoric in a biopolitical state reinforces existing structures—it would be absurd and self-contradictory for me to end with an optimistic demand for change.

At the same time, my hope is that this book might still serve a purpose. When I make the point that in a biopolitical state the woman citizen is the neutral citizen, I am not trying in an intellectually dishonest way to undermine the work of the feminist theorists who have so effectively and persuasively critiqued liberal patriarchy. I do, however, want to suggest that "equal citizenship" *per se* is not necessarily the incontrovertible solution to inequitable structures that many seem to assume it to be. In a state founded on the sovereign exception, wed to the maintenance of a healthy population, and preoccupied above all with personal and political security, equal citizenship may mean simply equality of regulation, equality of bodily invasion, and equality of biological intrusion. It may mean simply that every individual's bodily borders are equally subject to sovereign reinforcement or to sovereign violation. If this book does serve a purpose, therefore, it is to prompt those who do choose to agitate or who do call for change to be aware of the implications of the rhetoric they are invoking—to think carefully about what it means to demand progress in the name of the rights and duties of modern and post-modern women citizens.

Bibliography

Abreu, V.C. (2005), "Women's Bodies as Battlefields in the Former Yugoslavia: An Argument for the Prosecution of Sexual Terrorism as Genocide and for the Recognition of Genocidal Sexual Terrorism as a Violation of Jus Cogens under International Law," *The Georgetown Journal of Gender and the Law* **6**, 1-20.

Abu-Lughod, L. (ed.) (1998), *Remaking Women: Feminism and Modernity in the Middle East* (Princeton: Princeton University Press).

Afsaruddin, A. (ed.) (1999), *Hermeneutics and Honor: Negotiating Female* "Public" *Space in Islamic/ate Societies* (Cambridge: Harvard Center for Middle East Studies).

Agamben, G. (1998), *Homo Sacer: Sovereign Power and Bare Life* trans. Daniel Heller-Roazen (Stanford: Stanford University Press).

——(2005), *State of Exception* trans. Kevin Attell (Chicago: University of Chicago Press).

Alexander, L. (1986), "Consent, Punishment, and Proportionality," *Philosophy and Public Affairs* **15**:2, 178-182.

Altınay, A.G., "Talking and Writing our Sexuality: Feminist Activism on Virginity and Virginity Tests in Turkey," in Ilkkaracan (ed.), 403-411.

Anker, D.E. (2002), "Boundaries in the Field of Human Rights: Refugee Law, Gender, and the Human Rights Paradigm," *The Harvard Human Rights Journal* **15**, 133-154.

Arat, Y. (1996), "On Gender and Citizenship in Turkey," *Middle East Report* 198, 28-31.

Arendt, H. (1976), *The Origins of Totalitarianism* (New York: Harcourt).

Arıkan, E.B. (1999), "The Programme of the Nationalist Action Party of Turkey: An Iron Hand in a Velvet Glove?" in Kedourie (ed.), 120-135.

Asad, Talal. (2003), *Formations of the Secular: Christianity, Islam, Modernity* (Stanford: Stanford University Press).

Aswad, Evelyn Mary. (1996), "Torture by Means of Rape," *Georgetown Law Journal* **84**, 1913-1943.

Avcı, M. (2005), "Töre cinayetleri açısından sosyal-hukuki düzenlemelerin Evrimi," *Ekev Akademi Dergisi* **9**:22, 1-27.

Baines, Beverley and Rubio-Marin, Ruth. (eds.) (2005), *The Gender of Constitutional Jurisprudence* (Cambridge: Cambridge University Press)

Bartlett, R.C. (2001), "On the Politics of Faith and Reason: The Project of Enlightenment in Pierre Bayle and Montesquieu." *Journal of Politics* **63**:1, 1-28.

Bataille, G. (1986), *Erotism, Death, and Sensuality* (San Francisco: City Lights Books).

Bergelson, V. (forthcoming), "The Right to be Hurt: Testing the Boundaries of Consent," *George Washington Law Review* **75**.

Bergoffen, D. (2003), "February 22, 2001: Toward a Politics of the Vulnerable

Body," *Hypatia* **18**:1, 116-136.

Beyani, C. (1995), "The Needs of Refugee Women: A Human Rights Perspective," *Gender and Development* **3**:2, 29-40. [PubMed 12290124]

Blunt, F.J. and Lane Poole, S. (1878), *The People Of Turkey: Twenty Years' Residence Among Bulgarians, Greeks, Albanians, Turks, and Armenians*, (London: John Murray, Albemarle St.).

Boose, L.E. (2002), "Crossing the River Drina: Bosnian Rape Camps, Turkish Impalement, and Serb Cultural Memory," *Signs* **28**:1, 71-96.

Bowen, D.L. (1997), "Abortion, Islam, and the 1994 Cairo Population Conference," *International Journal of Middle East Studies* **29**:2, 161-184.

Briggs, L. (2002), *Reproducing Empire: Race, Sex, Science and U.S. Imperialism in Puerto Rico* (Berkeley: University of California Press).

Brockopp, J.E. (ed.) (2003), *Islamic Ethics of Life: Abortion, War, and Euthanasia* (Columbia: University of South Carolina Press).

Brown, T.A. (1995), "Forced Abortions and Involuntary Sterilization in China: Are The Victims of Coercive Population Control Measures Eligible For Asylum in the United States?" *San Diego Law Review* **32**, 745-769. [PubMed 16086515]

Brown, W. (1992), "Finding the Man in the State." *Feminist Studies* **8**:1, 7-34. [DOI: 10.2307/3178212]

Brownmiller, S. (1975), *Against Our Will: Men, Women and Rape* (New York: Simon and Schuster).

Cahill, A.J. (2000), "Foucault, Rape, and the Construction of the Feminine Body," *Hypatia* **15**:1, 43-64.

Caldwell, L. (1981), "Abortion in Italy," *Feminist Review* **7**, 49-63. [DOI: 10.2307/1394759]

Calloni, M. (2001), "Debates and Controversies on Abortion in Italy," in Stetson (ed.).

Campbell, K. (2003), "Rape as a 'Crime Against Humanity': Trauma, Law, and Justice in the ICTY," *Journal of Human Rights* **2**:4, 507-518. http://dx.doi.org/10.1080/1475483032000137093

Chamallas, M. (1987-1988), "Consent, Equality, and the Legal Control of Sexual Conduct," *Southern California Law Review* **61**, 777-862. [PubMed 11658947,11658941,11655852,11655851]

Cındoğlu, D. (2000), "Virginity Tests and Artificial Virginity in Modern Turkish Medicine," in Ilkkaracan (ed.), 215-229.

Clark, H. (1865), "On the Supposed Extinction of the Turks and the Increase of the Christians in Turkey," *Journal of the Statistical Society of London* **28**:2, 261-293. [DOI: 10.2307/2338418]

"Code Pénal,"*Legifrance—Le service public de l'accès au droit* [website], (updated 2006). http://admi.net/code/CPENALLL-222-23.html.

Cohen, J.L. (2002), *Regulating Intimacy: A New Legal Paradigm* (Princeton: Princeton University Press).

Conaghan, J. (2005), "Extending the Reach of Human Rights to Encompass Victims of Rape: M.C. v. Bulgaria," *Feminist Legal Studies* **13**, 145-162. [DOI: 10.1007/s10691-005-1462-5]

Cornell, D. (1995), *The Imaginary Domain: Abortion, Pornography, and Sexual*

Harassment (New York and London: Routledge).
Davidson, N. (1994), "Theology, Nature, and the Law: Sexual Sin and Sexual Crime in Italy from the fourteenth through the seventeenth Century," in Dean and Lowe (eds.), 74-99.
Dean, M. (1999), *Governmentality: Power and Rule in Modern Society* (London: Sage Publications).
Dean, T. and Lowe, K.J.P. (eds.) (1994), *Crime, Society, and the Law in Renaissance Italy* (Cambridge: Cambridge University Press).
Duben, A. and Behar, C. (2002), *Istanbul Households: Marriage, Family, and Fertility, 1880-1940* (Cambridge: Cambridge University Press).
Dunlop, W.B. (1889), "Railways—Their Future in China," *The Eclectic Magazine of Foreign Literature* **49**:4, 516-524.
Edgerton, R.B. (1999), *Death or Glory: The Legacy of the Crimean War* (Boulder, Co: Westview Press).
Elver, H. (2005), "Gender Equality from a Constitutional Perspective: The Case Of Turkey," in Baines and Rubio-Marin (eds.), 284-304.
Engle, K. (2005), "Feminism and its (Dis)contents: Criminalizing Wartime Rape in Bosnia and Herzegovina," *The American Journal of International Law* **99**:778, 778-816. [DOI: 10.2307/3396669]
Everhart, A.J. (1998), "Predicting the Effect Of Italy's Long-Awaited Rape Law: Reform in 'The Land of Machismo,'" *Vanderbilt Journal of Transnational Law* **31**, 671-718.
Faizan, M. (1993), "Islamic Law of Confession—A Comparison with Western and Indian Laws," *Islamic and Comparative Law Review* 131, 27-37.
Foord, J. (1900), "The Root of the Chinese Trouble," *North American Review* **171**:76, 401.
Foucault, M. (1990), *History of Sexuality: An Introduction* trans. Hurley, R. (New York: Vintage).
——(1995), *Discipline and Punish* (New York: Vintage).
——(2003), *Society Must Be Defended* trans. Macey, D. (New York: Picador Press).
Fraser, N. (1989), *Unruly Practices: Power, Discourse, and Gender in Contemporary Social Theory* (Minneapolis: University of Minnesota Press).
Fuchs, R.G. (2000), "Seduction, Paternity, and the Law in Fin de Siècle France," *Journal of Modern History* **72**:4, 944-989. [DOI: 10.1086/318550]
Gerber, H. (1994), *State, Society, and Law in Islam: Ottoman Law in Comparative Perspective* (Albany: State University of New York Press).
Giladi, A. (1990), "Some Observations on Infanticide in Medieval Muslim Society," *International Journal of Middle East Studies* **22**:2, 185-200.
Gözaydın, İ. (2006), "Adding Injury to Injury: The Case of Rape and Prostitution in Turkey," in Parry (ed.), 59-71.
Grewal, I. (1996), *Home and Harem: Nation, Gender, Empire, and the Cultures of Travel* (Durham: Duke University Press).
Grossmann, A. (1995), "A Question of Silence: The Rape Of German Women by Occupation Soldiers," *October* **72**, 42-63. [DOI: 10.2307/778926]
Hanley, S. (1997), "Social Sites of Political Practice in France: Lawsuits, Civil

Rights, and the Separation of Powers in Domestic and State Government," *The American Historical Review* **102**:1, 27-52. [DOI: 10.2307/2171265]

Hardt, M. and Negri, A. (2004), *Multitude: War and Democracy in the Age of Empire* (New York: Penguin Books).

Harris, J.P. (2000), "Refugee Women: Failing to Implement Solutions," *Human Rights Brief* 7, 30-31.

Hatem, Mervat. (2000), "The Professionalization of Health and the Control of Women's Bodies as Modern Governmentality in Nineteenth-Century Egypt," in Ilkkaracan (ed.), 67-81.

Hengehold, L. (1994), "An Immodest Proposal: Foucault, Hysterization, and the 'Second Rape,'" *Hypatia* **9**:3, 88-108.

HM Stationery Office. (1931), *Penal Code of the Kingdom Of Italy, as Approved by Royal Decree of October 19, 1930* (London: HM Stationery Office).

Hyde, A. (1997), *Bodies of Law* (Princeton: Princeton University Press).

İçduygu, A. (1996), "Correlates of Timing of Induced Abortion in Turkey," *Demography India* **25**:1, 131-146.

Ilkkaracan, Pınar. (ed.) (2000), *Women and Sexuality in Muslim Societies* (Istanbul: Kadının Insan Hakları Projesi).

Kalosieh, A. (2003), "Consent to Genocide?: The ICTY's Improper Use of the Consent Paradigm to Prosecute Genocidal Rape in Foca," *Women's Rights Law Reporter, Rutgers* 24, 121-135.

Kandiyoti, D.A. (1987), "Emancipated but Unliberated? Reflections on the Turkish Case," *Feminist Studies* **13**:2, 317-338. [DOI: 10.2307/3177804]

Kandiyoti, D.A. and Robert, M. (1998), "Photo Essay: Transsexuals and the Urban Landscape in Istanbul," *Middle East Report* 206, 20-25.

Katz, M.H. (2003), "The Problem of Abortion in Classical Sunni Fiqh," in Brockopp (ed.), 25-51.

Kazancı, Faruk. (ed.) (1994), *Türk Ceza Kanunu* (Istanbul: Kazancı).

Kedourie, *Sylvia*. (ed.) (1999), *Turkey Before and After Ataturk: Internal and External Affairs* (London: Routledge).

Kellor, F.A. (1898), "Sex in Crime," *International Journal of Ethics* 9:1, 74-85.

Kennedy, Ellen. (1997), "Hostis not *Inimicus*: Toward a Theory of the Public in the Work of Carl Schmitt," *Canadian Journal of Law and Jurisprudence* **10**, 35-47.

Kipris, L. (1998), "Adultery" *Critical Inquiry* **24**:2, 289-327. [DOI: 10.1086/448876]

Klepp, S.E. (1998), "Revolutionary Bodies: Women and the Fertility Transition in the Mid-Atlantic Region, 1760-1820," *Journal of American History* **85**:3, 910-945. [DOI: 10.2307/2567216]

Koğacıoğlu, D. (2004), "The Tradition Effect: Framing Honor Crimes in Turkey," *differences: A Journal of Feminist Cultural Studies* 15:2, 118-148.

Kritz, F. (2005), "Doctors Not Fans of Tom Cruise's Baby Gift: Sonogram machines aren't meant for living rooms, experts say," *MSNBC* [website] (updated December 6, 2005) <http://www.msnbc.msn.com/id/10309963/.

Labarthe, Napoléon Bacqua. (ed.) (1849), "Code pénal Napoléon," *Codes de la législation française* (Paris: Auguste Durand).

Lai, S.Y. and Ralph, R.E. (1995), "Female Sexual Autonomy and Human Rights,"

Harvard Human Rights Journal **8**, 1-32.

Lansing, C. (1997), "Gender and Civic Authority: Sexual Control in a Medieval Italian Town," *Journal of Social History*, 33-59.

Leroy-Beaulieu, P. (1899), "Le problême Chine," *Revue des Deux Mondes* **54**, 43-74.

Levin, Scott A. (2003), "U.N. Report: Sexual Exploitation of Refugee Children By U.N. Peacekeepers," *New York Law School Journal of Human Rights* **19**, 833-843.

Lombardi, Daniela. (1994), "Intervention by Church and State in Marriage Disputes in Sixteenth and Seventeenth Century Florence," in Dean and Lowe (eds.), 142-159.

Lombardo, P.A. (2005), "Phantom Tumors and Hysterical Women: Revising our View of the Schloendorff Case," *Journal of Law, Medicine and Ethics, Winter* 33, 791-800.

Lütfi, A. (1888), *Mirat-ı Adalet, yahud Tarihçe-i Adliye-yi Devlet-i Aliyye* (Istanbul: Kitapçı Ohannes Lütfi).

MacKinnon, C.A. (1989), *Toward a Feminist Theory of the State* (Cambridge: Harvard University Press).

——(2006), "Women's September 11th: Rethinking the International Law of Conflict," *Harvard International Law Journal* **47**, 1-31.

Marramao, G., (2000), "Schmitt and the Categories of the Political: The Exile of the Nomos: For a Critical Profile of Carl Schmitt," *Cardozo Law Review* **21**, 1567-1587.

Mazower, M. (1998), *Dark Continent: Europe's Twentieth Century* (New York: Vintage).

McBride, T. (1992), "Public Authority and Private Lives: Divorce After the French Revolution," *French Historical Studies* **17**:3, 747-768. [DOI: 10.2307/286570]

McCormick, J.P. (1997), "The Dilemmas of Dictatorship: Carl Schmitt and Constitutional Emergency Powers," *The Canadian Journal of Law and Jurisprudence* **10**, 163-187.

McCormick, J.P. (2000), "Poststructuralism Meets Schmitt: Schmittian Positions on Law and Politics?: CLS and Derrida," *Cardozo Law Review* 21, 1693-1722.

McLaren, A. (1978), "Abortion in France: Women and the Regulation of Family Size 1800-1914," *French Historical Studies* **10**:3, 461-485. [DOI: 10.2307/286340]

Meixler, L. (2004), "Lawmakers Confirm that Turkish Government has Shelved Proposal to Criminalize Adultery," *Associated Press Worldstream* (15 September 2004).

Murray, R.B. (2000), "Sex for Food in a Refugee Economy: Human Rights Implications and Accountability," *Georgetown Immigration Law Journal* **14**, 985-1025.

Oaks, L. (2000), "Smoke-Filled Wombs and Fragile Fetuses: The Social Politics of Fetal Representation," *Signs* **26**:1, 63-108.

Omran, A.R. (1992), *Family Planning in the Legacy of Islam* (New York: Routledge).

Parla, A. (2000), "The 'Honor' of the State: Virginity Examinations in Turkey," *Feminist Studies* **27**:1, 65-88.

Parrish, M.J. (2000), "Redefining the Refugee: The Universal Declaration of Human Rights as a Basis for Refugee Protection," *Cardozo Law Review* **22**, 223-267.

Parry, J.T. (ed.) (2006), *Evil, Law, and the State: Perspectives on State Power and State Violence* (Amsterdam: Rodopi Press).

—— (forthcoming) "Terrorism and the New Criminal Process," *William and Mary Bill of Rights Journal* **15**.

Pateman, C. (1980), "Women and Consent," *Political Theory* **8**:2, 149-168.

——(1988), *The Sexual Contract* (Stanford: Stanford University Press).

——(1989), *The Disorder of Women: Democracy, Feminism and Political Theory* (Stanford: Stanford University Press).

Payne, J.P. (1998), "The Criminal Use of Chloroform," *Anaesthesia* **53**, 685-690.http://eutils.ncbi.nlm.nih.gov/entrez/query.fcgi?cmd=Retrieve&db=pubmed&dopt=Abstract&list_uids=9771177http://dx.doi.org/10.1046/j.1365-2044.1998.528-az0572.x

Pedersen, J.E. (1996), "Regulating Abortion and Birth Control: Gender, Medicine, and Republican Politics in France, 1870-1920," *French Historical Studies* **19**:3, 673-698. [DOI: 10.2307/286640]

Peirce, L. (1997), "Seniority, Sexuality, and Social Order: The Vocabulary of Gender in Early Modern Ottoman Society," in Zilfi (ed.), 169-197.

——(1999), "The Law Shall Not Languish: Social Class and Public Conduct in Sixteenth Century Ottoman Legal Discourse," in Afsaruddin (ed.), 140-154.

——(2003), *Morality Tales: Law and Gender in the Ottoman Court of Aintab* (Berkeley: University of California Press).

Peters, R. (1994), "The Islamization of Criminal Law: A Comparative Analysis." *Die Welt Des Islams* **34**, 246-260. [DOI: 10.2307/1570932]

Philipose, L. (1996), "The Laws of War and Women's Human Rights," *Hypatia* **11**:4, 46-62.

Primariantari, R. (1999), "Women, Violence, and Gang Rape in Indonesia," *Cardozo Journal of International and Comparative Law* **7**, 245-276.

Rains, R.E. and Benedetti, G. (2001), "A Discursive Essay on the Nature of Marriage and Divorce in Italy and the United States," *National Italian American Bar Association: The Digest* 10, 1-28.

Rao, R. (2000), "Property, Privacy, and the Human Body," *Boston University Law Review* **80**, 359-460. [PubMed 16523588]

Ray, A.E. (1997), "The Shame of It: Gender-Based Terrorism in the Former Yugoslavia and the Failure of International Human Rights Law to Comprehend the Injuries," *American University Law Review* **46**, 793-840.

Reagan, L.J. (1991), "About to Meet Her Maker: Women, Doctors, Dying Declarations, and the State's Investigations of Abortion, Chicago, 1867-1940," *Journal of American History* **77**:4, 1240-1264. [DOI: 10.2307/2078261]

Red Cross. (1922), *Annual Report* (Washington D.C.: American Red Cross).

Reggiani, A.H. (1996), "Procreating France: The Politics of Demography, 1919-1945," *French Historical Studies* **19**:3, 725-754. [DOI: 10.2307/286642]

Rispler-Chaim, V. (2003), "The Right not to be Born: Abortion of the Disadvantaged Fetus in Contemporary Fatwas," in Brockopp (ed.), 81-97.

Rizzo, J.A. (ed.) (1927), *Code pénal Turc* (Istanbul: J.A. Rizzo).

——(1996)(ed.) (1939), *Code pénal Turc* (Istanbul: J.A. Rizzo).
Robinson, J.C. (2001), "Gendering the Abortion Debate: The French Case," in Stetson (ed.), 87-111.
Ruhl, L. (2002), "Dilemmas of the Will: Uncertainty, Reproduction and the Rhetoric of Control," *Signs* **27**:3, 641-663.
Said, E. (1979), *Orientalism* (New York: Vintage).
Sanger, M. (1920), *Woman and the New Race* (New York: Brentemos).
Sarat, A. (2001), *When the State Kills: Capital Punishment and the American Condition* (Princeton: Princeton University Press).
Sassatelli, R. (1998), "Justice, Television and Delegitimation: On the Cultural Codification of the Italian Political Crisis," *Modern Italy* **3**:1, 108-115.
Scarry, E. (1990), "Consent and the Body: Injury, Departure, and Desire," *New Literary History* fall, 867-896. [DOI: 10.2307/469190]
Schmitt, C. (1985), *Political Theology: Four Chapters on the Concept of Sovereignty* trans. Schwab, G. (Chicago: University of Chicago Press).
——(1996), *Concept of the Political trans. Schwab, G.* (Chicago: University of Chicago Press).
——(2004), *Legality and Legitimacy* trans. Seitzer, J. (Durham: Duke University Press).
Senlet, P., Curtis, S.L., Mathis, J., and Ragges, H. (2001), "The Role of Changes in Contraceptive Use in the Decline of Induced Abortion in Turkey," *Studies in Family Planning* **32**:1, 41-52. [DOI: 10.1111/j.1728-4465.2001.00041.x]
Seral, G. (2000), "Virginity Testing in Turkey: The Legal Context," in Ilkkaracan (ed.), 413-417.
Sidahmed, A.S. (2001), "Problems in Contemporary Applications of Islamic Criminal Sanctions: The Penalty for Adultery in Relation to Women," *British Journal of Middle Eastern Studies* 28:2, 187-204.
(1997), "Being Secure in One's Person: Does Sexual Assault Violate a Constitutionally Protected Right?" *Boston College Law Review* **38**, 1011-1049.
Sohn, AM.-A. (1995), "The Golden Age of Male Adultery: The Third Republic," *Journal of Social History* spring, 469-490.
Sonbol, A. (2000), "Rape and Law in Modern Ottoman Egypt," in Ilkkaracan (ed.), 309-325.
Spotts, F. and Wieser, T. (1986), *Italy: A Survey of Italian Politics*. (Cambridge: Cambridge University Press).
Stetson, Dorothy McBride. (ed.) (2001), *Abortion Politics, Women's Movements, and the Democratic State* (Oxford: Oxford University Press).
Stoianovich, T., (1960), "The Conquering Balkan Orthodox Merchant," *Journal of Economic History* **20**:2, 234-313.
——(1962), "Factors in the Decline of Ottoman Society in the Balkans," *Slavic Review* **21**:4, 623-632. [DOI: 10.2307/3000577]
Stoler, A.L. (1995), *Race and the Education of Desire* (Durham: Duke University Press).
——(2002), *Carnal Knowledge and Imperial Power: Race and the Intimate in Colonial Rule* (Berkeley: University of California Press).
Stormer, N. (2000), "Prenatal Space," *Signs* **26**:1, 109-144.

Taub, N. (1999), "Why Afford Constitutional Protection of Reproduction?" in Taylor, Rush, and Munro (eds.), 497-459.

Taylor, B.W., Rush, S., and Munro, R.J. (eds.) (1999), *Feminist Jurisprudence, Woman, and the Law: Critical Essay, Research Agenda, and Bibliography* (Buffalo, NY: Wm. S. Hein Publishing).

Temkin, J. (1998), "Medical Evidence in Rape Cases: A Continuing Problem for Criminal Justice," *Modern Law Review* **61**, 821-850. [DOI: 10.1111/1468-2230.00180]

Terrade, O. (2001), "Projet relatif à l'interruption volontaire de grossesse et à la contraception, N° 200, Sénat, Session Ordinaire de 2000-2001," French Senate [website], . http://www.senat.fr/rap/r00-200/r00-2000.html

Tezcan, S. (1980), *"Türkiye'de Çocuk Düşürme"* (Ankara: Hacettepe Üniversitesi Toplum Hekimliği Enstitüsü).

Tezcan, S. and Omran, A.R. (1981), "Prevalence and Reporting of Induced Abortion in Turkey: Two Survey Techniques," *Studies in Family Planning* **12**:6/7, 262-271. [DOI: 10.2307/1965874]

Triolo, N. (1994), "Fascist Unionization and the Professionalization of Midwives in Italy: A Sicilian Case Study," *Medical Anthropology Quarterly* **8**:3, 259-281. [DOI: 10.1525/maq.1994.8.3.02a00010]

Tucker, J. (1998), *In the House of the Law: Gender and Islamic Law in Ottoman Syria and Palestine* (Berkeley: University of California Press).

van Boeschoten, Riki (**2003**), "The Trauma of War Rape: A Comparative View on the Bosnian Conflict and the Greek Civil War," *History and Anthropology* 14:1, 41-54.

van Kammen, J. (1999), "Representing Users' Bodies: The Gendered Development of Anti-Fertility Vaccines," *Science, Technology and Human Values* **24**:3, 307-337.

Watson, C. (1952), "Birth Control and Abortion in France Since 1939," *Population Studies* **5**:3, 261-286. [DOI: 10.2307/2172430]

Weiler, S. (1998), "Bodily Integrity: A Substantive Due Process Right to be Free from Rape by Public Officials," *California Western Law Review* **34**, 591-610.

White, L. (1997), "The Traffic in Heads: Bodies, Borders, and the Articulation of Regional Histories," *Journal of South African Studies* 23:3, 325-338.

"Yeni Türk Ceza Kanunu—Yeni TCK 5237 sayılı kanun, 29.9.2004," *Yeni Türk Ceza Kanunu* [website], <http://www.hukuki.net/kanun/5237.15.text.asp>

Young, G. (ed.) (1905-1906), "Code pénal ottoman," *Corps de Droit Ottoman* (Oxford: Clarendon Press).

Zilfi, M.C. (ed.) (1997), *Women in the Ottoman Empire: Middle Eastern Women in the Early Modern Era* (Leiden: Brill).

Notes and Anonymous Articles

"Chinese Punishment Methods." (1894), *New York Times* (28 November 1894), 5.

"Council of Europe: 'Make Birth Control Available." (1976), *International Family Planning Digest* **2**:3, 16.

"How China is Governed." (1892) *New York Times* (26 January 1892), 2.

"Reproductive Freedom for Refugees." (1993), *Lancent* **341**, 929-30. [DOI: 10.1016/0140-6736%2893%2991216-9]

"Saving Amina Lawal: Human Rights Symbolism and the Dangers of Colonialism." (2004), *Harvard Law Review* **117**, 2365-2386.

"Secret of Crispi Favor: Africa is the Answer to the Vexing Italo-English Enigma—Aggression, Adventure, and Ruin: Most Cruel, Inquisitorial, and Harrowing of All Imposts." (1898), *New York Times* (21 September 1898), 2.

"Sexual Violence as Genocide: The Developing Law of the International Criminal Tribunals and the International Criminal Court." (2003), *Michigan Journal of Race and Law* **8**, 503-527.

"Torture in Chinese Trial: Peking Officials Use Forbidden Methods." (1908), *New York Times* (11 May 1908), 4.

Index